The Way into Narnia

A READER'S GUIDE

Peter J. Schakel

William B. Eerdmans Publishing Company

Grand Rapids, Michigan / Cambridge, U.K.

© 2005 Wm. B. Eerdmans Publishing Co.

Wm. B. Eerdmans Publishing Co.
255 Jefferson Ave. S.E., Grand Rapids, Michigan 49503 /
P.O. Box 163, Cambridge CB3 9PU U.K.
www.eerdmans.com

Printed in the United States of America

10 09 08 07 06 05   7 6 5 4 3 2 1

ISBN 0-8028-2984-8

The material in Chapter 2 of this book previously appeared in a slightly different
form in Peter J. Schakel's *Imagination and the Arts in C. S. Lewis: Journeying to Narnia
and Other Worlds*, copyright © 2002 by the Curators of the University of Missouri,
and is reprinted here by permission of the University of Missouri Press.

To my colleague and good friend

Charles Huttar,

to whom I owe so much

Contents

Preface

This is the third book I've written dealing primarily with the Chronicles of Narnia. In the first, *Reading with the Heart: The Way into Narnia* (1979), I discussed universal themes and traditional literary structures created by the archetypal symbols and patterns Lewis used in the Chronicles, and the specifically Christian themes Lewis developed through establishing parallels between the Chronicles and Lewis's *Mere Christianity*. In the second, *Imagination and the Arts in C. S. Lewis: Journeying to Narnia and Other Worlds* (2002), I examined Lewis's theory of imagination, especially as it bears upon the Chronicles, and showed the importance of the imaginative arts — music, dance, art, architecture, and clothing design — in Lewis's life and as motifs in the Chronicles.

Perhaps, as the most basic of the three books, this is the one I should have written first: the "guide" pointing out the "way" into Narnia and preparing for the journey. But I needed to write the others first to get to know the Chronicles well enough to do this one. This book reuses some material from those earlier studies, but it is a new book in approach, emphasis, and insights. Its unifying theme is that the best way to enter Narnia is to read the Chronicles as fairy tales. The book brings out the influence on the Chronicles of the ideas about Faërie developed by Lewis's friend J. R. R. Tolkien in his essay "On Fairy-Stories." A chapter on each of the Chronicles walks readers through the work, pointing out fairy-tale features, considering literary strategies and structures, and examining universal themes, particularly religious ones.

The opening section explores questions such as these: How did a middle-aged professor with no children come to write books that have become classics of children's literature? What is the best order for reading the Chronicles? What differences exist between different editions? This provides a necessary framework for the middle section, which contains the chapters on the Chronicles themselves. The final section supplies marginal notes for each of the Chronicles, clarifying unfamiliar words, highlighting allusions and significant details, and offering interpretive comments for problematic passages. Such notes provide valuable help to parents and teachers for answering questions, and enrich the imaginative experience with the Chronicles for other readers as well.

Sources of citations in the chapters and annotations can be found on pages 163-91. For help in locating passages in the Chronicles, see the table on pages 192-94, which correlates page numbers with chapters.

As I worked on the chapters and annotations, I was helped by the interest, enthusiasm, and questions of my freshman composition class in the fall semester of 2004. I am indebted especially to Anne Hoekstra for assistance with the annotations. Charles Huttar, Susan Palwick, and Jack Ridl read the chapters in typescript and offered valuable corrections and suggestions; I am deeply grateful for their help and their friendship. Chuck Huttar also provided generous help with the annotations. Myra Kohsel, office manager for the Hope College English department, assisted me graciously and willingly in many ways. And I am grateful, as always, to my wife, Karen, for her love, assistance, and encouragement.

I want to acknowledge also the assistance of Mary Hietbrink, Project Editor at Eerdmans Publishing Company. Mary edited the manuscript with great care and imagination, offering many suggestions that have improved the book significantly. About twenty years ago Mary did an excellent job of editing *Reason and Imagination in C. S. Lewis: A Study of "Till We Have Faces"*; it has been a pleasure to work with her again.

The Chronicles:
The Author and the Books

Chapter 1

The Story-maker
and His Stories

I am sure that some are born to write as trees are born to bear leaves.

In the late 1940s, a fifty-year-old Oxford professor named Clive Staples Lewis began writing a fairy story for children. He was unmarried, had no children, and had never before written a children's book. This all seems a recipe for failure, but the book turned out to be a huge success. It and its six sequels have sold millions of copies and are now regarded as classics. How did this happen? Why would a middle-aged man even conceive of writing *The Lion, the Witch and the Wardrobe* and the other books that later came to be called the Chronicles of Narnia? How does one account for this surprising turn of events? Many aspects of his life make his attempt and success seem most unlikely; however, on closer examination other parts make it seem almost inevitable.

Lewis's preparation to be a "story-maker" creating imaginary worlds began in his childhood. He was born in Belfast, Ulster (now Northern Ireland), on 29 November 1898, to well-educated parents who loved books and were voracious readers. His father, Albert, was a lawyer; his mother, Florence (Flora) Augusta Hamilton, graduated with honors from Queen's University, Belfast, at a time when most women did not consider pursuing a college education. They married in 1894 and had one other child, Warren, born in 1895.

Growing up in a house filled with books, Lewis not surprisingly learned to read early, perhaps when he was three, and became a constant reader, devouring nearly everything he could lay his hands on. In his auto-biography, *Surprised by Joy*, he says that "dressed animals" and "knights in armour" were the chief literary pleasures of his boyhood. He remembers with affection Beatrix Potter's books, Jonathan Swift's *Gulliver's Travels* (1726), and Edith Nesbit's stories as they were serialized in the *Strand*, especially the Psammead series: *Five Children and It* (April to December 1902), *The Phoenix and the Carpet* (July 1903 to June 1904), and *The Story of the Amulet* (May 1905 to April 1906).

Of particular importance was his reading, around 1906, of "Tegnér's Drapa," a poem by Henry Wadsworth Longfellow, specifically the opening lines, "Balder the beautiful/Is dead, is dead." Balder, the god of beauty, goodness, and wisdom in Norse mythology, was killed by a dart of mistletoe (the only thing that could harm him), thrown by his blind brother Hoth. His death was a turning point in the history of the Northern gods, leading to the coming of evil and their death. These lines lifted Lewis into "huge regions of northern sky," awakening a deep sense of longing for something unidentifiable at the time, but associated with the North. Lewis carried that love of Northernness into the Chronicles, especially as a prominent theme in *The Horse and His Boy* but present also as an underlying theme throughout the series.

When he was about six, Lewis began writing stories, undoubtedly influenced by his reading, about an imaginary country, Animal-Land. He wrote in school notebooks, with ink or ink-and-watercolor illustrations. The settings were medieval, with castles, heroes, and battles. The characters were dressed animals, like King Benjamin VIII (a rabbit); Lord John Big (a frog), the "Little-master" (the equivalent of Prime Minister) of the country; and Viscount Puddiphat (an owl), the fashion plate of the land and, because he was owner of a chain of music halls, a bit disreputable.

The plots were about politics and war. At the time, Lewis had no interest in politics (and not much interest later), but adults in early twentieth-century Ireland talked about politics constantly, so he concluded that politics must be important and what one ought to write about. His boyishness came through often: he would dash off a long battle or political campaign in one paragraph, then spend five or six paragraphs describing a practical joke one character played on another. The stories even had a history (he constructed a timeline of events) and a geography, with maps, such as one of the railway system in Animal-Land. Eventually the Animal-Land stories evolved into stories about "Boxen," the country formed through the merger of Animal-Land with his brother Warren's imaginary India.

The Animal-Land and Boxen stories are not proper fantasies: their characters are essentially humans with animal faces, and the action is located on earth, not in an imaginary world, though it is an imaginary earth where India is an island with its north coast backed up to the Himalayas. The stories lack the magic and enchantment of fairy stories, and they are more unlike the Chronicles than similar to them. Yet, they clearly are the forebears of the Chronicles: without them, the Narnian tales probably would not have been written. The stories appear to have been among Lewis's most cherished childhood memories. On two visits to his father, made in September 1927 and April 1928, he began an *Encyclopedia Boxoniana,* which he never completed. Later, in *Surprised by Joy,* he spends nearly eight pages fondly reminiscing about the stories. If he spent time in his late twenties revisiting this childhood enthusiasm, no wonder he eventually returned to the format and tried to do something more with it.

Having the imaginary world of Animal-Land as a place to retreat to helped Lewis cope with a traumatic event: his mother dying of cancer in 1908. In *Surprised by Joy* he writes, "With my mother's death all settled happiness, all that was tranquil and reliable, disappeared from my life." More than forty years later he constructed *The Magician's Nephew* around a touching story of a mother near death and the struggle of a boy (about the age Lewis was when his mother died) to deal with it.

Prior to her death, Lewis was educated at home, learning French and Latin from his mother and other subjects from a governess, Annie Harper. After her death, he — like Warren before him — was sent to a boarding school in England, in part because English schools afforded greater social mobility than Irish schools. Both boys went first to Wynyard School in Watford, outside London, Warren in 1905 and Lewis in 1908, only a few weeks after his mother's funeral. The school had by then only a handful of students left and a headmaster who was both tyrannical and abusive, though somehow the Lewis boys were spared the beatings other boys received. The theme of education that runs through the Chronicles, especially the negative attitude toward schools, was shaped by his unhappy experience at Wynyard, which he referred to in his autobiography as a concentration camp, "Belsen."

In these early years the foundations were laid for the Christian themes that run through the Chronicles. Lewis was raised in a home with deep Christian roots on both sides. Albert Lewis's grandfather was a religious enthusiast who became a Methodist minister, and Albert's father wrote evangelical pamphlets. Flora Lewis was the daughter and granddaughter of clergymen. Albert, Flora, and their sons regularly attended St. Mark's Church, Dundela, where Flora's father was rector. But except for the introduction to the doctrines of Christianity he received at Saint John's Anglo-Catholic church in Watford while he was a student at Wynyard, little was built on these foundations until the 1930s.

Wynyard School closed in 1911. Lewis spent one term at Campbell College in Belfast, then entered Cherbourg School in Malvern, in western England. Here his real education began, under some excellent teachers, and here he ceased to be a Christian. Lewis attributes his departure from his childhood faith to several factors: the influence of two tutors at Cherbourg House (one who taught him worldliness and another who dabbled in the occult), the burden of performing private devotions daily, and his inability to accept (as he was being taught) that one religion — Christianity — was true and all others false. However, his mother's untimely death and the brutality of his first school surely contributed as well, perhaps even more than the causes he acknowledged. Whatever the explanation, the attitude toward religion he held at that point makes it surprising that he later came to write the Chronicles as we know them, with the underlying Christian themes that add to the richness of their effect.

Lewis probably completed the last of the Boxen stories before the autumn of 1913, when, after two happy years at Cherbourg, he won a scholarship to prestigious Malvern College, one of the British schools that prepare students for university entrance exams. By inclination private and solitary, Lewis did not fit into the boarding-school environment, with its emphasis on social life and sports. He was deeply unhappy at Malvern and soon began insisting that he be allowed to leave, even mentioning suicide. As a result, his father arranged for him to study for the entrance exams to Oxford with W. T. Kirkpatrick, a former schoolmaster now retired to rural Surrey, south of London. For two-and-a-half almost idyllically happy years (from fall 1914 through spring 1917), Lewis lived with Kirkpatrick and his wife and thrived under Kirkpatrick's tutelage, embracing especially his instructor's rigorous insistence on logic. The increasingly skeptical and rationalistic outlook that Lewis developed in those years also makes it surprising that in later years he would become the author of a series of fairy tales embodying Christian themes.

But the years with Kirkpatrick also added two important elements contributing to the sense that the writing of the Chronicles was almost inevitable. First, he came to love Edmund Spenser's romance *The Faerie Queene* (1590-96), which was not included in his set lessons but was part of his leisure reading. Decades later, he pointed out that until the early twentieth century, this was "everyone's poem — the book in which many and many a boy first discovered that he liked poetry; a book which spoke at once . . . to every reader's imagination." Its appeal, he added, is to the most naïve and innocent tastes: "It demands of us a child's love of marvels and dread of bogies, a boy's thirst for adventures, a young man's passion for physical beauty." These qualities, which could characterize the Chronicles, come together in Spenser's plots, which deal with knights, magicians, dragons, and damsels in distress, and with the world Spenser created, the land of Faërie. A place "seeming to have a life of its own," Spenser's imaginary world is lifelike in its inner consistency and its breadth, all of it resonant with Christian imagery and meaning. Lewis was enchanted by Spenser's work, except for its Christianity. As he wrote to his friend Arthur Greeves in 1916, "I have at last come to the end of the Faerie Queene: and though I say 'at last,' I almost wish he had lived to write six books more as he hoped to do — so much have I enjoyed it." For the rest of Lewis's life it shaped his mental picture of what Fairy-land is.

Second, he discovered the works of George MacDonald. On a Saturday evening in 1915 or 1916, while waiting for a train in Leatherhead station, Lewis came across a copy of *Phantastes: A Faerie Romance* (1858), bought it almost by chance, and began reading it that evening. "A few hours later," he recalls in the preface to *George MacDonald: An Anthology*, "I knew that I had crossed a great frontier." He already loved the Romantic imagination of nineteenth-century figures like William Morris. In *Phantastes* he found what he loved in Morris, but enriched by "a new quality," the numinous (an aura of spirituality, of the supernatural), that Morris lacked. Pervading *Phantastes* was a "bright shadow" that he later recognized as "Holiness." That night, he writes in *Surprised by Joy*, "my imagination was, in a certain sense, baptized." Without that baptism, he would never have come to write the Chronicles, at least not in the form we know them.

Well prepared by Kirkpatrick, Lewis began his studies at Oxford in January 1919, after military service in France during World War I. From autumn of that year until 1951, he shared a home with the mother and sister of an army buddy of Irish descent, Paddy Moore, who had died in action in France. This turned out to be crucially important in his life and his writing. The mother, Janie Moore, was very different from Lewis and not an easy person for him to live with: she was not a Christian; she was not well-educated; she was autocratic, demanding, and controlling. But she was also an outgoing, kind, hospitable person whose house was always open to guests and people in need. Living with Mrs. Moore kept Lewis from the isolation and solitariness to which he was inclined by nature and helped him learn a great deal about people and everyday life outside the ivory towers of academia, experiences on which he drew in his nonfiction writings and in his fiction for both adults and children. It seems very likely that, if Lewis had not lived with Mrs. Moore and her daughter and mingled with the people who passed through their home, he would not have been able to write the Chronicles.

Throughout his years in Surrey and at Oxford, as a student and later as a young don, creative writing was so important to Lewis that it seemed inevitable that he would be an author of some sort. His genre then was poetry, not fairy tale or even fiction generally. "If you thought of Lewis" in his teens and twenties, his close friend Owen Barfield has said, "you automatically thought of poetry." As an undergraduate at University College, Lewis established a brilliant academic record, winning the vice chancellor's essay prize in 1921 and earning first-class honors in Greek and Latin, classical philosophy, and English language and literature. After filling a one-year position tutoring philosophy from 1924 to 1925, he applied for and was elected to a position as fellow at Magdalen College, Oxford, a position he held for almost thirty years.

In 1925, the year Lewis became a fellow at Magdalen, J. R. R. Tolkien was elected to the Professorship of Anglo-Saxon at Oxford. He and Lewis first met on 11 May 1926 at a gathering of the English faculty. In his diary Lewis describes Tolkien as "a smooth, pale, fluent little chap . . . thinks language is the real thing in the school. . . . No harm in him: only needs a smack or so." Only several years later, in December 1929, did a close association develop, when Lewis invited Tolkien to his rooms at Magdalen after an evening meeting and they talked until half past two about Norse gods and mythology and their shared interest in Northernness generally. The two soon became personal friends, spending a morning with each other most weeks during the 1930s and meeting as part of the group of friends Lewis called the Inklings (members took turns reading aloud pieces they were working on and received criticism as well as support and encouragement).

Lewis's friendship with Tolkien, a devout Roman Catholic, and with others in Oxford who were Christians or were on their way toward religious faith was one factor that played a part in his return, in his early thirties, to the Christian faith of his childhood. There were other contributing factors as well. One was his study of English literature, in which he found that the authors he loved most, such as Spenser, Donne, Herbert, and Milton, were Christians. Also, his philosophical studies led him to belief in moral law and a lawgiver behind the law (something he explains in the first section of *Mere Christianity*), and he came to regard the pagan religions not as false but as incomplete, precursors to Christianity rather than contrary to it. Perhaps most important, he finally recognized the romantic longings he had experienced throughout his life as a yearning for the divine.

All these factors led him, in 1929, to believe in the existence of God. He became a theist, but not yet a Christian. The further step, to Christian belief, was influenced directly by changes in his understanding of myth. A key event was a late-night conversation with Tolkien and another close friend, Hugo Dyson, who showed Lewis the importance of myth to the

Christian faith. Lewis came to understand that the story of Christ's sacrifice works on us the same way as pagan myths, the difference being that it
really happened. "It is God's myth," Lewis wrote in a letter soon afterward,
"where the others are men's myths." This revised outlook on myth would,
almost two decades later, have a direct bearing on Lewis's development of
mythical motifs, both borrowed and invented, in the Narnian Chronicles.

The nature of Lewis's work as a literary scholar also ended up contributing to the Chronicles. In his teaching and in such books as *The Allegory of
Love* (1936) and *English Literature in the Sixteenth Century, Excluding Drama*
(1954), he was a literary historian, helping his students and other readers to
enter, to some extent, the imagination and world — both very different
from ours — of persons living in the Middle Ages or the Renaissance, and
to read their literary works as nearly as possible the way they read them. In
the Chronicles and his other fantasy writing, he sought to do the same
thing: to enable readers to enter other worlds and imagine what life in
those worlds was like for their inhabitants.

The fact that Lewis began writing adult fiction in the 1930s might
make it seem surprising that he soon turned to fairy tales suitable for children, but the adult fiction in some ways helped equip him to write the
Chronicles. His first work in the fantasy genre, *Out of the Silent Planet* (1938),
grew out of and responded to Lewis's love of early science fiction, especially, Lewis himself said, "the 'scientifiction' of H. G. Wells." Although the
book does involve space travel, it is not strictly (or mainline) science fiction, since there is little emphasis on science or technology; it seems closer
to "space fantasy" than "science fiction." The story takes us with the hero,
Elwin Ransom, out of our own world and enables us to live for a while,
imaginatively, in a fantasy world; at the same time, it enables us to look
back at our world from a fresh perspective and to reassess our familiar life
and values.

In the sequel, *Perelandra*, Lewis created his most perfect imaginary
world, a world almost totally water-covered, with floating islands moving
about its surface; a world covered by a golden dome, as the sun causes the
dense atmosphere to glow warmly; a world of fresh, vibrant colors and delightful smells; a world with mostly unique vegetation, animals, and
foods, rather than ones belonging to our planet. Ransom discovers that

this is a new world — not that the planet is new, but that human life on it is. It is a paradisal world, a global Garden of Eden. Among all his books, *Perelandra* was one of Lewis's favorites. In fact, he seems to have fallen in love with the fantasy world he created in it. His friend Roger Lancelyn Green recalls an evening walk when they saw Venus shining brightly in the sky and Lewis said "Perelandra!" with passionate longing in his voice, as if he wished he could go there as Ransom had.

Just when Lewis began trying to write fairy tales suitable for children isn't clear, but it is clear that he did not succeed until the late 1940s, during a very busy time in his life. He was under a good deal of pressure, working hard at researching and writing his massive scholarly undertaking for the Oxford History Series, *English Literature in the Sixteenth Century*, and caring for Mrs. Moore, who now was an invalid. As a creative outlet, a diversion from his scholarly work and his responsibilities at home, he wrote *The Lion, the Witch and the Wardrobe* and the rest of the Chronicles.

During the years in which the Chronicles were published, significant events were occurring in Lewis's personal life. First, Mrs. Moore died in January 1951, three months after the publication of *The Lion, the Witch and the Wardrobe*. Then, in September 1952 (the month in which *The Voyage of the "Dawn Treader"* was published), Lewis met Joy Davidman Gresham, an American who had become a Christian through reading his books and with whom he had been corresponding since 1950. She moved to England with her two sons, David and Douglas (nine and seven years old), in November 1953 (about two months after *The Silver Chair* was published), and she and Lewis became close friends. The following year he dedicated *The Horse and His Boy* to David and Douglas. Lewis and Joy were married in a civil ceremony on 23 April 1956 (about a month after publication of *The Last Battle*) and by an Anglican priest in March 1957. Between the two ceremonies, in October 1956, doctors discovered that Joy was seriously ill with cancer and said they expected her to live only a few months longer. However, the cancer went into remission, which both regarded as a miracle, and she and Lewis spent three very happy years together before the cancer returned. Joy died in July 1960, at the age of forty-five, the same age Lewis's mother had been when she died of cancer fifty-two years before.

At the time of Joy's death, Lewis himself was in poor health. He had suffered from osteoporosis since the late 1950s, and a kidney infection pre-vented him from teaching in the fall of 1961. His health improved in 1962 and the first half of 1963, but he suffered a heart attack on 15 July 1963 and was so near death that last rites were administered. However, he recovered and in August returned home. Despite his poor health, his interest in the future of the Chronicles continued. On 20 November 1963 he received a visit from Kaye Webb, editor of Puffin Books, which had at that point brought out paperback editions of the first three Chronicles. Lewis prom-ised her "to re-edit the books (connect the things that didn't tie up)." Those revisions were never made. Lewis died two days later, on 22 November, the same day as author Aldous Huxley and President John Fitzgerald Kennedy.

Chapter 2

Controversies over Texts
and Reading Order

The series was not planned beforehand. . . . So perhaps it does not matter very much in which order anyone reads them. I'm not even sure that all the [books] were written in the same order in which they were published. I never keep notes of that sort of thing and never remember dates.

A t the time of Lewis's death, the Chronicles were gaining in popularity and selling briskly. In Britain a paperback edition was being released, and in the United States a paperback edition would be published two years later. It must have seemed unlikely that books as acclaimed and beloved as the Chronicles would become the subject of controversy. But that has turned out to be the case: some recent editorial decisions about publishing them have been contested vigorously. This chapter examines conflicts involving textual editing of the Chronicles and the currently suggested order for reading them.

Originally, the Chronicles were published in two editions. One was a clothbound edition produced in Britain and sold throughout the English-speaking world except in the United States. The first five books were issued by Geoffrey Bles, the last two by The Bodley Head. Legal regulations then in effect required that books sold in the United States be typeset in this country. Thus, a second edition of the Chronicles appeared, clothbound books published by Macmillan, very close to the British edition, but with some significant differences.

First, there were some textual revisions. Because of the new typesetting, Lewis had to correct a second set of proofs. As he did, he made some changes — mostly minor corrections, but also a few significant revisions, especially in *The Lion, the Witch and the Wardrobe* and *The Voyage of the "Dawn Treader."* Lewis could have — perhaps should have — made those changes in later printings of the British edition and brought the two into conformity; but he didn't. Thus, British readers were told that Eustace, in *The Voyage of the "Dawn Treader,"* was "far too stupid to make anything up himself," while readers in the United States, until 1994, were told that he was "quite incapable of making anything up himself."

British and U.S. editions were brought into conformity in the 1990s, but in a way that has proved controversial. HarperCollins, which held publication rights outside the United States, secured publication rights within the U.S. as well, and in 1994 issued a uniform worldwide edition of the seven Chronicles. If you buy new copies of the Chronicles today, this is the edition you are purchasing. The controversial aspect is that this edition does not use the revised United States versions but goes back to the initial British texts. Standard editorial practice, followed in most cases when a text is reissued, incorporates an author's corrections and revisions. An authoritative edition usually seeks to embody an author's latest thoughts, except when it deliberately and explicitly reproduces the first version of a work in order to bring out contrasts with the later changes. The 1994 edition of the Chronicles goes against such principles, relying on the earliest text even though there is broad agreement among scholars that most of the revisions are improvements. In this book, the significant changes Lewis made in the Macmillan edition are described and discussed in the Annotations section (pages 121-62).

Another difference between the British and the Macmillan editions appears in the illustrations. Each of the original British clothbound books contains at least 34 (up to 46) pen-and-ink illustrations by Pauline Baynes, plus full-page color frontispieces in *The Lion, the Witch and the Wardrobe* and *Prince Caspian,* and maps in *Prince Caspian, The Voyage of the "Dawn Treader," The Silver Chair,* and *The Horse and His Boy.* The experiencing of a children's book is significantly affected by the illustrations, especially when children first encounter the books by hearing a parent or teacher read them aloud.

These children "read" the illustrations, which are an integral part of the text, before they read the words. The illustrations not only establish specific visual images but also shape the way the entire story will be imagined. Thus, to read an edition with fewer or different illustrations is in fact to read a different work. The original Macmillan clothbound edition of the Chronicles omitted many of the illustrations (in some books almost half of them); this edition, as a result, is significantly different from the British edition in ways that most readers in the U.S. were not even aware of.

A paperback reprint of the seven books was issued in Britain between 1959 and 1965 as Puffin books, published by Penguin. They contain the full texts of the first British editions and all the illustrations and maps except the frontispieces for *The Lion, the Witch and the Wardrobe* and *Prince Caspian,* the end-paper map for *The Voyage of the "Dawn Treader,"* and four full-page plates in *The Horse and His Boy.* A paperback reprint in the United States was published in 1970 by Collier Books, a division of Macmillan, but it was much less satisfactory. It reprinted the texts of the Macmillan edition, but it included only one illustration per chapter and none of the frontispieces or the end-paper maps. While the British paperback of *The Lion, the Witch and the Wardrobe* had 43 illustrations, the Collier paperback had 17. Eight of those 17 were cropped versions of the originals (the loss of details of the interior of the Beavers' house is particularly sad), and four of the 17 were the result of dividing two original full-page drawings in half. Thus, millions of readers in the United States (myself included), as we used the Collier texts, had severely impoverished reading experiences compared to readers of copies published in Britain.

A larger controversy has emerged concerning the order in which the books should be read. For those who read the Chronicles in the 1950s as each book appeared, one per year from 1950 to 1956, there was only one order in which to read and experience them — the order of publication. Most reprintings of the books in the 1960s, 1970s, and 1980s numbered them in that order:

1. *The Lion, the Witch and the Wardrobe: A Story for Children*
2. *Prince Caspian: The Return to Narnia*
3. *The Voyage of the "Dawn Treader"*

4. *The Silver Chair*
5. *The Horse and His Boy*
6. *The Magician's Nephew*
7. *The Last Battle: A Story for Children*

So they were listed in the Geoffrey Bles and Bodley Head editions in Britain and the Macmillan editions in the United States once *The Last Battle* was completed, as well as in the later Collins clothbound reprints in Britain, the Puffin paperback edition in Britain until the mid-1970s, and the Collier paperback edition in the United States until the mid-1980s.

At the same time, quiet but persistent voices began urging that they be renumbered in the order in which events occur in the stories (or nearly so: the events of *The Horse and His Boy* actually occur during, not after, those of *The Lion, the Witch and the Wardrobe*):

1. *The Magician's Nephew*
2. *The Lion, the Witch and the Wardrobe*
3. *The Horse and His Boy*
4. *Prince Caspian*
5. *The Voyage of the "Dawn Treader"*
6. *The Silver Chair*
7. *The Last Battle*

The uniform, worldwide edition of 1994 is numbered in this order. People who purchase new copies of the Chronicles now may never become aware that *The Magician's Nephew* was not always treated as Book 1 and that there is an alternative order for reading the series, one which produces quite different imaginative effects, especially the first time one reads the series. (The order for rereading the books does not matter much, once the strategies for initial reading have been encountered.) In the rest of this chapter I will consider how the new ordering developed and compare the effects of the different orderings.

The first time the stories were published with the new numbering was the set of "Fontana Lions" issued by Collins in 1980. Lewis biographer Walter Hooper asserts that "for the first time the books were given the order

Lewis said they should be read in." They were listed in that order several years earlier, opposite the title page of the Puffin paperback edition of *Prince Caspian*. The earliest I have seen is a 1974 reprint, with this intriguing heading: "All seven stories of Narnia are published in Puffins, and the correct reading order is. . . ." Other Puffin reprints of *Prince Caspian* from the mid-1970s on list this ordering, but without the explanatory statement. What does "correct" mean here? Correct by what criteria? The 1994 uniform edition includes the following statement on the copyright page: "The HarperCollins editions of The Chronicles of Narnia have been renumbered in compliance with the original wishes of the author, C. S. Lewis." Again the wording is puzzling. Why "original wishes"? Does "original" mean from the time at which *The Magician's Nephew* was completed? If so, why did Lewis not request The Bodley Head to include this renumbering in the new book, or in *The Last Battle* the following year, or have Geoffrey Bles change the order in later reprints of the other books? If it had been a matter of importance to Lewis, surely his publishers would have complied with his wishes, or included the renumbering in the paperback editions that appeared a few years later. Thus any strong evidence that these were deeply held wishes of the author is missing.

Lewis gave qualified approval to the chronological arrangement in a letter to a young boy, Laurence Krieg, dated 23 April 1957. Laurence believed, after publication of *The Magician's Nephew*, that it should be read first, but his mother thought the books should continue to be read in order of publication. Laurence wrote to Lewis asking whether he or his mother was right. Lewis replied, "I think I agree with your order for reading the books more than with your mother's. . . . [But] perhaps it does not matter very much in which order anyone reads them." Walter Hooper reports that Lewis had him take out his notebook and that he dictated to Hooper "the order in which the stories should be read [beginning with *The Magician's Nephew*]." But Lewis himself said that an author "is not necessarily the best, and is never a perfect, judge" of a book's meaning or effect. Note that Lewis, despite expressing agreement with Laurence, does not say this is the *correct* order for reading them. When he says, "perhaps it does not matter very much," he probably means that more than one order, or perhaps any order, is acceptable to him for reading the Chronicles. If, however, he is suggesting that the order doesn't make any difference to the reading experience, then he is simply mistaken. In that sense, the order of reading matters a great deal. Considered in terms of the imaginative reading experience, the new arrangement deprives readers of effects Lewis worked carefully to achieve.

The only reason for putting *The Magician's Nephew* first is to have readers encounter events in chronological order, and that, as every storyteller knows, is quite unimportant as a reason. Often the early events in a sequence have a greater impact or effect as a flashback, told after later events that provide background and establish perspective. Beginning a story *in medias res* — "in the middle of things" — is one of the oldest and most basic of narrative strategies, going back at least to the *Iliad* and the *Odyssey*, two of the earliest stories in the Western literary tradition. Lewis had used it before in *Perelandra* and would use it later in *Prince Caspian* and in *Till We Have Faces*.

To read one of the other books before *The Lion, the Witch and the Wardrobe* sacrifices strategies used by Lewis to lead readers into the world of Narnia and to help them share imaginatively in the experiences of Lucy and, later, the other Pevensie children as they discover what that world is like. Consider, for example, how the careful use of details enables readers to share Lucy's experience as she enters Narnia for the first time. In an ordinary-seeming house in the country, Lucy steps into an ordinary-seeming wardrobe, to smell and feel the long fur coats hanging in it. The vivid details enable readers to share Lucy's experience as she reaches ahead into the darkness of the wardrobe, hears a crunching underfoot, feels the cold snow and the prickliness of the trees, and glimpses the light of the lamppost ahead of her. Readers share her bewilderment and uncertainty about where she is and what she has gotten into, and her surprise as she hears footsteps and comes face to face with not another human, but a creature which, though having the body of a man from the waist upwards, has legs shaped like a goat's, goat's hoofs, two horns, and a tail.

The careful introduction continues with the first mention of the name *Narnia* and the initial reference to Aslan. Tumnus the faun asks Lucy how she came into Narnia, and Lucy in turn asks what readers also want to know: "Narnia? What's that?" Tumnus replies, "This is the land of Narnia,

. . . where we are now; all that lies between the lamp-post and the great castle of Cair Paravel on the eastern sea." Readers will want and need to know more, of course, but for now they have been supplied the necessary basic information and given adequate orientation. Mr. Beaver makes the first reference to Aslan when he meets the children in the woods: "They say Aslan is on the move — perhaps has already landed." The following sentence is very important to the imaginative experience of reading the book for the first time: "None of the children knew who Aslan was any more than you do; but the moment the Beaver had spoken these words everyone felt quite different." In a long paragraph that follows, Lewis sought directly and intentionally to help readers share imaginatively the Pevensie children's experience as each feels "something jump in his inside." For readers fully to participate imaginatively in this paragraph, to feel something mysterious jump "inside," requires that it be the first book in the series to be read. Readers experience the power of Aslan's name but — like the Pevensie children — are left to wonder who and what this person is. The wondering and the eventual discovery form one of the great pleasures of reading the story. The fact that Lewis wrote other books later, including a book describing events prior to these, does not change the artistic strategy of this passage.

The imaginative experience of the opening sentences of *The Magician's Nephew* is very different: "This is a story about something that happened long ago when your grandfather was a child. It is a very important story because it shows how all the comings and goings between our own world and the land of Narnia first began." For those who have previously read *The Lion, the Witch and the Wardrobe,* this evokes immediate recognition: *Narnia* itself immediately connects readers with their earlier imaginative experiences and awakens a flood of memories. The word will not be used again in *The Magician's Nephew* until Chapter 9, but that doesn't matter: knowing that this story will connect with earlier ones engages readers' imaginations and emotions and evokes their eager and watchful anticipation.

The opening sentence takes for granted knowledge of things that those who come to *The Magician's Nephew* first don't have. Reading this story first leaves readers asking, What comings and goings? What is the land of Narnia? Neither question is answered in the opening chapter or indeed in the first half of the book. Instead, the second paragraph abruptly shifts to a different story, one set in London and the land of Charn.

The word *Narnia* does not reappear until the final lines of Chapter 9: "Narnia, Narnia, Narnia, awake. Love. Think. Speak. Be walking trees. Be talking beasts. Be divine waters." Consider the difference in the imaginative experiencing of these words for those who are reading this book first, and those who have previously read one or more of the other Chronicles. If *The Magician's Nephew* is read first, the account of the creation of Narnia is a beautiful, powerful story, told in vivid detail. It draws readers into the events and enables them to experience the excitement, emotions, mystery, and magic of what is occurring. For a lion to bring a new world into being and breathe life into it is something readers will never forget. And yet the imaginative experience is limited because the world being created has at that point no meaning for them. "Narnia" is merely a name. It lacks the experiential context that readers who have read other Chronicles bring to the chapter. The many rich memories, emotions, and associations from other stories intensify the significance of Narnia's creation much more than is possible for those who begin with *The Magician's Nephew.*

Readers who have shared with Lucy the mysterious experience of encountering a lamppost unaccountably placed in the middle of a forest have the pleasure, upon seeing the lamppost grow in *The Magician's Nephew,* of recognition: "Oh! That's how the lamppost got there!" (For those who watch the birth of the lamppost before reading *The Lion, the Witch and the Wardrobe,* there is no mystery about it when they encounter it with Lucy, and mystery is crucial to the fairy-tale genre.) Likewise, readers who have already encountered the White Witch in *The Lion, the Witch and the Wardrobe* experience surprise and recognition in *The Magician's Nephew* as they gradually figure out who Jadis is and realize the long-term significance of the events in Charn. Readers who were first introduced to Aslan in *The Lion, the Witch and the Wardrobe* experience the thrill of recognition as the lion comes into view, and perhaps the pleasure of accurate anticipation if they guess that the voice is Aslan's before he comes into view or before his name is mentioned. The fullest imaginative experiencing of *The Magician's Nephew* comes through reading it as a flashback, for that is the way Lewis thought of it as he wrote it, and those are the narrative strategies he consciously or unconsciously built into it. Thus, there is no introduction to Aslan in *The Magician's Nephew*, no explanation that he is the king of the wood or the son of the great Emperor-Beyond-the-Sea; there was no need for it — Lewis expected readers to know all that already from earlier books.

In one sense, then, as Lewis said, the order in which the Chronicles are read doesn't really matter, but it unquestionably does make a difference — which he didn't acknowledge, and perhaps didn't recognize fully. The decision to renumber and rearrange the Chronicles in current editions may or may not be considered unfortunate. But it is definitely unfortunate that the publishers do not disclose that a different arrangement existed in earlier versions, that it remains an alternative order for reading the books, and that it is preferred by a number of Lewis scholars. Principles of textual editing, past and present, call for signaling textual variants so readers can evaluate the difference the variants make, and perhaps choose between the alternative readings. Failure to indicate variants — of wording within the texts and of the numbering of the books — has the regrettable effects of wiping out the past and imposing a single, "authoritative" reading upon the Chronicles. It is a decision that detracts from — not enhances — recognition and appreciation of the artistry and meaning of Lewis's best-known books.

The Chronicles
as Fairy Tales

Chapter 3

The Storytelling:
Fairy Tale, Fantasy, and Myth

I wrote fairy tales because the Fairy Tale seemed the ideal Form for the stuff I had to say.

In *A Preface to "Paradise Lost"* Lewis asserts that "the first qualification for judging any piece of workmanship from a corkscrew to a cathedral is to know *what* it is — what it was intended to do and how it is meant to be used." As we consider what is most useful to bring to the Chronicles of Narnia in order to enter into and richly appreciate them, it is wise to begin by giving attention to the kind of literature they are, and to the influence on that form of Lewis's close friend J. R. R. Tolkien.

Fairy Tales

Lewis says that the origin of the Chronicles goes back to mental images. "All my seven Narnian books," he wrote in an essay, "and my three science fiction books, began with seeing pictures in my head. At first they were not a story, just pictures. The *Lion* all began with a picture of a Faun carrying an umbrella and parcels in a snowy wood. This picture had been in my mind since I was about sixteen. Then one day, when I was about forty, I said to myself: 'Let's try to make a story about it.'" He started not with a sense of narrative or a narrative form, but with deeply felt visual images he found intriguing. Only then did he begin to make an effort to place them in a narrative context.

It isn't clear when he first tried to turn the image of a faun into a story, even though he says "when I was about forty." Perhaps he was referring to a paragraph written on the back of the manuscript of another story, *The Dark Tower*:

> This book is about four children whose names were Ann, Martin, Rose and Peter. But it is mostly about Peter who was the youngest. They all had to go away from London suddenly because of the Air Raids, and because Father, who was in the army, had gone off to the war and Mother was doing some kind of war work. They were sent to stay with a relation of Mother's who was a very old Professor who lived by himself in the country.

The date of the *Dark Tower* manuscript is disputed — it was written perhaps in late 1939 (when Lewis had turned forty) or perhaps in the mid-1940s. In either case, Lewis went no further then, maybe because he found himself too busy, but probably because the right form for the story had not yet occurred to him. Lewis elsewhere notes that a story requires both ideas and a form:

> In the Author's mind there bubbles up every now and then the material for a story. For me it invariably begins with mental pictures. This ferment leads to nothing unless it is accompanied with the longing for a Form: verse or prose, short story, novel, play or what not. When these two things click you have the Author's impulse complete.

Initially he had an idea but not a form.

The images apparently remained in his mind, and he returned to them later. In August 1948 Lewis told his friend Chad Walsh that he was working on a children's book, and that the right form had finally come to him: the fairy tale. Describing the development of *The Lion, the Witch and the Wardrobe*, Lewis wrote,

> Everything began with images: a faun carrying an umbrella, a queen on a sledge, a magnificent lion.... As these images sorted themselves into

events (i.e., became a story) they seemed to demand no love interest and no close psychology. But the Form which excludes these things is the fairy tale. And the moment I thought of that I fell in love with the Form itself: its brevity, its severe restraints on description, its flexible traditionalism, its inflexible hostility to all analysis, digression, reflections and "gas." I was now enamoured of it.

Lewis's account is interesting and helpful, but it oversimplifies. Why did the form come to him in the late 1940s though it hadn't come earlier? What occurred in the interim that made the fairy tale seem the right form now?

Such a question cannot be answered with certainty, but a probable answer is the influence of J. R. R. Tolkien's ideas about fairy tales. In 1939 Tolkien used fairy stories — which he called "one of the highest forms of literature" — as the topic of the Andrew Lang Lecture he delivered at the University of St. Andrews in Scotland. The points Tolkien raised in that lecture have become central to the study of fairy tales and fantasy literature. There is no direct evidence that Lewis read Tolkien's lecture then, though it is difficult to believe that Tolkien would not have at least discussed with Lewis what he was going to say.

What is certain, however, is that Lewis came to know Tolkien's ideas well a few years later. In 1944 Lewis began gathering and editing a collection of essays intended to be presented to his friend Charles Williams when he and the rest of the Oxford University Press staff returned to London. The OUP offices had been moved to Oxford in 1939 for safety, and now, as the end of World War II approached, they were preparing to return. Before the volume could be completed, however, Williams died unexpectedly on 15 May 1945. The book then became a memorial volume, published in November 1947, and one of the essays in it is an expanded version of Tolkien's lecture entitled "On Fairy-Stories." The thorough familiarity with Tolkien's ideas that Lewis gained as he edited the essay surely helped him to become "enamoured" of the form and to bring it to mind when he returned to those mental images in or around 1948. Looking at the central points of that essay can help us gain a clearer understanding of the qualities Lewis embodied in the Chronicles.

It is important to understand, first, that Tolkien — and Lewis — did not mean by "fairy story" a short work of fiction about fairies. Rather, a fairy story is one that takes place in the realm of Faërie, an enchanted world, Fairy-land, a place that creates a sense of marvel and mystery by describing things that are beyond an explanation from nature. Such a world is epitomized for Lewis in one of his favorite poems, Edmund Spenser's romantic epic *The Faerie Queene*. The poem is set in a world that seems initially ordinary and everyday, but soon is revealed to be a magical realm, one where the hero meets creatures that are mythical in our world — elves, dragons, giants, enchanters, enchantresses, satyrs, nymphs, hamadryads, and naiads. In calling the Chronicles fairy tales, Lewis asserts that Narnia, like the world of Spenser's poem, is Faërie-land, an enchanted and enchanting place, full of adventure, mystery, wonder, and excitement.

A key point of Tolkien's essay that Lewis came to accept fully is that fairy stories are not intended for children. Because some adults prefer realistic fiction over fairy stories, they regard the latter as "children's literature," since children are supposedly naïve enough to enjoy stories dealing with creatures that are "unbelievable" or "untrue." But Tolkien argues that fairy stories are not literature just for children. Not all children enjoy them, and enjoyment of them is not limited to children. Some adults and some children have the taste for fairy stories; other adults and children do not. It is a taste that increases, not decreases, with age, and some adults develop a love of fairy stories only later in life. Thus, to determine the appeal and effect of fairy stories, we must look further than taking advantage of children's innocence and credulity.

Tolkien asserts further that the appeal of fairy stories lies chiefly in their ability to awaken and at least partially to satisfy a sense of longing, a longing inherent in the nature of Faërie itself. It is a "primal desire" to get outside the world of everyday experience, a desire to fly, to communicate with animals, to meet living things not present in our world. It is a desire for an Other-world, a world richer and more resonant than the world of everyday experience. Lewis, taking Tolkien's point further, says that the desire for an enchanted Other-world is in fact a longing for a spiritual Other-world, a "desire for our own far-off country," as he put it in his 1941 sermon "The Weight of Glory." In longing for elves, dragons, and the realm of Faërie, we are actually longing for God and the heavenly realm.

The heart of Tolkien's essay is his lengthy discussion of four qualities (he calls them "values and functions") that characterize fairy stories: Fantasy (to be discussed in the next section), Escape, Recovery, and Consolation.

Fairy tale and fantasy are often dismissed by "realistic" critics as escapist literature, valued by readers who, unable or unwilling to deal with aspects of everyday life, "escape" to made-up worlds. Tolkien denies that accusation emphatically. While "realists" tend to equate the "real world" with material objects and our experiencing of them, Tolkien, in contrast, calls that world a "prison." Who, he says, would not want to escape from "the noise, stench, ruthlessness, and aimlessness of the internal-combustion engine" and from "hunger, thirst, poverty, pain, sorrow, injustice, [and] death"? He explains "escape" not as cowardly but as heroic, not as deserting one's true home but as gaining freedom from an internment camp that prevents one from reaching home. Children and adults who read fairy stories do so in part in order to travel to realms where their deep desires find fulfillment, especially the deepest desire of all, to escape from death — or from the fear of death. As Frederick Buechner puts it, "Good and evil meet and do battle in the fairy-tale world much as they meet and do battle in our world, but in fairy tales the good live happily ever after. That is the major difference."

Fairy stories appeal to some adults and some children because the escape gained through fairy stories enables them to recover, or regain, a clear view of life, and to recover realities not recognized by those who limit reality to material objects. Fairy stories enable such readers to see things in the everyday world as they were meant to be seen, freed of the "drab blur of triteness or familiarity." We become so familiar with, so close to the people and things that surround us that we no longer really see them. We take them for granted, or accept deficiencies as inevitable, or cease to appreciate fully the beauty or richness of things and people. Tolkien says that spending time in an Other-world enables us as we return to see the everyday world renewed, noticing new mystery and complexity in creatures and objects we were taking for granted.

Escape and Recovery lead into the ultimate value of fairy stories: the Consolation afforded by a happy ending. "Ending," however, might not be the best word. Fairy stories, says Tolkien, have no true ending, but are always characterized by a "joyous 'turn,'" produced by a "sudden and miraculous grace." It is the nature of tragedy to result in a catastrophe; it is the nature of fairy stories to end in what Tolkien named *Eucatastrophe*, the good catastrophe. "The *eucatastrophic* tale is the true form of fairy-tale, and its highest function," he asserts. The presence of *Eucatastrophe* does not deny the existence of sorrow and failure. Rather, it denies universal final defeat and relates to what we said above about desire. In its denial of defeat it offers a basis for hope and is an instance of *evangelium*, of good news, "giving a fleeting glimpse of Joy, Joy beyond the walls of the world." A fairy story is not "untrue": "the peculiar quality of the 'joy' in successful Fantasy can thus be explained as a sudden glimpse of the underlying reality or truth" on which the fairy story is constructed. It shows us "a far-off gleam or echo of *evangelium*" in an imaginary world and helps us recover that gleam in the everyday world we inhabit.

Lewis nowhere says that in calling the Chronicles of Narnia fairy tales he has in mind the same characteristics Tolkien described in his essay. But as we look at each of the Chronicles individually in Chapters 4 through 10, we will find exactly the qualities just discussed: the stories take place in a Fairy-land, an enchanted Other-world; they appeal to both children and adults, but only those who love and desire such realms; they arouse and partially satisfy desire, specifically the longing for another world; they are characterized by both strangeness and wonder; they afford escape from the dreariness and everydayness of the "real world"; they lead to a sense of recovery, enabling us as we re-enter our own world to see it in fresh, more vivid ways; and they, both individual stories and the series as a whole, have eucatastrophic turns that offer a fleeting glimpse of Joy beyond the walls of our own world.

Fantasy

Integral to the three characteristics of fairy stories discussed above is Fantasy, which is of such importance to the works of Lewis and Tolkien that it deserves separate, detailed attention. One of the reasons Lewis was able finally to complete *The Lion, the Witch and the Wardrobe* in the late 1940s is the influence of a fairy tale, *The Wood that Time Forgot,* by a student at Oxford, Roger Lancelyn Green, that Lewis read in manuscript in 1945. He praised the story highly to Green and suggested a number of revisions. Lewis, who was famous for his retentive memory, very likely absorbed Green's descriptions of three children who pass through a tunnel into a wood in an Other-world, of a superhuman evil figure with magical powers, and of a sweet raspberry drink that tempts one of the children to join with him, until eventually they proved a spur to his own imagination. Green's fantasy world enabled Lewis to bring his own Other-world to life in a rich and compelling way.

At the heart of the desire raised by Faërie, Tolkien says, is the making or glimpsing of Other-worlds. Tolkien uses the word *Fantasy* not as the name of a literary genre or type, but to describe a quality inherent in the fairy-tale form. That quality involves both fantasy as fantasizing, as *invention* of the sort that gives free play to the mind's power to create images that are at odds with the world we know (a green sun is one of Tolkien's examples), and also fantasy as the *aura* that pervades the world of Faërie, an aura of both "strangeness" (strikingly different from the world of everyday experience) and "wonder" (that is, awe, reverence, or fear caused by the presence of something majestic, sublime, or sacred). Other-worlds of the kind Tolkien (and Lewis) especially enjoyed were ones that awaken and satisfy an acknowledged or unrecognized spiritual desire, ones that have a numinous quality and a spiritual or even mystical effect on the reader.

Tolkien calls Other-worlds "Secondary Worlds," in contrast to the "Primary World" in which we live our daily lives (he and Lewis avoided calling ours the "real" world). A Secondary World may have natural laws different from those of our world, but once those laws are established, they must be adhered to — if they are ignored or violated, the effect of the story will be broken. In the words of George MacDonald, the nineteenth-century Scottish preacher and story writer whom Lewis called his "teacher," man may, if he pleases, invent a little world of his own, with its own laws; for there is that in him which delights in calling up new forms — which is the nearest, perhaps, he can come to creation. . . . His world once invented, the highest law that comes next into play is, that there shall be harmony between the laws by which the new world has begun to exist; and in the process of his creation, the inventor must hold by those laws. The moment he forgets one of them, he makes the story, by its own postulates, incredible.

Tolkien calls the invention of a fantasy world an act of "sub-creation." Humans, made in God's image, have a creative bent akin to that of God. Making an Other-world — a subcreation — is, according to Tolkien, more difficult to do well than writing realistic fiction, and when it is achieved well he considers it the most potent and nearly pure mode of story-making, a higher form of art than realistic fiction.

Tolkien uses the contrast between Primary World and Secondary World to discuss the degree of believability we extend to each. If a Secondary World is so well created in its use of detail and inner consistency that it creates a spell of enchantment, readers can enter that world imaginatively and, while they are inside it, believe in its "truth" or reality the same way they believe in the truth and reality of the Primary World (Tolkien calls the latter "Primary Belief" and the former "Secondary Belief"). If the spell is broken, by an inconsistency in the fantasy world or by the intrusion of the Primary World into the Secondary World, readers will find themselves plunged back into the Primary World, no longer able to give unqualified belief to the Secondary World. It is possible to re-enter the Secondary World after the spell has been broken, but not to re-enter the spell. In that case, instead of *believing*, we must *set aside our disbelief*, engage in what Samuel Taylor Coleridge in 1817 called "that willing suspension of disbelief for the moment." As Tolkien puts it, "This suspension of disbelief is a substitute for the genuine thing [Secondary Belief], a subterfuge we use . . . when trying . . . to find what virtue we can in the work of an art that has for us failed."

The appeal of fantasy, for those who experience Secondary Belief, seems to be an extension of the primal desire discussed above. Embedded in most human beings, Tolkien believes, is a primordial desire to "survey the depths of space and time" and to "hold communion with other living things." Lewis said something similar in *An Experiment in Criticism*. Each of us seeks "an enlargement of our being. We want to be more than ourselves. . . . We want to see with other eyes, to imagine with other imaginations, to feel with other hearts, as well as with our own." That is what all stories (and plays and poems) enable readers to do: to get out of ourselves and our limited perspectives, to participate imaginatively in other lives and other places. Fantasy goes a step further, enabling readers to get outside the Primary World, to survey the depths of Other-worlds, and see through the eyes and feel with the hearts of living beings totally different from those in our world.

But Tolkien reminds us that the point is not just getting out (escape), but returning (recovery). As we return from a Secondary World, we see new things in the Primary World, and we see old things in new ways. Some of the enchantment and glory of the Secondary World returns with us and illuminates the Primary World. Lewis described such an experience after he read MacDonald's *Phantastes: A Faerie Romance* when he was sixteen or seventeen: "I saw the bright shadow coming out of the book into the real world and resting there, transforming all common things and yet itself unchanged. Or, more accurately, I saw the common things drawn into the bright shadow." That, for readers who love fantasy, describes its power and appeal: to take us to new worlds, yes, but also to bring us back from them transformed by that journey into a world that also seems transformed by what we have experienced outside it.

The Chronicles appeal as fantasy in part because of the Secondary World Lewis creates in them. Narnia is a pastoral paradise, incorporating features of the Carlingford Mountains of Ireland, which Lewis considered the loveliest countryside he had ever seen. Narnia is a land of grassy slopes, heathery mountains, plashy glens, mossy caverns, and deep forests, unspoiled by the side effects of urbanization and industrialization. It is a world that many readers are able to enter through Secondary Belief and to live in imaginatively. The Chronicles as fantasy enlarge our being by taking us out of the Primary World and enabling us to see it in new ways as we look back at it from Narnia and as we re-enter it after being in Narnia. The Chronicles do for many readers what *Phantastes* did for Lewis: baptize their imaginations. Readers encounter in Narnia a bright shadow, a divine aura, a world aglow with a divine spirit, that continues with them as they return to our world and find it transformed by that radiance.

Myth

An additional factor that contributed to the success of the Chronicles was the emergence of the great lion, Aslan. In January and February 1949, besieged by problems at home, Lewis had a series of dreams that added a deeper dimension to the narrative: "I had very little idea how the story would go," Lewis recalls; "but then suddenly Aslan came bounding into it. I think I had been having a good many dreams of lions about that time. Apart from that, I don't know where the Lion came from or why He came. But once He was there He pulled the whole story together." As he pulled the narrative together, he also brought a mythical dimension into it.

In the field of literature, *myth* usually does not mean a "fictitious story, or unscientific account, theory, belief, etc." (literary critics do not dismiss something as just a myth). Instead, to Lewis and Tolkien, myths deal with matters beyond and above everyday life, concerning origins, endings, aspirations, purpose, and meaning, in conceptions or narratives that appeal to the imagination and the emotions rather than the intellect. They are nonrational and nonintellectual, not irrational or anti-intellectual. Thus Tolkien says that myth has a "total (unanalysable) effect." Myth, Lewis adds, "deals with impossibles and preternaturals." The experiences that myths generate are serious and awe-inspiring, conveying a sense of the numinous. Myths open huge vistas, plumb depths of the emotions and the spirit. The sheer imaginativeness of such stories, like that of much poetry, adds to life, creates sensations we never had before, and enlarges our conception of possible experience.

Myth deals, in Tolkien's phrase, with the "permanent and fundamental," not as abstract ideas or theories or "truths," but through imaginative and appealing stories. Myth conveys realities that are universal and feel inevitable to the human heart or the spirit, enabling us not to *think* about them but to *taste* them, to use Lewis's metaphor in "Myth Became Fact": In experiencing myth, he writes, you are "not knowing, but tasting." That is, "in the enjoyment of a great myth we come nearest to experiencing as a concrete what can otherwise be understood only as an abstraction." Our temptation is to try to express in nonimaginative terms what a myth "means," instead of seizing the opportunity myth offers to "taste" a reality. As Lewis puts it, "What flows into you from the myth is not truth but reality (truth is always *about* something, but reality is that *about which* truth is)."

Myths reach back to the earliest stories people told in ancient cultures, to stories of gods or heroes that have a religious or moral purpose, "panning the vein of spirit out of sense," in Tolkien's phrase. The tellers and the hearers regarded those stories as expressing reality and accepted them as real, as describing the way things are in nature, in their world as a whole, and in their world's relationship with the supernatural. That is, they could *accept* the myths as equal in reality to the physical world and as a continuation of it, extending to them the same Primary Belief they did to the Primary World.

Most people today no longer regard most ancient myths as expressing reality but accept them at best through Secondary Belief, and more often as folklore. Some people, however, continue to accept some myths — the biblical myths, for example — as reality and extend Primary Belief to them, or at least parts of them. Tolkien and Lewis regarded the New Testament stories about Jesus' birth, death, and resurrection as Reality, and accepted them with Primary Belief. In his important late-night conversation with Lewis in 1931 (see above, pp. 9-10), Tolkien convinced Lewis that "the story of Christ is simply a true myth: a myth working on us in the same way as [pagan myths], but with this tremendous difference: that *it really happened*." Lewis incorporated that idea in "Myth Became Fact": "The heart of Christianity is a myth which is also a fact. The old myth of the Dying God, *without ceasing to be myth*, comes down from the heaven of legend and imagination to the earth of history. . . . By becoming fact it does not cease to be myth: that is the miracle."

That sense of the continuing immediacy and impact of myth enabled

Tolkien and Lewis to produce stories with an unusual degree of mythical power. They created fairy tales whose mythical resonance is so deep that their effect on readers approaches Primary Belief, approaches the power and authority of ancient myths. Lewis describes writers with that ability in the preface to his anthology of writings by George MacDonald: occasionally, he says, a genius appears who can achieve one of the greatest arts, the ability to create stories that carry the power of myth. Such a story "arouses in us sensations we have never had before, . . . hits us at a level deeper than our thoughts or even our passions, troubles oldest certainties till all questions are re-opened, and in general shocks us more fully awake than we are for most of our lives." Lewis cites Kafka, Novalis, and MacDonald as examples of writers of such mythopoeic art. Today we can add Lewis and Tolkien to the list.

It is important to understand that fairy tales, fantasy, and myth are different from allegory. Many readers are inclined to call the Chronicles *allegories* and to search them for biblical parallels and "Christian meanings." But that is incompatible with what MacDonald, Tolkien, and Lewis believed about fairy tales. "A fairytale is not an allegory," MacDonald insists; "there may be allegory in it, but it is not an allegory." Tolkien says in a letter to the poet W. H. Auden that he is open to allowing appreciative readers a variety of "interpretations" in *The Lord of the Rings*, "always excepting, of course, any 'interpretations' in the mode of simple allegory: that is, the particular and topical." Lewis's views concurred with Tolkien's: "Tolkien's book is not an allegory — a form he dislikes. . . . *My* view wd be that a good myth (i.e. a story out of which ever varying meanings will grow for different readers and in different ages) is a higher thing than an allegory (into which *one* meaning has been put). Into an allegory a man can put only what he already knows: in a myth he puts what he does not yet know and cd not come to know in any other way."

An allegory is a literary form, often a narrative, in which objects, persons, and actions make sense on a literal level but also are equated in a sustained way with things or meanings that lie outside the story, things or meanings of deeper significance than those in the literal story. The problem in approaching MacDonald, Tolkien, and Lewis in this way is clear: to read a fairy tale as an allegory, one must repeatedly leave the Secondary

World in order to identify the parallel in the Primary World. The fairy tale could not then function as faërie: the spell would be broken.

Today many readers come to the Chronicles aware that they have Christian overtones, and they are tempted to look for one-to-one parallels between characters, objects, and events in Narnia and corresponding ones in the Bible. However, that is not the way Lewis wanted the Chronicles to be read. "You are mistaken when you think that everything in the books 'represents' something in this world," he wrote to a fifth-grade class in Maryland. "Things do that in *The Pilgrim's Progress* but I'm not writing in that way. I did not say to myself 'Let us represent Jesus as He really is in our world by a Lion in Narnia': I said, 'Let us *suppose* that there were a land like Narnia and that the Son of God, as He became a Man in our world, became a Lion there, and then imagine what would happen.' If you think about it, you will see that it is quite a different thing." In another letter a few years later, he explained that he was using not allegory but "supposition."

The Chronicles do definitely contain Christian meanings, but Lewis intended that readers stay within the story and absorb broad patterns of meaning, not move in and out of the story seeking "allegorical" parallels. Doing so violates the principle of the independence of fantasy worlds upon which the stories' full effect depends. In the chapters that follow, I point out broad patterns of Christian meaning that Lewis wove mythically into his stories, along with other thematic patterns that for him were nearly as important as the religious ones. Those thematic patterns can best be recognized when the Chronicles are approached as fairy tales: that is the starting point for understanding and enjoying the books fully, and for allowing them to appeal to and work upon the imagination and the emotions. "We spoil countless precious things by intellectual greed," MacDonald wrote as part of his protest against allegorizing. "The best way with music [and with a fairy tale is] . . . to be still and let it work on that part of us for whose sake it exists."

Lewis quoted Roger Lancelyn Green as once saying that the reading of Rider Haggard romances was to many people a "sort of religious experience." Lewis agreed, but qualified the statement: "It would have been safer to say that such people had first met in Haggard's romances elements which they would meet again in religious experience if they ever came to have any." That is, fairy stories, fantasy, myth, and religious experience all create a powerful imaginative and emotional appeal, a sense of wonder and longing, that can be satisfied only by something beyond the realm of this world. That, for many people, is the effect they experience as they read the Chronicles of Narnia.

Chapter 4

Magic and Meaning in
The Lion, the Witch and the Wardrobe

When I say "magic" I am not thinking of the paltry and pathetic techniques by which fools attempt and quacks pretend to control Nature. I mean rather what is suggested by fairy-tale sentences like: "This is a magic flower, and if you carry it the seven gates will open to you of their own accord."

"Faërie," says Tolkien, "may perhaps most nearly be translated by Magic — but it is magic of a peculiar mood and power, at the furthest pole from the vulgar devices of the laborious, scientific magician." There are magicians in Fairy-land, a land full of enchantments of various sorts; but there is also the magic of the storyteller, the magic that "produces a Secondary World into which both designer and spectator can enter." Magic of both types lies at the center of *The Lion, the Witch and the Wardrobe*, permeating its world and words and unifying its events and images, attitudes and atmosphere, method and meaning.

The story's first words are "once there were," a paraphrase of the typical fairy tale's opening "Once upon a time." However, this story doesn't begin in a vague never-time but in actual rock-hard reality: the Blitz of 1940-41. That profoundly influences its tone and details. For children old enough in 1950 to remember the Blitz, this was a time of great turmoil, fear, and anxiety; and if they weren't old enough to remember the Blitz, they had probably heard their parents talk about it. This "once," therefore, was a real time, a decade earlier, with bombs dropping on London and the city's children, for safety's sake, being transported to country homes (often the homes of strangers). There was certainly nothing magical or enchanting about that world, dominated as it was by fear, tyranny, oppression, and the danger of defeat and subjugation.

Within a few pages, however, the war story turns into a fairy story. From the Blitz and a strange house in our world, Lucy stumbles unexpectedly into an enchanted Other-world. In line with the way fantasy commonly makes use of something ordinary, like a door, as a portal, or entrance, to the extraordinary world beyond it, Lucy steps into an ordinary-looking wardrobe to smell and feel the fur coats in it, but finds beyond the ordinary coats something extraordinary: a different world, a strange and wonderful place beyond anything she could have imagined or dreamt of. Portals are always magic, and part of the magic of this one is that most of the time the wardrobe is just an ordinary piece of furniture. Lucy discovers later that it serves as a portal only when magic from the other world opens it and draws her and her siblings through it.

Through that portal Lucy passes without realizing it into Faërie-land, a mysterious and exciting realm that Lewis makes believable for readers through the "elvish craft," the storyteller's magic, of providing abundant detail appealing to all five senses. When Lucy hears crunching underfoot, feels snow and tree branches, and sees instead of darkness the light far off, the reader is able to share her bewilderment and uncertainty about where she is and what she has gotten into. Lewis continues to make the world she has entered real and believable by the detailed descriptions of Tumnus's cave and tea and his struggle over whether to lull Lucy to sleep and turn her over to the White Witch. The details carefully mix the familiar (European types of plants and animals, the customs and decor of Edwardian England as well as its foods and language, including its school-age slang) with the unfamiliar (animals who think and talk, mythical beings that actually exist, the lack of other humans) in order to help readers, especially young readers, adjust to and accept that world.

Its reality is ironically reinforced by the skepticism of the other children. The first to enter Narnia is the youngest and the most impressionable child. Edmund sneers at Lucy's account of what lies beyond the wardrobe, but his ridicule soon turns to realization when he follows Lucy into

Narnia and discovers that her imaginary country is not imaginary at all. The older, clear-headed realists Susan and Peter are certain that there could not be any such world beyond the wardrobe, but that certainty is shaken when the Professor exposes their logical errors and opens their minds to wider possibilities. Their doubts are thoroughly blown away when all four children enter Narnia together. If we as readers doubt the reality of Narnia, we find ourselves in the position of the three older children, sharing their discredited disbelief. The empirical evidence of watching Edmund, Peter, and Susan lose their skepticism when they enter Narnia should convince us skeptical readers as well.

The opening chapters are used to establish the atmosphere of enchantment that permeates the story. The wardrobe strikes the first note: in the words of Lucy, "It's — it's a magic wardrobe." The wardrobe's magic works next for Edmund, who encounters in Narnia a different kind of magic: a great lady in white who, by dropping a potion into the snow, produces a cup of hot drink and a box of enchanted Turkish delight. Later, a still different magic propels all four children through the wardrobe into Narnia. To keep away from the housekeeper, Mrs. Macready, and a gang of sightseers who seem to be following wherever they go, the children enter the wardrobe room and then the wardrobe itself as if "some magic in the house had come to life and was chasing them into Narnia."

Readers are almost a third of the way into the book (in the sixth of seventeen chapters) before all four children enter Narnia and the main plot can begin. This would be a slow, ineffective way to begin the second book in a series, but it is an appropriate way to start a first book, carefully establishing the credibility of the Secondary World before initiating the adventures in that world. In Chapter 6 the children set out on a mission to reach Aslan, the great lion king, in hopes of rescuing Tumnus, the faun who befriended Lucy when she first found herself in Narnia. The adventures that follow clearly occur in a Fairy-land, a world filled with wonder and magic. A robin leads them to a talking beaver who warns them against trees that are untrustworthy, that would betray them to the White Witch. They receive a warm reception and a wonderful supper at Mr. Beaver's home, and they learn about the great lion Aslan, the King of Beasts, and more about the White Witch and her magical powers.

The Fairy-land atmosphere established by the presence of magic and enchantment is confirmed by a stock element of fairy stories: the theme of good versus evil. Evil appears first in what seem to be minor ways: Edmund's snapping at one sister and putting down the other, grumbling, acting spiteful, lying, and betraying Lucy's trust. Minor though each may be individually, they reveal a disposition in Edmund that needs to be changed. Evil then appears in a much more threatening form: a witch who has enslaved Narnia and made it always winter, but without Christmas. She is a tyrant. Those who oppose her rule she executes or turns into stone, and she dominates Narnia so completely that animals like Mr. Beaver live in fear of being overheard saying something against her. (The actual historical setting of the book certainly intensified the effect of those traits for initial readers of the book, living only some five years after the defeat and death of Hitler.)

In the middle chapters Edmund moves from being a bad-tempered boy with behavior problems to being a traitor. Still under the influence of the enchanted Turkish delight, he sneaks off to the Witch's house, ready to betray his siblings to the enemy. (Here too the story would strike initial readers even more strongly than it does readers today, their minds still fresh with the memory of collaborators assisting the German cause.) He receives a frosty welcome and, instead of more Turkish delight, is fed crusts of dry bread. As Peter, Susan, and Lucy flee from the Witch with Mr. and Mrs. Beaver, Aslan's coming is signaled by the arrival of another Fairy-land figure — Father Christmas, from whom the three children receive gifts, including an enchanted horn and a magic cordial for healing. Edmund, meanwhile, travels toward the Stone Table with the White Witch. When it is clear that they cannot reach it before the others, the Witch plans to execute Edmund but is thwarted when Aslan's forces rescue him.

In Chapter 14 the book takes a new, decidedly religious direction. Until now, Aslan has been presented in the heroic terms fitting an adventure story, as the King of the Wood, the son of the great Emperor-Beyond-the-Sea. In Chapter 11, where his arrival causes winter to turn to spring, he could be assumed to be some sort of nature god appropriate to a Faërie world, the Witch's magic power being superseded by a greater power. And even in Chapter 12 when the children meet him as a powerful but benevolent king, one who is "good and terrible at the same time," his true identity is not revealed — that *Aslan* is the name for the person known in our world as Jesus the Christ, the Second Person of the Trinity. Lewis intended that connection to come as a realization, if readers recognize it at all; and he was delighted when they did not.

The basis for Christian significance in the story is laid in Chapter 13, when the Witch approaches Aslan to claim Edmund as hers. Because the Witch is the *de facto* ruler in Narnia, holding power as its Queen, she can declare that she has the right, even the obligation, to execute him: "Every traitor belongs to me as my lawful prey and . . . for every treachery I have a right to a kill." In keeping with the fairy-tale genre, Lewis has the Witch base her claim on magic — "Deep Magic from the Dawn of Time." Deep Magic is what in our world is known as the moral law, or the Law of Nature. In *Mere Christianity* Lewis calls it "the Law of Human Nature," the law or rule about right and wrong — the rules of fair play and straight dealing — that "every one [knows] by nature and [does] not need to be taught." Deep Magic, like the Law of Nature, is universal. It is written on the Stone Table, recalling the Old Testament tablets of stone with their statement of natural law, and it is carved "in letters deep as a spear is long on the trunk of the World Ash Tree," a symbol of the origin and foundation of the world in the Icelandic myths. It is of divine origin — the "Emperor's magic," "engraved on the sceptre of the Emperor-Beyond-the-Sea" — but it is not co-existent with the Emperor: it has existed only from the Dawn of Time. It was created with the universe as a power that makes moral and social order in the universe possible.

Aslan himself ranks adherence to and preservation of it very high: "'Work against the Emperor's magic?' said Aslan turning to [Susan] with something like a frown on his face. And nobody ever made that suggestion to him again." In Narnia as on Earth, undermining the law will lead to chaos: "Unless I have blood as the Law says," the Witch declares, "all Narnia will be overturned and perish in fire and water." What is clear in this chapter immediately is the seriousness of Edmund's treachery: it is not just a matter of bad behavior. Throughout Europe during the recent war, and through most of human history, traitors must die. By that standard, Edmund's life is forfeit.

Even to this point, however, the story has not turned specifically Christian. Deep Magic lays out a standard of expected moral and civil behavior, and the Witch's comments on it clarify the consequences of failure to live up to that standard. But the moral law itself is not the property of one religion. Only when Aslan volunteers to take Edmund's place does Christian significance emerge. Again the story treats the matter in terms of magic. Transcending Deep Magic is "Deeper Magic from *before* the Dawn of Time," a magic inherent not in created things but in their creator, the greater magic of God's grace, love, and forgiveness.

That Deep Magic appears in the story before Deeper Magic is important. Lewis had said in his radio talks that for the latter to make sense they must be considered in that order: "It is after you have realised that there is a real Moral Law, and a Power behind the law, and that you have broken that law and put yourself wrong with that Power — it is after all this, and not a moment sooner, that Christianity begins to talk." So it is too in Narnia. Readers of *The Lion, the Witch and the Wardrobe* are first made aware of the fundamental moral law — by recognizing Edmund's treachery first to Lucy and then to the others — *in order that* Aslan's death may convey its full meaning.

The account of Aslan's death is the only section of *The Lion, the Witch and the Wardrobe* that can justifiably be said to invite an allegorical reading. The willing sacrifice, the biblical tone and imagery (with its similarity to Isaiah 53:7: "He was oppressed and afflicted, yet he opened not his mouth"), and Aslan's subsequent return to life clearly associate him with Christ. Yet, even so, Aslan's death does not parallel Christ's death in the Bible as closely as "allegory" would require. Aslan's death saves all of Narnia from destruction, but he does not die to save all Narnians from their failures to keep the law: in that sense he dies only for Edmund. He dies by stabbing, not crucifixion; he is dead only overnight, not for two nights; he comes back to life, but the next morning, not on the third day. Allegory is simply not the best way to explain what Lewis is trying to achieve. Lewis himself called it not *allegorical* but *suppositional:* "The Passion and Resurrection of Aslan are the Passion and Resurrection Christ might be supposed to have had in *that* world — like those in our world but not exactly like." Using Tolkien's language, "God is the Lord, of angels, and of men — and of elves" and of talking animals. The Chronicles are about his lordship over Narnia, not over planet Earth.

From a suppositional approach, the meaning of Aslan's death should be comprehensible in terms of the Secondary World that Lewis created and not be dependent on reference to the Primary World for clarity or effect. The general meaning of Aslan's death is very similar to the meaning of the death of Christ in our world, but one does not need to know or refer to the biblical account of Christ to gain that meaning. The story itself, by its structural movement from Deep Magic to Deeper Magic, from catastrophe to eucatastrophe, conveys the magic of grace. Aslan does not "stand for" Christ; in Lewis's suppositional world he *is* Christ. His death in Narnia is similar to his death in our world because both are examples of the myth of the dying and returning god, one that appears in many cultures. The story of Aslan's death, like the similar pagan myths, conveys truth (the need for sacrifice), but is not factual — it did not really happen. The account of Jesus' death in the Bible also is myth, conveying that same truth, but with the enormous difference, Lewis believed, that it is also fact: it really did happen.

Although Lewis asserted emphatically that he did not want his stories to be read as religious allegories, he did admit to "smuggling theology" into them. In a letter to a friend discussing *Out of the Silent Planet*, Lewis concludes, "Any amount of theology can now be smuggled into people's minds under cover of romance without their knowing it." In several instances he introduces difficult and problematical theological issues into the Chronicles. *The Lion, the Witch and the Wardrobe* includes such an issue — that of the meaning of the truth being conveyed by the myth of the dying and returning god, the meaning of sacrifice.

As he constructed the episode of Aslan's death, Lewis inevitably found himself dealing with the question "Why did Aslan die?" just as the cover story of the 12 April 2004 issue of *Time* magazine asked "Why Did Jesus Die?" The *Time* article summarized three theories of atonement: (1) the good versus evil theory: that by incarnation, death, and resurrection, Christ triumphed over Satan and rescued humanity from evil; (2) the paying-a-debt theory: Christ sacrificed himself to make amends for sins against God; and (3) the role-model theory: by his example, Christ inspires people to live in obedience to God's ways. The writers use Lewis as a contemporary reference for the third theory: "C. S. Lewis, the Christian thinker and author of the *Narnia* series . . . was not a doctrinaire exemplarist, but the lion Aslan, who stood in for Christ, was clearly a figure to be emulated."

The writers of the article definitely miss the point. *The Lion, the Witch and the Wardrobe* illustrates the second theory: Aslan gives himself to the Witch as a sacrifice to make amends for Edmund's disobedience. By focusing on that theory, Lewis takes a stronger stand than he does in *Mere Christianity*. There he acknowledges that "a good many different theories have been held as to how [Christ's death] works," but he goes on to say that the theories are less important than the fact that it does work: "We are told that Christ was killed for us, that His death has washed out our sins, and that by dying He disabled death itself. That is the formula. That is Christianity. That is what has to be believed. Any theories we build up as to how Christ's death did all this are, in my view, quite secondary."

He notes, however, that one theory is most familiar, and he clearly leans toward that one. He initially seems to dismiss it because it appears "on the face of it . . . a very silly theory," and he describes it using unfavorable language: "According to that theory God wanted to punish men for having deserted and joined the Great Rebel, but Christ volunteered to be punished instead, and so God let us off." Assuming that Christians have to believe in this theory of atonement seems to have been one of the things that hindered his acceptance of Christianity as a young man, but he admits that he has come to see it in a more positive way. "What possible point could there be in punishing an innocent person instead [of a guilty one]? None at all that I can see, if you are thinking of punishment in the police-court sense. On the other hand, if you think of a debt, there is plenty of point in a person who has some assets paying it on behalf of someone who has not."

At first glance *The Lion, the Witch and the Wardrobe* may seem to exemplify the police-court model Lewis dismissed in *Mere Christianity*. Consider the Witch's words, "For every treachery I have a right to a kill." Throughout the episode, however, Lewis uses financial images that point in a different direction: "His life is forfeit to me," the Witch continues. "His blood is my property." The terms "forfeit" and "property" are commonly used together in instances of inability to keep up payments on a mortgage. After Aslan talks to the Witch, he reports that the Witch has "renounced the claim on your brother's blood" — again, "renounce" and "claim" are associated more with business law than with criminal law. Edmund owes a debt that he cannot pay, and Aslan offers to pay it for him, "footing the bill" or helping him climb out of the hole he has fallen into, to use other metaphors Lewis included in *Mere Christianity*.

Lewis's purpose was far deeper than creating characters and situations that remind readers of persons or actions in the Bible. His aim, beyond telling a story well, was to present in a fresh way and on a level available even to children a representation of central elements of the Christian faith. He was seeking through a fairy tale to recover the crucifixion, to regain a clear view of it, to free it from the "blur of triteness or familiarity" for readers who were no longer able to experience its full potency. But the episode of Aslan's death can convey a powerful message about love and sacrifice even to readers who do not pick up on the similarity to the New Testament. The story achieves those effects by coming alive in the imaginations of readers, not by creating connections to be grasped by the intellect. Lewis believed in a deeper sense of knowing, one that comes through the language of story even more meaningfully than through conceptual language.

Aslan's death has two dramatic effects. First, it puts the law in a new perspective. At Aslan's resurrection, "the Stone Table was broken into two pieces by a great crack that ran down it from end to end," an echo of the veil in the Temple tearing as Christ died, thus changing the nature of people's relationship to God. Previously the Witch could claim that the "proper use" of the Stone Table was the execution of traitors; a broken table cannot be effective for, or symbolic of, that old use. Law by itself, in New Testament terms, inevitably leads to death; it is grace that gives life.

Second, it changes the meaning and effect of death. As Aslan romps with Susan and Lucy after his return to life, he explains that, if the White Witch had known about Deeper Magic, "she would have known that when a willing victim who had committed no treachery was killed in a traitor's stead, the Table would crack and Death itself would start working backwards." The effect of Deeper Magic, then, is to give life. The direct recipient of this life is, of course, Edmund, whose life is saved by Aslan's sacrifice. Before Aslan goes to his death, he walks apart with Edmund for a "conversation which Edmund never forgot." It apparently was not about the arrangement Aslan was soon to make with the Witch; he apparently learned about that only later. The important thing is that Edmund comes to know Aslan, and to love him.

As a result of that and of his experiences in Narnia, Edmund gets past "thinking about himself" and just goes on "looking at Aslan." Edmund's life is spared physically and healed spiritually: Lucy finds him "not only healed of his wounds but looking better than she had seen him look — oh, for ages. . . . He had become his real old self again and could look you in the face." Edmund's experiences continue to have a significant influence upon his character thereafter, one that is reflected in the name he is given later as one of the monarchs of Narnia: "Edmund was a graver and quieter man than Peter, and great in council and judgement. He was called King Edmund the Just." He who has had a personal experience with justice — and its counterpart of grace — is best able to appreciate its proper use and value.

The meaning and method of the first Chronicle of Narnia are epitomized shortly after Aslan's resurrection when he and the two girls rush to the Witch's castle and Aslan begins to breathe on the "courtyard full of statues" they find there. "Everywhere the statues were coming to life. The courtyard looked no longer like a museum; it looked more like a zoo." Those who were trapped in stone by the demands of the Stone Table are given new life by the effects of the Deeper Magic. Lewis echoes here his own analogy in *Mere Christianity*, where he says that receiving *Zoe*, the spiritual life which is in God from all eternity, would be comparable to a statue being changed from carved stone to a real man: "And that is precisely what Christianity is about. This world is a great sculptor's shop. We are the statues and there is a rumour going around the shop that some of us are some day going to come to life." What was metaphor in *Mere Christianity* becomes reality in Narnia — the idea is transformed into image.

And that is what happens in *The Lion, the Witch and the Wardrobe* as a whole. In telling the story about Aslan, Lewis presents the basic ideas of the Christian faith in our world, transformed into the images and actions of another world. The structure of the story captures, for the imagination, the shape of the Christian message and presents it as true in Narnia as well as our world: first law, then release, through sacrifice and love; first Deep Magic, then Deeper Magic. *The Lion, the Witch and the Wardrobe* conveys a message about divine love in a form that children can grasp and identify with more easily than the biblical account, and in a way that revitalizes for older readers as well truths and feelings that have become obscured by familiarity and repetition. Seeing such divine love in action through fresh, vital images invites a response of love and trust, and that response becomes the focus of the next Chronicle Lewis wrote, *Prince Caspian*.

Chapter 5

Believing and Seeing in
Prince Caspian

I believe there is such a place as New York, [though] I have not seen it my-self.

"**M**any of the elements commonly found embedded in fairy-stories," Tolkien points out, such as wicked stepmothers, en-chanted bears, and cannibal witches, are "relics of ancient customs once practised in daily life." Part of the effect of these "relics" is precisely that "they are now *old*, and antiquity has an appeal in itself." The appeal of an-tiquity is partly that it takes us beyond realms where we can know to a realm where we can, at best, believe. We attempt to verify and see clearly, but ultimately we must trust the accuracy and reliability of that which is passed on to us from the past. *Prince Caspian*, with its beginning in the ru-ins of an ancient castle and its pervasive sense of antiquity, of the past, of the old days, of old stories, raises the question of believability: How can we believe in what we cannot see?

Belief is also challenged by the Faërie elements in the story. Unlike *The Lion, the Witch and the Wardrobe*, this story does not begin with a portal (though it does end with one). It begins instead with the four Pevensie chil-dren experiencing a strange, magic conveyance, being pulled off a train platform as if by the suction of a gigantic vacuum cleaner and deposited in Narnia. It would be hard for them, and for readers, to recognize and ac-cept what happened if this were their first adventure. But after all that happened their first time in Narnia, they immediately recognize what it is, as do we: "This is magic." That they are in a world of Faërie is clear from their surroundings — a thick wood on an island, with a dwarf in distress and in need of their assistance.

References to magic extend throughout the rest of the book, sustaining the aura of enchantment. First, within a trove of ancient treasures the children find the diamond bottle of magic cordial given to Lucy by Father Christmas on their earlier visit. Soon we learn that Caspian's new tutor, Doctor Cornelius, is a magician, though a very minor one, who teaches Caspian the theory of magic, but not the practical applications, and who finds Caspian in the forest by "a little use of simple magic." Aslan's How, the location of the Stone Table, is now considered "a very magical place," the "most deeply magical of all," and the table itself is too magical to be put to ordinary uses. Later, Caspian employs "White Magic" to summon help, while Nikabrik urges the use of black magic and initiates incantations to call up evil spirits. Good magic calls the tree-people to life, exudes from Aslan's mane, creates the feast of plenty, and is bestowed by Aslan on the first Telmarine to walk through the magic door out of Narnia into our world. The fairy-tale quality of the book is created in large part through the aura of enchantment that hovers over and permeates its world. This joins with the feeling of age and antiquity to focus on the theme of believing.

An emphasis on ancient times and old stories pervades the opening of the book. Although the first three chapters occur in the present and describe the arrival of the Pevensies in Narnia, the discovery of the ruins of Cair Paravel, and the rescue of Trumpkin the dwarf, their concern lies primarily with the past. The setting, the ruins of an old castle, reminds the children of former days: "How it all comes back," Lucy exclaims. A feeling of pastness, of antiquity, is created by the discovery of the gold chess piece the children had used centuries before ("It brought back — oh, such lovely times"), of the apple orchard they had helped plant, and of the ancient treasure chamber containing the gifts Father Christmas gave them long ago. The details and reminiscences take the children and the readers back to "the Golden Age in Narnia," with its "battles and hunts and feasts."

The "old days" also dominate the chapters that introduce the hero of the story. In a four-chapter flashback, Trumpkin recounts Caspian's childhood at the new castle, his escape when a son is born to the usurper Miraz, his reception by the Old Narnians in the forest, his early, unsuccessful efforts in the war against Miraz's forces, and his decision to blow the ancient horn of Queen Susan in hope of summoning Aslan's help. Again a sense of and nostalgia for the past dominate the tone. "I wish — I wish — I wish I could have lived in the Old Days," Caspian remarks to his uncle, and Doctor Cornelius urges Caspian to try to be "a King like the High King Peter of old." The past is also emphasized as the Old Narnians establish their headquarters in a mound "raised in very ancient times," one that seems "to belong to an even older Narnia" than what Caspian had been told about before. While the opening seven chapters are important, then, for filling in the background of Caspian's story, they are equally important in creating "a great longing for the old days when the trees could talk in Narnia."

At first glance the first half of the book, with its four-chapter flashback, might seem cumbersome. But, beyond allowing the action to begin "in the middle of things," that structure has a purpose. The opening three chapters provide readers a touchstone by which to judge the stories of the past referred to in the following four chapters. Some characters do not believe in those old stories about talking animals and a supernatural lion. King Miraz dismisses accounts of such things as "fairy tales," and Trumpkin calls them "old wives' tales." By having Miraz and Trumpkin use those dismissive words, Lewis confronts head on the issue of believability, not just for the Narnians and their stories of the past, but also for us as we read this story (the credibility of its Secondary World) and as we encounter the stories of our own past, such as the biblical stories that some people dismiss as fairy tales or old wives' tales. The way the book opens is crucial to the issue of believability. The relics of the past that the children discover, as well as their very presence in Narnia, attest to the truth of the old stories, unlikely as they may seem.

Although some characters always believed the old stories ("We don't change," says Trufflehunter. "I believe in the High King Peter . . . as firmly as I believe in Aslan himself"), many experience doubt to a greater or lesser extent. But readers know, because of what they have seen in the opening three chapters, how groundless all those doubts, and perhaps all such doubts, really are. The word *believe* is used twice when Trumpkin comments on the story he has been told all his life, that the woods are as full of ghosts as they are of trees: "I never quite believed in the ghosts. But those two cowards you've just shot believed all right." "Belief" or "believed" is repeated at least twenty-eight times thereafter, establishing it as a major, constant theme running throughout the book.

In contrast to Trufflehunter is a series of characters who disbelieve. One is Caspian's uncle, the usurper, King Miraz. When Caspian tells his uncle about the stories he has heard — of a witch and a long winter, of two boys and two girls who became kings and queens, and of a great lion called Aslan — Miraz declares, "There never were those Kings and Queens.... And there's no such person as Aslan.... And there never was a time when animals could talk. Do you hear?" Later, Caspian is informed by his tutor, Doctor Cornelius, that all this is not an inability to believe but a rejection by Miraz of what he knows to be true. As a part of this rejection of truth, this obscuring and hiding of reality, the Telmarines have made up stories about ghosts haunting the Eastern woods and the ocean beyond them because in the old stories Aslan always comes from the East and is the son of the Emperor-over-the-Sea. In their efforts to avoid belief and to usurp the truth, the Telmarines have created falsehoods and, ironically, have begun to believe them.

Another example of disbelief is the black dwarf Nikabrik, who, Caspian remarks later, has "gone sour inside from long suffering and hating." When Caspian asks if he believes in Aslan, Nikabrik replies that he will believe in anything that drives the Telmarines out of Narnia. Such "belief," however, is in fact disbelief, born not out of denial, as in Miraz's case, but out of despair. Lewis pairs and contrasts him with the red dwarf Trumpkin, who says he doesn't believe in walking trees or in magic or in Aslan, though he shows more doubt than disbelief. Out of despair, Nikabrik brings a hag and a werewolf to the leaders' council and prepares to have them call up the White Witch of old: "We want power: and we want a power that will be on our side." In the ensuing skirmish, Nikabrik is killed, and Caspian expresses regrets, thinking that Nikabrik might have turned out better if Caspian's forces had won a quick victory. Perhaps so. But central to the book's development of this theme is that belief leads to trust, and that trust not only endures the hard times but is shown to be trust only by enduring the hard times.

Initially this story may seem like a traditional initiation tale, the story of a young person leaving a sheltered environment to encounter hardships and through them grow to maturity. However, it soon becomes clear that in this book the most important maturation involves not the title character but those who are searching for him. After Trumpkin decides to believe in the children, Peter declares that they must set out immediately to join Caspian. Their efforts to reach Caspian turn out to be not only a physical journey but also a journey of personal growth. They leave the island by boat, choosing their own course — along the coast and up Glasswater Creek — and relying upon their own resources: their memories of the Narnian landscape and Peter's pocket compass. However, things have changed since the children's previous visit to Narnia, and Peter eventually has to admit, "We're lost." At that point Lucy, the youngest of the children and the one least involved in making the decisions, sees Aslan, indicating by his expression that he wants them to go in the opposite direction from the one they have chosen. The others prefer, however, to rely on their own judgments and to go their own way: the result is a long, tiring walk, an attack by some sentries of Miraz, and a time-wasting return along the way they had come.

That night, in one of the most beautiful and numinous episodes of the Chronicles, Aslan awakens Lucy from a deep sleep by calling her to him in the moonlight. The extended, detailed description of the mysterious voice, the dancing trees, and finally the magnificent lion shining in the moonlight creates a deep sense of wonder and awe in most readers. The physical description is enhanced by a marvelous passage that develops explicitly the theme of personal growth implicit throughout the Chronicles. Lucy says to Aslan, "You're bigger," to which Aslan replies, "That is because you are older. . . . Every year you grow, you will find me bigger." The word *grow* here is crucial: It doesn't mean just getting older or taller. Lucy's *capacity for knowing* Aslan must grow larger. Lewis clarifies this in *Mere Christianity*, commenting on Christ's words that only those who receive the Kingdom of God like a little child will enter that kingdom: "Christ never meant that we were to remain children in *intelligence*. . . . He wants a child's heart, but a grown-up's head. . . . [You must not] be content with the same babyish ideas [of God] which you had when you were a five-year-old."

Lucy goes on to learn a valuable lesson about trust. When Aslan says that much time was wasted that day, Lucy begins defending herself for going along with the others and ends up realizing that often, in crucial matters, one must go it alone. At first she says, "I couldn't have left the others and come up to you alone, how could I?" But she soon admits that she could have, and that she wouldn't have been alone, "not if I was with you." Aslan then tells her to act upon that lesson: "Go back to the others now, and wake them up; and tell them you have seen me again; and that you must all get up at once and follow me — what will happen? There is only one way of finding out." The episode, with the allusion to Christ's words directing his disciples to "follow me," conveys the essence of commitment, especially in the instructions Aslan gives to Lucy: if the others will not come, Aslan says, "then you at least must follow me alone."

As Lucy tries to get the other children and Trumpkin to accompany her, they fall back on the old adage "Seeing is believing." They don't see Aslan, so they don't believe he is there. That underlies earlier and later examples of disbelief as well. Trumpkin does not believe in Aslan because he has never seen him, just as he doesn't believe in the High King Peter and the others who reigned at Cair Paravel because he hasn't seen them. Only when he is shown — by being disarmed by Edmund in a fencing match, outdone by Susan in an archery contest, and cured by a drop of Lucy's magic cordial — will he accept the children as the true kings and queens of old. An ironic inversion on Trumpkin's situation occurs later, after Edmund has delivered the challenge from Peter to King Miraz. Miraz asks his advisors Glozelle and Sopespian if they believe the old stories about Peter and Edmund, and Glozelle answers, "I believe my eyes, your Majesty." But Glozelle and Sopespian do not really see, neither who Edmund is (though they have seen him outside the tent) nor what the situation truly is. Seeing is not always believing, but Glozelle's use of the phrase is sufficient to trick Miraz into accepting the challenge that leads directly to his death.

In Lewis's thinking, the old adage must be reversed: Believing is seeing. Those who believe are able to see; those who do not believe cannot see. When Aslan instructs Lucy to go to the others and tell them to follow him, she asks, "Will the others see you too?" His reply is, "Certainly not at first. . . . Later on, it depends." The image is the same one Lewis would use later in *The Last Battle* and again in *Till We Have Faces*. In the former, the dwarfs do not see Aslan or the feast he offers them because they do not believe in him or his gifts. In the latter, Orual is unable to see the palace in which Psyche lives with her divine spouse because Orual does not believe in the gods or in the palace.

What a person sees depends on who he or she is and what he or she is looking for (as the experience of Uncle Andrew demonstrates in *The Magician's Nephew*). Because Lucy's companions do not believe Aslan is present, they do not see him. They are greatly confused and even angry at their inability to see Aslan, but at last they do decide to go with Lucy, a first step in faith. Of course, at first they are just following Lucy. She fixes her eyes on Aslan, and the others keep their eyes on her. As they follow her and are led successfully down a steep cliff and across a roaring river, their trust increases, and first Edmund and Peter, then Susan, and finally even Trumpkin are able to see him.

Susan and Trumpkin provide an interesting contrast in the way sight is transformed into belief and belief into trust. Susan believed all along in Aslan's existence, but her emotions kept her from seeing and putting her trust in him at that moment: "I really believed it was him," she admits later, but she could think only of getting out of the woods and wouldn't let herself admit that he was there. Aslan recognizes and ministers to her problem: "'You have listened to fears, child,' said Aslan. 'Come, let me breathe on you.'" Trumpkin, on the other hand, did not believe until he saw, and still does not fully trust. Doubting Thomas that he is, he must experience Aslan's presence before he will believe, and Aslan deals with him accordingly. By picking Trumpkin up and tossing him high into the air, as one might do with a child, Aslan makes the dwarf physically dependent upon him: "The Dwarf flew up in the air. He was as safe as if he had been in bed, though he did not feel so." Having seen Aslan, Trumpkin believes; having, without choice, been forced to rely upon Aslan, he finally comes to trust him and is ready to move on and act upon his faith.

After meeting Aslan, the company divides, Peter, Edmund, and Trumpkin going to the assistance of Caspian, while Susan and Lucy accompany Aslan. Realizing that his army is outnumbered and unlikely to defeat Miraz's forces, Peter issues a challenge to Miraz to settle the matter by single combat. The challenge itself is another reminder of the past, of the old days, as Peter remembers the language he had used for such documents long ago. The scene — from the wording of the challenge, to the assignment of marshals, to the fight itself, to Peter's courtesy as "a Knight" — is straight out of the romance tradition, with its stories of heroes. The combat ends, however, very unheroically — through villainy on the part of the Telmarines: "'To arms, Narnia. Treachery!' Peter shouted." In a story whose theme has been belief and trust, the decisive incidents, ironically, proceed through a series of violations of trust: the insubordination and rebellion of Nikabrik, the treachery of Glozelle and Sopespian in goading Miraz to fight and in attacking the Narnians before the combat has ended, and the infidelity of Glozelle in stabbing the fallen Miraz in the back. The Telmarines' lack of belief in Aslan is reflected in their lack of respect for their fellow creatures, as shown by the way they have treated talking animals and other non-human creatures ever since they entered Narnia.

Meanwhile, Aslan is leading a campaign of subversion against Miraz and the Telmarines who had "silenced the beasts and the trees and the fountains, . . . killed and [driven] away the dwarfs and fauns," and enslaved the spirits of their own people by wiping out the very memory of Aslan and all that he stood for. Aslan's campaign is conducted not through battle but through revelry, in passages that use mythical overtones to enlarge still further our knowledge of who Aslan is and what he does. Dance has appeared throughout the story as a symbol of order, harmony, and a proper response to Aslan — the dance of the heavens as the planet Tarva salutes the planet Alambil in Chapter 4, the dance of the fauns in Chapter 6, and the dance of the trees in Chapter 10 all anticipate the wild romp that begins in Chapter 11 and concludes in Chapter 14. Dance imagery is common in Lewis's fiction, but here it is complicated by the introduction of "a youth, dressed only in a fawn-skin, with vine-leaves wreathed in his curly hair." He is Bacchus, the Greek god of wine and revelry, who, as Lucy was told earlier, had been a frequent visitor in Narnia in its heroic age, with his strange company of maenads, satyrs, and sileni. During their visits "the streams would run with wine instead of water and the whole forest would give itself up to jollification for weeks on end."

Lewis introduces Bacchus here to reinforce and expand the sense and experience of joy and freedom as the invaders liberate the occupied territories. The use of Bacchus presents dangers: the Greeks, recognizing the harmful potential of wine, characterized Bacchus by drunken frenzy and cruelty as well as by release and mirthmaking. With Bacchus under the restraints of Aslan's greater power, however, he can be used to convey the meaning of Aslan's coming. With his usual eclecticism, Lewis uses pagan rites to clarify Christian theology. Part of what Bacchus adds is described in Edith Hamilton's account of the Bacchic festivals in later Greek history: "No other festival in Greece could compare with it. It took place in the spring when the vine begins to put forth its branches, and it lasted for five days. They were days of perfect peace and enjoyment. All the ordinary business of life stopped. No one could be put in prison; prisoners were even released so that they could share in the general rejoicing." Lewis draws on the joy, change, and freedom traditionally associated with Bacchus to celebrate the restoration of the "long-lost days of freedom" in Narnia, but also and more importantly to signal the effect of putting one's full trust in Aslan.

The celebration begins with a wild romp, with everyone seeming to be playing a different game: "It may have been Tig, but Lucy never discovered who was It. It was rather like Blind Man's Buff, only everyone behaved as if he was blindfolded." Later Aslan declares a holiday, and the whole party moves off, leaping, rushing, and turning somersaults, with animals frisking around them. The freedom within that company soon reaches out to others — first to the Great River, as strong trunks of ivy and other vegetation break down the bridge that impedes its flow to give it freedom.

Aslan then offers freedom to two schoolteachers. The revelers first come upon a girls' school, where Telmarine confinement and repression are epitomized by tight hairdos, tight collars, and thick, tickly stockings. Miss Prizzle, the teacher, after reprimanding one girl, Gwendolen, for looking out the window and talking nonsense about a lion, sees her tidy schoolhouse dissolve into a forest glade and flees from nature and freedom with her class — except for Gwendolen, who joins the dance and is released from some of the "unnecessary and uncomfortable" clothes she was wearing. In contrast to Miss Prizzle's response is that of "a tired-looking girl" at another school who "was teaching arithmetic to a number of boys who looked very like pigs." When she looks out of the window and sees the revelers, a stab of joy goes through her heart. After Bacchus frightens off her insolent, belligerent pupils and turns them externally into the pigs they already were internally, she yields to the divine longing within her and joins the celebration. The coming of Aslan liberates ("Chained dogs broke their chains"), comforts ("The boy, who had been crying a moment before, burst out laughing and joined them"), and heals ("Why I do declare I feel *that* better. I think I could take a little breakfast this morning").

In the final chapter, the celebration of the victory of the Old Narnia over the New concludes with a dance and a feast, and the earlier themes are reiterated. The theme of magic is extended even further as Aslan describes the cave, "one of the magical places" of our world, through which the ancestors of the Telmarines blundered into the Land of Telmar. The theme of skepticism is reasserted by the reaction of the Telmarines to the door Aslan set up as a portal, through which they can return to the island in the Pacific from which their ancestors came: they don't see another world and won't believe there is one, unless someone else goes through the door first. And the theme of trust is re-emphasized by Reepicheep's quick response, offering to lead his company "through that arch at your bidding without a moment's delay."

The ending, while unifying the plot and themes of the book, does not complete the story of the title character's growth. *Prince Caspian* describes Caspian's initiation and the first steps toward his maturity: he rides off from his sheltered, secure home life "to seek adventures," and as a result his face began to wear "a kinglier look." But he is not yet ready to be king; on the whole his leadership of the army is unsuccessful. When Peter arrives, he takes command, and he, not Caspian, fights the decisive, character-testing duel. Lewis subordinates his title character in the second half of the book in order to allow his continued growth — in maturity, knowledge of Aslan, and trust in Aslan — to occur in *The Voyage of the "Dawn Treader,"* the second book of the "Caspian trilogy." As a result, the theme of this story, the quality that gives the book its distinctive flavor, is not that of heroism, the reliance on human efforts, but that of trust, of handing everything over and relying completely on Another.

Chapter 6

Longing and Learning in
The Voyage of the "Dawn Treader"

*There have been times when I think we do not desire heaven; but more often
I find myself wondering whether, in our heart of hearts, we have ever desired
anything else.*

Fairy-stories, Tolkien claims, are centrally concerned with longing: if
they awaken desire, "satisfying it while often whetting it unbearably,"
they succeed. In his childhood, he writes, he "desired dragons with a profound desire." Thus he longed to experience Other-worlds, Faërie worlds,
for only in them were dragons to be found. Longing was also a central
thread in Lewis's life. From early years he felt sensations of "intense longing" for an "unnameable something." In his autobiography, *Surprised by Joy*,
he calls such longing "Joy," defined as "an unsatisfied desire which is itself
more desirable than any other satisfaction." In addition to longing, *Surprised by Joy* is about learning, especially the process through which Lewis
learned that his longing for an Other-world was, in fact, a desire for
heaven and that God implants such longings in people as a way of drawing
them to their heavenly home. Since longing is at the heart of Faërie, it is
not surprising that Lewis came to love the fairy-tale form and to write a series of fairy stories himself. And, given Lewis's life story, it is not surprising that one of them, *The Voyage of the "Dawn Treader,"* would have longing
and learning as its central themes.

The story opens with Edmund and Lucy in an ordinary bedroom in

Cambridge, longing to be in Narnia. "Most of us," the narrator supposes, "have a secret country," but it is "only an imaginary country." Edmund and Lucy are luckier than we are, for "their secret country [is] real." By having his characters long for Narnia, Lewis incorporates into the plot the effect a fairy tale should have on its readers: the awakening of a desire to be in Fairy-land (here, Narnia) and the satisfying of that desire, at least partially or temporarily. Clearly the Chronicles do have that effect. Millions of children and adults not only read them but, more significantly, read them over and over. As Lucy and Edmund long for Narnia, so do readers. For them, too, Lucy and Edmund's secret country is real. It is *there* in the books, not a figment of their imaginations. And like Lucy and Edmund, they have limited access to Narnia: they can enter it only through a portal, the books, only when the text enables them to.

A few moments later, Edmund and Lucy enter Narnia again, this time through a picture frame. The picture in the frame, with a Narnian-type ship, comes to life, and Edmund, Lucy, and their cousin Eustace fall through the frame into Fairy-land. Readers accompany them — imaginatively, of course — but the text assumes the possibility that they could enter it on their own: using second-person pronouns and past-tense verbs, the narrator says, "If you spent a hundred years in Narnia," you would return the same moment you left in our time, and if you went back a week later, a thousand Narnian years or none at all may have passed. That's all hypothetical. But a shift away from "if" clauses makes getting there a real possibility: "You never know till you get there."

The portal takes us not to the country of Narnia, as in the previous books, but to the seas east of Narnia and a ship, the *Dawn Treader*. The magic of the portal, the presence of a talking mouse, a silver lamp fashioned by dwarfs, and references to fauns and giants signal that again we have entered an enchanted realm, full of adventure, wonder, and "arresting strangeness." Again the adventure entails a journey, but instead of a journey by land, as in the previous books, this one is a journey by sea, borrowing and adapting a different traditional story type. Its predecessors include the classical voyages of Odysseus, Jason, and Aeneas; Celtic legends like the *Voyage of Bran* and the *Voyage of Maeldúin*; and the imaginary voyages of the seventeenth and eighteenth centuries, which are best known through their satirical counterparts such as *Gulliver's Travels*. The voyage to scattered islands was a characteristic of the Old Irish *imram*, exemplified by the *Voyage of St. Brendan*.

The story of a voyage generates a quality of response different from that of a journey by land. Partly, of course, the voyage gives to the story the peculiar flavor of the sea, the taste of the salt on the lips. Beyond that there is the sense of mystery and excitement that oceans have always engendered, the wild stories of strange creatures and mysterious places told by old sailors. In this case the voyage is a quest story, as Caspian sets out to find the seven noble lords whom King Miraz sent off to explore the unknown Eastern Seas beyond the Lone Islands. And, typical of voyage stories, the book is episodic in form, a series of linked but unrelated adventures held together by the ship, the quest, and the characters.

The adventures start with the ordinary: an encounter with slave traders and a storm that could also happen in our own world. But as the ship sails on, the adventures turn extraordinary, leaving no doubt that this is a voyage through a Faërie sea, not a previously undiscovered area of the Pacific Ocean. The Other-worldly includes an encounter with a dragon, an attack by the great Sea Serpent, an island where the water turns whatever touches it into gold, an island inhabited by invisible, one-legged people and ruled by a magician, a dark island where dreams (including nightmares) come true, an island where a magnificent banquet is served each morning and where a celestial being resides (a star at rest), and a passage through the Last Sea, where the water is sweet and Lucy has a glimpse of a race of Sea People who live on the ocean floor. As the voyage proceeds, there is an increasing sense of mystery, strangeness, wonder, and excitement, culminating with the arrival at "The Very End of the World," the title of the last chapter. Each stage takes the characters — and the readers — deeper into the world of Faërie.

In addition to a search for lost lords, the voyage turns out to be an occasion for growth and learning. A voyage is particularly well suited for depicting a journey into experience, as the ship (a "little bit of a thing") becomes a little world, a microcosm compressing the tensions and difficulties of personal and social life and forcing them upon the hero, carrying him through a symbolic journey to encounter other difficulties and dangers and to prove his worth. Caspian, like Ulysses (to whom he is compared in Chapter 16), Aeneas, Huckleberry Finn, and many other predecessors, is on a voyage that involves physical, emotional, and spiritual testing and maturation: a journey through and beyond his kingdom and a journey toward manhood. Some of the adventures on the journey are described briefly, but each of those treated at length focuses on the growth and maturation of one of the main characters.

The earliest adventure, on the Lone Islands, is crucial for the development of the young king, Caspian. Although he learned a great deal through his flight to the wilderness and his military service with the old Narnians, he was left at the end of *Prince Caspian* a new king with a great deal more to learn about himself and the world. When the ship reaches Felimath and Caspian suggests that the children walk across the island, for example, the narrator comments, "If Caspian had been as experienced then as he became later on in this voyage he would not have made this suggestion." By being captured and sold as a slave, he gains an understanding of the slave trade from the inside, in contrast to the purely pragmatic view of Governor Gumpas. He learns military strategy from Lord Bern, gaining control of Avra through a show of power greater than they actually possess. And he learns to conduct himself as a noble king, deposing Gumpas, installing Bern as Duke of the Lone Islands, freeing all slaves, and rescuing his friends.

He still has more to learn. Later in the voyage he is gripped by greed on Deathwater Island and by jealousy when he learns he is not to go on to the End of the World. But in a series of episodes, he grows in wisdom, learning increasingly to rely on his mind rather than his passions. The final and perhaps decisive lesson is Aslan's rebuke to his surliness and quick temper near the end of the world. Caspian emerges from his encounter with Aslan in the ship's cabin a more humble and mature person. That he is ready to confront life is expressed in terms of a journey: "You're to go on — Reep and Edmund, and Lucy, and Eustace; and I'm to go back." His journey into experience completed, Caspian is to return and marry the princess, which traditionally symbolizes maturity, readiness to encounter life as an adult. The others, having not yet completed their journeys, must travel on.

The second extended episode, on what comes to be called Dragon Island, deals especially with the growth and maturation of the boy who was "called Eustace Clarence Scrubb, and . . . almost deserved it." To show that he needs to change, Lewis depicts him as someone absorbed completely in modern, materialistic culture and values. He has been influenced by his parents, Harold and Alberta, "very up-to-date and advanced people" who, unlike Lewis, were "vegetarians, non-smokers and teetotalers." Eustace himself is characterized as a pseudo-intellectual, fond of animals only if "they were dead and pinned on a card," and liking only informational books with "pictures of grain elevators or of fat foreign children doing exercises in model schools." Eustace's own intellectual training was at a modern, experimental school, and his tastes are summed up by his preference for "liners and motor-boats and aeroplanes" over the trim and graceful *Dawn Treader.*

From the first, Eustace is disagreeable and selfish, bossing and bullying other characters and taking more than his share of the water rations. The ultimate — and most humiliating — indication of his character is the inability of the slave traders to get rid of him, even when he is thrown in free with other lots. When the ship reaches land after the great storm, Eustace characteristically slips away to take a nap instead of doing his share of the work. He gets lost, takes shelter in a dragon's cave, and by sleeping on the dragon's hoard, turns into a dragon, a transformation typical of the fairy-tale genre.

Cut off now from his shipmates, he comes to appreciate them and eventually to realize that throughout this voyage he has been "pretty beastly," behaving like a "monster." When he attains that realization, Aslan — in his first appearance in the story — comes to him and takes him to a pool in a garden on a mountain. Eustace understands somehow that if he could get into the pool, the water would soothe his pains, but Aslan tells him he must first undress. Three times Eustace peels off his dragon skin, and three times it grows right back. Then Aslan asks Eustace to let him do it, and Eustace agrees. After Aslan pulls "the beastly stuff" off and throws Eustace in the water, Eustace finds that he has turned back into a boy. Aslan dresses him in new clothes and returns him to the seashore to rejoin the others.

The episode is filled with Christian overtones. The inability of Eustace to change himself, the assistance given him by Aslan, the water into which he is plunged, and the new clothes he is given unite to make this event a Narnian conversion story. Eustace is "reborn," and he begins to be "a different boy." Water, as an element in the sacrament of baptism, symbolizes death and rebirth because of the traditional associations of water as being necessary to sustain life but also capable of taking life. This stage of Eustace's spiritual journey, then, which began when he fell into the briny waters of a picture at home, culminates with his baptism in the well of life on a mountain in Narnia. He, like Caspian, will have more to learn as the voyage continues, but the change has begun.

Lucy is the focal character in the next extended episode, on the magic-filled Island of Voices, where invisible characters, the Dufflepuds, threaten to kill Caspian and his friends unless Lucy will enter the house of a supposedly fearsome magician and find a spell that will make the Dufflepuds visible again. At first glance Lucy might not seem to have much to learn. As Edmund says in telling Eustace about Aslan, "Lucy sees him most often." She is unselfish to all, generous to a fault with Eustace, brave and even potentially sacrificial when she agrees to enter the house and say the spell. But Lucy, like the others, is young; she too needs to gain maturity through experience. Her most important growth occurs in the Magician's house, especially as she looks in the Magician's book.

Several details suggest that the book, at one level, is a symbol of life. There was, for example, "no title page or title." Also, "You couldn't turn back. The right-hand pages, the ones ahead, could be turned; the left-hand pages could not." More specifically, it symbolizes Lucy's life. As Lucy gazes at a page, she sees a picture of "a girl standing at a reading-desk reading in a huge book ... dressed exactly like Lucy." What she sees in the book is "much more than a picture. It [is] alive." Within that book of life is a set of temptations hinging on the theme of false power, of doing things only God should do (changing the weather) or knowing things only God should know (what your friends are saying about you). For Lucy this becomes a Fall story, since she yields to a temptation and comes to know things she can't forget, the things her friend said about her.

But the fall and loss of innocence are quickly followed by grace and redemption. This is not only a book of life, of experience and temptation; it is also a Book of Life. Lucy encounters a series of pages that are more like a story than a spell. In them she reads "the loveliest story" she has ever heard. She does not remember the story after she finishes reading it, but she can recall a few details in it, specifically a cup, a sword, a tree, and a green hill. These symbols, clearly Christian, suggest that "the loveliest story" is the story of Christ. And when she asks Aslan if she will ever hear that story again, he gives her the comforting assurance that she will indeed, that he will keep telling it to her for the rest of her life.

In this chapter Lewis clarifies the nature and effect of myth. In the earlier books he has established that the mythic figures of our world can be realities in Narnia, as with Father Christmas and Bacchus. Here he reverses the formula: what is reality in our world becomes fairy tale or myth in Narnia. For Lucy to read the story of Jesus is a useful part of her spiritual maturation in Narnia. But if she were to stay in Narnia, reading that story would not be enough: she would need to grow closer to God in his Narnian incarnation as Aslan.

For readers of the Narnian fairy tales, the situation is just the reverse. The Narnian stories can be a means — but no more — of drawing us nearer to the divine realities in our world. They can be a beginning, a useful part of our spiritual growth, as Lucy's reading of the story of Christ in Narnia was for her. But for us, as for Lucy, reading the myths of an Otherworld is not enough. Further progress toward spiritual maturity requires getting to know Aslan by his earthly name and learning to know him better as a reality in our own world.

Still another figure for whom the voyage is a life-changing experience is Reepicheep, the focal figure in the extended episode describing the arrival at the end of the world. Throughout the book, Reepicheep has continued the theme of longing introduced in the first chapter by Edmund and Lucy's desire for Narnia. All his life Reepicheep has longed to reach Aslan's country, ever since a Dryad said over his cradle that he would find all he seeks in the utter East. What Reepicheep feels seems close to the pangs of longing Lewis experienced throughout his early life, as he wanted acutely "something that cannot be had in this world." Eventually he recognized this as a "desire for my true country, which I shall not find till after death." Lewis then realized that he — like Reepicheep — must "make it the main object of life to press on to that other country and to help others to do the same."

Such longing is felt most often by persons with romantic inclinations. It is significant, therefore, that Reepicheep is a romantic hero. He is brave — "the most valiant of all the Talking Beasts of Narnia" — and idealistic, accompanying Caspian on the journey not "to look for things useful but to seek honour and adventures." His mind is "full of forlorn hopes, death or glory charges, and last stands." Although Reepicheep is on a pilgrimage, it is not toward maturity: his faith in Aslan is sure; his commitment is total. Rather, his goal, his heart's desire, is to "go on into the utter east and never return into the world," but instead to live with Aslan in Aslan's country.

The strength of that commitment makes Reepicheep, in a sense, even more than Caspian, the guiding spirit of the expedition. He is the first to approach the dragon when it lands by their camp, the one who is consulted about whether Lucy should look for the Magician's book, and the one whose idea saves the ship from the Sea Serpent. It is Reepicheep who replies to the terrifying voice that comes out of the blackness near the Dark Island.

Perhaps it is inevitable, given his commitment and his spirit, that he should be the first to partake of the magnificent banquet they find on the last island to the east. The feast, spread on Aslan's table, seems the Narnian equivalent of the Eucharist of Christianity. It is a table of remembrance (the stone knife lying on it, the same one "the White Witch used when she killed Aslan at the Stone Table long ago," has been "brought here to be kept in honour while the world lasts") and a table of nourishment, physically (for "all were very hungry") and spiritually (for only those who believe in its goodness are to eat at it). And it is a magic table, "eaten [by birds from the East], and renewed, every day." The table appears at the end of the voyage: "It is set here by [Aslan's] bidding" as a reward for those who have come this far in their pilgrimage, but it is also a source of strength for those who desire to journey further, to — and beyond — the very end of the world.

Reepicheep, of course, does desire to go further, and as he nears his goal, the images of sea and ship expand in importance. The sea is the Silver Sea, a body of sweet water covered with lilies, a traditional symbol of life.

The ship is replaced first by a rowboat and then by a coracle, a tiny boat with room only for Reepicheep: in this final stage of his journey toward spiritual fulfillment, toward union with Aslan, he must "go on alone."

As the boat approaches the world's end, the sense of Otherness is enhanced by descriptions of the light ("a brightness you or I could not bear even if we had dark glasses on") and a wall of water, a long, tall wave that marks the boundary between worlds. Beyond the wave and beyond the sun is a range of mountains so high that it was impossible to see the top, though even so there was no ice and snow on them. "No one in that boat doubted that they were seeing beyond the end of the world into Aslan's country." And with the Otherness comes a renewed sense of longing, intensified by a musical sound, so overwhelming that the children would never talk about it later.

As Reepicheep says good-bye to the children, he tries to be sad for their sakes, but he quivers with happiness. Then he gets into the coracle and paddles until he reaches the current, which carries him away swiftly. The coracle ascends to the top of the wall of water at the world's end, pauses a moment at the top, and then disappears. And after that moment, the narrator tells us, no one in Narnia has seen Reepicheep; but he believes Reepicheep did reach Aslan's country safely and has lived there ever since. His journey is complete, and his longing for Aslan's country and Aslan himself has been perfectly fulfilled.

The voyage for Edmund, Lucy, and Eustace ends as they leave the boat, wade to the shore, and step into one of the most powerfully numinous episodes in the Chronicles, a stunning blend of fairy tale and deeply resonant myth. The sense of Otherness is profound: they are at the end of the world, a point at which the sky — solid and real, like a bright blue wall, or a panel of blue glass — comes down and joins the earth. They find a lamb, so white they can hardly look at it, cooking fish over a fire on the grass. After they eat a meal (the most delicious food they have ever tasted), Lucy asks if this is the way to Aslan's country, and the lamb replies that for them the door into Aslan's country is from their own world. Here the image of a door — that Fairy-land portal between worlds — becomes the point of entry to the ultimate Other-world, heaven.

The lamb then turns into a lion, and the children realize he is Aslan. In contrast to his active roles in *The Lion, the Witch and the Wardrobe* and *Prince Caspian*, Aslan does very little in *The Voyage of the "Dawn Treader,"* except with Eustace. Characters are aware of his presence on seven occasions. They see him on the horizon or through the page of a book; he answers Lucy's prayer by providing help to escape from the terrors of the Dark Island; and he talks to Caspian, Lucy, and Edmund. He empowers, encourages, restrains, and guards the children, filling a spiritual more than a physical role. Although they are aware of his presence on those specific occasions, he actually seems to be present all the time, in a protective way, even though they are not conscious of his proximity. Here and later in the Narnian chronology, Aslan's physical presence is more and more withdrawn from the world. Just as Christ in the Gospels turned over more and more responsibility to his disciples, so does Aslan following his resurrection. This concept grew as the series developed, however, since Aslan is still active as a physical presence in the world in *Prince Caspian*.

The sense of longing for Narnia that opened the book returns at the end, when Aslan tells the children that he will "open the door in the sky" through which they must return to their own country, and that Edmund and Lucy will not return to Narnia. Lucy begins to sob, not from longing for Narnia itself, but for Aslan: "How can we live, never meeting you?" she cries. Aslan replies that she *will* meet him in our world: "But there I have another name. You must learn to know me by that name"; as they learn to know him there by that name, he will tell them "all the time" how to reach his country. He then adds, "This was the very reason why you were brought to Narnia, that by knowing me here for a little, you may know me better there." What Aslan says to the children, Lewis offers to readers as a brilliant explanation of his ultimate goal in writing the Chronicles.

It is a powerfully evocative passage, full of Christian symbols (light, lamb, lion, river, door), biblical allusions (the passage as a whole echoes John 21:4-19), and universal symbolism (Aslan says that the way into his country from our world lies across a river, a traditional symbol of death and passage to another world). In reading it, however, one does not tend to isolate such features and consider their individual effects: its components unite to create a passage that appeals directly to the emotions and the imagination. It contains, as great myth always does, more than the author could have intended. It conveys, through story and symbols, things the author could not have put in any other way.

The final pages leave many readers longing even more acutely to return to Narnia, and, unlike Edmund and Lucy, they can return. With each return journey, they learn more about Aslan and the Narnian world, and about themselves. The longing each successive book in the series creates builds toward a reprise of longing as a theme in the final book, where Lewis shows that the deep desire of the characters is — as he came to understand about his own longings — not for the world of Narnia but for Aslan's country. Before Edmund and Lucy reach Aslan's country as their ultimate destination in *The Last Battle*, however, Eustace will visit it briefly in the next of the Chronicles to be published, the concluding volume of the Caspian trilogy, when Caspian, though not permitted to go there with Reepicheep in this book, will be welcomed there also.

Chapter 7

Freedom and Obedience in
The Silver Chair

Obedience is the road to freedom.

Tolkien says that in using fantasy, a writer has the freedom to create whatever physical laws a Secondary World demands — a world in which the sun is green, for example. But the writer also is required to remain obedient to such laws, for the story to be credible. "Few attempt such difficult tasks," he continues. "But when they are attempted and in any degree accomplished then we have a rare achievement of Art . . . story-making in its primary and most potent mode." In *The Silver Chair* Lewis did not create a green sun, but he did create a credible Secondary World without a sun. And he achieves some of his most skillful and imaginative fantasy effects in this story, which explores at several levels the complicated relationship between personal freedom and the need for obedience.

The story's almost perfectly symmetrical structure begins in an ordinary setting, the grounds of a British boarding school, but the particular school itself was one that Lewis would prefer to be seen as out of the ordinary. It is called "Experiment House," a "progressive," co-educational school, and Lewis uses it to continue the satire on modernism he began with his descriptions of the Scrubb family in *The Voyage of the "Dawn Treader."* It is the kind of school Harold and Alberta would naturally want for their son. The people who run the school, the narrator tells us, have the idea that "boys and girls should be allowed to do what they liked." Unfortunately, what some boys and girls like best is bullying other boys and girls.

When Eustace Scrubb finds a classmate, Jill Pole, reduced to tears by a group of bullies, he tells her about Narnia, "a place where animals can talk and where there are — er — enchantments and dragons — and — well, all the sorts of things you have in fairy tales," and suggests that they try to go there together. In this case the portal for reaching Fairy-land is a door in the wall of the school grounds. It is usually locked, but this time it opens, not onto the ordinary grey, heathery moor they expected, but onto "a different world." When Jill hesitates, Eustace grabs her hand and pulls her "through the door, out of the school grounds, out of England, out of our whole world into That Place."

They emerge not into the Other-world of Narnia but into the most otherly of Other-worlds, the incredibly high mountains that Edmund, Lucy, and Eustace glimpsed beyond the sun when they reached the end of the world in *The Voyage of the "Dawn Treader,"* the mountains of Aslan's country. Here Eustace, attempting to save Jill from falling over the edge of a cliff, loses his balance and falls himself. He is seemingly plunging to his death, until a huge lion appears and with his breath gives him a gentle flight to a landing somewhere far below.

After a long cry, Jill finds herself "dreadfully thirsty." Hearing a stream nearby, she goes toward it but finds the lion lying in her path. He says to her, "If you are thirsty, come and drink." His invitation echoes Christ's words, "If any man thirst, let him come unto me, and drink." In literary terms this is *allusion,* not *allegory.* The verbal echo, for those who recognize it, may also recall the episode at Jacob's well, where the Samaritan woman had come to fill her pitcher. There, when she meets Christ, he offers her spiritual water instead, and later he explains: "Whosoever drinketh of the water that I shall give him shall never thirst; but the water that I shall give him shall be in him a well of water springing up into everlasting life." In order to drink, Jill must walk past the lion, trusting him not to harm her. Finally she does so and drinks the "most refreshing water she had ever tasted."

The lion, who of course is Aslan, calls her to him and assigns her a task. This story, like *Prince Caspian* and *The Voyage of the "Dawn Treader,"* involves a quest, this time to search for a prince who disappeared from Narnia ten years ago and bring him back to his father's house. Then, to help her and Eustace find Prince Rilian, Aslan gives Jill four signs. First, Eustace will meet an old friend when he arrives in Narnia and must greet him at once. Second, Eustace and Jill must travel north until they find the ruins of an ancient city of the giants. Third, they must look for some writing on stone in those ruins and do what it tells them. And fourth, they will recognize the prince by the fact that he will ask them to do something in Aslan's name. Aslan then directs Jill to memorize the signs and to keep repeating them: to think of them first thing in the morning and last thing at night — and even during the night if she wakes up, much as Moses told the children of Israel to keep God's statutes always before them, to think of them "when thou liest down and when thou risest up." The signs become for Jill what the words of the law were for Israel: a source of direction and guidance, and she must keep them before her at all times. As the Israelites found freedom through obedience to the law, so obedience to Aslan's directives will lead to inner freedom for Jill and Eustace and freedom from slavery for the prince.

Starting with the incredible height of Aslan's country, Lewis constructs his plot as a series of descending and ascending movements, what literary critic Northrop Frye calls the most basic of narrative patterns: "First, the descent from a higher world; second, the descent to a lower world; third, the ascent from a lower world; and fourth, the ascent to a higher world." In this case the higher and lower worlds are Faërie worlds, above and below another Faërie world, Narnia. The first stage of the descent is from the cliff into Narnia: Jill follows Eustace, as Aslan sends her down safely on his breath as well and she joins Eustace.

Because Eustace does not know what Aslan told Jill and does not recognize the frail old king they see embarking as his friend Caspian, they quickly muff the first sign. But they then receive help from the owl Glimfeather and his folk, who fill in the background for the story. While out maying in the north parts of Narnia, the Queen, Caspian's wife, was bitten and killed by a great, shining serpent, "as green as poison." Lewis complicates the structure by introducing a second quest, a quest within a quest: there is the children's search for Prince Rilian, but the prince, when he disappeared, was himself on a quest, seeking revenge for the death of his mother. Rilian spent his days riding the northern marches, hunting for the serpent, "to kill it and be avenged." But he soon mentioned to Lord Drinian that he encountered, by the fountain where his mother was killed, "the most beautiful thing that was ever made," a lady, "tall and great, shining, and wrapped in a thin garment as green as poison," whom Drinian is sure is "evil" and who beckoned for the prince to join her. A few days later Prince Rilian rode out again, and he has never been seen since.

That a mother is killed while maying provides significant clues to the nature of the beautiful lady. She is an evil temptress. The wise owls recognize similarities between her and the White Witch who came out of the North long ago and for a hundred years bound Narnia in snow and ice: "We think this may be one of the same crew." Like the White Witch, she dislikes motherhood, creativity, and men. Thus, on May Day, a holiday that celebrates the return of growth and fertility after the dearth of winter, she kills a mother and makes plans to entice and enslave a sterling example of young manhood. The witch's hatred, however, goes beyond the royal family to the nation itself: there lingers on in her the animosity the White Witch felt toward Narnia as a place of life, beauty, and freedom. She plans, therefore, to rule the Narnians through Rilian, who will murder their natural lords and dominate the land as a ruthless tyrant.

When the owls hear that the children plan to travel to the land of the ancient giants, they carry Jill and Eustace to the northern border of Narnia and entrust the children to Puddleglum, the Marsh-wiggle. *The Silver Chair* ranks as the most creative of the Chronicles because, for the first time, Lewis invents a race of characters. Marsh-wiggles have bodies about the size of a dwarf but are taller than most men because of their very long legs and arms, which have webbed toes and fingers. They hold a gloomy, serious outlook on life. Puddleglum, like Fred Paxford, Lewis's gardener of many years, is "an inwardly optimistic, outwardly pessimistic, dear, frustrating, shrewd countryman of immense integrity."

With Puddleglum as companion and guide, the children set out across Ettinsmoor in search of the ruined city mentioned in the second sign. Puddleglum's prognosis is typical of his outlook: he warns them they will encounter winter, giants, mountains, rivers, hunger, and sore feet. All those difficulties they are able to cope with. However, as they travel northward and cross an ancient bridge spanning a deep ravine, they meet their first serious danger: an internal threat.

A beautiful lady, wearing "a long, fluttering dress of dazzling green," riding with a knight in black armor, advises them to stop for the winter, or at least for a rest, with the gentle giants at the castle of Harfang, where they will find "steaming baths, soft beds," and big meals four times a day. Her words affect the children in a way that the weather, roads, and giants were not able to — they become able to think about nothing else but "how lovely it [will] be to get indoors." They forget about the lost prince, and Jill stops reviewing the signs. By yielding to the temptation of relaxation, of decreased vigilance, they miss the second sign, even as they stumble across the squares and oblongs of the ruined city on a flat hilltop, and the third sign, the written message, although Jill falls into one of its letters. Instead of obeying Aslan's instructions and concentrating on his signs, they have now begun to think of themselves and to rely on their own judgment. They have put themselves into the hands of symbolic giants, of emotional forces that could enslave and devour them, even before they walk into the hands of the literal giants at Harfang. Puddleglum tries to get them to stop, review the signs, and look around them, but the children can think only of creaturely comforts.

Although the internal threat Harfang poses is a greater danger than the physical threat, the latter is great enough: the Gentle Giants come very close to literally *having* the travelers "for [their] Autumn Feast," in the more sinister meaning of Eustace's naive greeting. Fortunately, the travelers escape through an open pantry door during the cook's nap, and the giant king's fears are realized: "We'll have no man-pies to-morrow." Meantime, they have had to confront the inner threat as well. Jill, during their night at Harfang, dreams that a lion tells her to go through the signs, but she has forgotten them all. As her dream continues, the lion shows Jill, through the window, "written in great letters across the world or the sky (she did not know which) . . . the words UNDER ME."

Her seeing words across the world or the sky is another sign — an affirmation that everything under the sky and under the world is controlled by a higher authority, one in which they need to place their trust. Next morning, the children look out a palace window and see, "spread out like a map," the second sign, "the ruins of a gigantic city." And across the center of the city is the third sign: in large, dark lettering, the same words as in Jill's dream, "UNDER ME." Now the travelers must begin again to rely on the signs, to follow the "map" they have been given in order to find the prince, and, when they do, to meet the threats still to come.

After the travelers slip out of the castle of Harfang and escape from the giants, they begin the second stage of the narrative descent used as plot structure, from the Narnian world to a fantasy world below it. The portal to this world is a small crevice beneath the steps in the ruined city, the steps telling the children and Puddleglum they literally must go "under me." In total darkness, they slide down a long incline — perhaps for a mile — and land in the Deep Realm, a wonderfully conceived underground fantasy world, complete with its own oceans, roads, cities, palaces, ports, ships, and trade. There is no sun, but parts of the Deep Realm are illuminated mysteriously. It has its own vegetation (tall, flabby plants with branches like trees), its own animals (mostly dragon-like or bat-like), and its own inhabitants: gnomes, or "Earthmen," of many different sorts — tall, short, with tails or not, with beards or without, some with trunks, others with horns. All are sad as can be, and silent. Here is no talking, no laughter, no music.

The journey to the Deep Realm is reminiscent of the traditional trip to the underworld in classical literature, usually the greatest test of the hero's character. It images the descent into the depths of despair, the pilgrimage into the dark night of the soul, which must either crush the spirit or force it to rise from the worst with new strength and courage. As Jill, Eustace, and Puddleglum are led through cavern after cavern and a lengthy voyage over an underland sea, they reassure themselves, in Puddleglum's words, that they are "back on the right lines. We were to go under the Ruined City, and we *are* under it. We're following the instructions again."

Even as they reach the underworld city and meet the Black Knight, they feel they must continue to follow instructions. When they meet the prince, he instructs them not to be influenced by his pleas while he is bound to the silver chair (and is, ironically, un-enchanted), and they resolve to remain "steady." They do so even when the prince himself says, loud and clear, "Quick! I am sane now. Every night I am sane. If only I could get out of this enchanted chair, it would last. I should be a man again." And when the fourth sign appears, with the prince making his plea in the name of the great Lion Aslan, they have no trouble recognizing it: "It's the Sign," says Puddleglum, and Jill replies, "Oh, what *are* we to do?"

Their real difficulty, now, is to remember and follow the sign given them at the castle of Harfang, that everything is "UNDER ME." They wonder, for example, if the reference to Aslan is not a mere accident. But they must recall what Puddleglum had said but an hour or so before, that "there *are* no accidents." And once again it is Puddleglum who puts the proper emphasis on trust: "You see, Aslan didn't tell Pole what would happen. He only told her what to do. That fellow will be the death of us once he's up, I shouldn't wonder. But that doesn't let us off following the Sign."

They do trust. They follow the signs, and for the moment everything does come right. Half of the children's quest has been achieved: they were brought to Narnia by Aslan first to find and free the prince. Now they must carry out the other half: to escape with him and bring him back to his father.

The conclusion of Rilian's quest, following shortly after Jill, Eustace, and Puddleglum have released him from the silver chair, focuses on the theme of identity: his ordeal had forced him to lose his identity and leads him now to find or regain it. By yielding to a witch's temptations to follow her, Rilian lost touch with reality. He was deceived about the witch: "She is a nosegay of all virtues." And he was deceived about his own identity: "How do you call him? — Billian? Trillian? . . . There is no such man here." His enchantment made him "the toy and lap-dog" of a thoroughly evil sorceress. Only after the others free Rilian from his enchantment and imprisonment can he affirm that "I know myself. . . . I am the King's son of Narnia."

The prince has recovered his identity, but his quest has not yet been completed. All four must face one more test of consciousness and alertness. A bit later the witch returns, and she begins to work an enchantment by incense and hypnotic music. The sweet smell and the thrumming sound overwhelm their minds as the witch chants again and again that the overworld is but a dream, a figment of imagination: "There never was any world but mine." Her words nearly overcome their vigilance with relaxation and comfort: "'Tis a pretty make-believe. . . . There is no Narnia, no Overworld, no sky, no sun, no Aslan."

As Lewis ridicules modernist ideas about education in Chapter 1, so he undermines modernist ideas about myth and meaning in this chapter. What the Witch says assumes that only things we can see and touch are real. She tells the children, Rilian, and Puddleglum that the sun and Aslan are only myths. Having seen a lamp lighting a room, they projected a greater "lamp" that lights the world and called it *sun*, and having seen cats, they imagined a greater cat and called it a *lion*. "The lamp is the real thing; the *sun* is but a tale." Such materialism leads to a "bottom up" theory of myth which says that the "higher" conceptions in myths are generated from the lower. It is, in fact, a modernist means of explaining away that which is regarded as "mythological."

Once he became a Christian, Lewis accepted an older, "top down" theory of mythology. Tolkien convinced him that myth, far from being projected falsehood, is "invention about truth," in biographer Humphrey Carpenter's paraphrase: "We have come from God . . . and inevitably the myths woven by us, though they contain error, will also reflect a splintered fragment of the true light, the eternal truth that is with God." Starting with acceptance of the reality of nonmaterial things, Lewis believed that lower things are the reflections of the higher things, even if, inevitably, only inadequate reflections. As he put it in *Miracles*, myth is "a real though unfocussed gleam of divine truth falling on human imagination."

As on the plains outside Harfang, the temptation is to forget the signs — in this case, signs of reality. Puddleglum, fighting hard against the enchantment, recalls them: "I've seen the sky full of stars," he says, and the sun coming up in the morning and setting in the evening, and these experiences testify to the reality of the overworld and of its maker. The words of the previous night's dream should serve as a new sign: the world and even the underworld are under Aslan. The children, Puddleglum, and Rilian are saved from the enchantment by Puddleglum's rejection of the Witch's materialism. After stamping out the fire, he affirms his faith in the "signs": "Suppose we *have* only dreamed, or made up, all those things — . . . in that case, the made-up things seem a good deal more important than the real ones. . . . I'm going to live as like a Narnian as I can even if there isn't any

Narnia." At that the witch transforms herself back into the serpent form in which she attacked Rilian's mother, and, as the others combine their efforts to kill her, the objectives of both quests are achieved: Rilian's mother is avenged, and Rilian is freed from being a slave of his mother's slayer.

Having completed their ordeal, the characters have reached the end of the downward stages of their journey. But before they begin their ascent from the underworld, they are given a glimpse of another Other-world, deeper still, a truly extraordinary subterranean world. Although it is not developed in detail, only sketched out, it is in its originality and creativity one of Lewis's most impressive achievements as a fantasy writer, on a par with the amazing fantasy world of Perelandra. Upon the witch's death, a chasm opens in the floor of the Deep Realm, exposing, deep below it, the world of Bism. From there the witch had brought the Earthmen to work as her slaves, and to it they now descend as rapidly as possible — a world dazzling in its brightness from the river of fire that runs through it, a river inhabited by white-hot salamanders that are also witty, eloquent speakers. Alongside the river are planted fields and groves in which grow living gold, silver, and gems. One of the Earthmen, Golg, invites the prince, Eustace, Jill, and Puddleglum to accompany him to Bism, where he can give them bunches of rubies to eat and cups of diamond-juice to drink. It is a marvelous Secondary World, and when the prince reluctantly declines the invitation, he admits that he leaves "half of [his] heart" in Bism. Many readers do as well.

As the Earthmen descend to reach their land, the prince, Eustace, Jill, and Puddleglum must ascend to reach theirs. That ascent is neither simple nor sure, but once again they are given a sign. Rilian's shield, hitherto black and without a device, now turns bright as silver, and on it appears the figure of a lion, which signifies, the prince believes, that "Aslan will be our good lord," regardless of what may happen to them. Their ability to accept that sign, to trust in Aslan as they begin their long, slow climb and soon find themselves in utter darkness, illustrates the extent to which they have, through their ordeal, come to know themselves and to trust in Another. The first stage of their ascent is complete when they realize that they have not only emerged into the outer world but have come out "in the heart of Narnia."

They arrive on the evening of the Great Snow Dance, a festive celebration in which fauns and dryads do complicated steps and figures with a ring of dwarfs circling them and throwing snowballs between them in perfect time with the music and with aim so careful that no one is hit. It is fitting that, at the end of a quest that required following directions and placing full trust in their giver, the heroes and heroine are greeted by a dance which, in its complex pattern and need for complete cooperation, symbolizes such adherence and trust.

The nearly perfect symmetry of the book is evident as the prince and the travelers who left Narnia earlier now return to it. It continues as the king, who was departing from Cair Paravel in Chapter 3, comes back in Chapter 16. In the background "solemn, triumphal music" conveys a tone of celebration. But Lewis replaces the traditional marriage of the prince (used as a symbol of harmony and celebration in *The Voyage of the "Dawn Treader"*) with the death of the king: "Suddenly the King's head fell back," and the musicians stopped. When they resumed playing, it was "a tune to break your heart."

The ending seems at this point appropriate to tragedy, not fairy tale. But the story does not end with death. It moves on to the second phase of ascent, the return to Aslan's mountain, continuing the symmetrical and circular structure of the story. When Aslan tells the children he has come "to bring [them] Home," his words apply to King Caspian as well, for he takes the dead king to Aslan's mountain, and Aslan, Eustace, and Jill weep over him. The Christian imagery present in Chapter 2 reappears in Chapter 16, and catastrophe turns to eucatastrophe.

The imagery begins with water, the king lying in the same stream from which Jill drank living water in Chapter 2. It continues with Aslan's blood being mingled with the water, resulting in new life: the king's white beard turns to grey, then to yellow, then disappears; his cheeks grow fresh and smooth, his eyes open, and he leaps up and stands before them — "a very young man, or a boy." The depiction of a new life of youth and vigor in another country, of the reversal of youth's normal decline into age, provides for children (as well as adults) a beautiful picture of death: it makes death less fearful and unnatural, for, after all, as Aslan tells Eustace, "most people have [died], you know." And the rebirth completes the movement of the story, as Caspian, having descended in death, ascends to live forever in the idyllic world of Aslan's country.

The movements of descent and ascent that give structure to the story as a whole and provide a suitable vehicle for the themes of revenge and rescue, words and signs, obedience and freedom, and identity and instruction, appear also, in reversed order, in the frame story. The symmetry of the book is concluded as Eustace and Jill return to Experiment House. At the beginning of the story, Jill and Eustace scramble *up* "the steep, earthy slope" to escape the persecution of the likes of Adela Pennyfather, Cholmondely Major, Edith Winterblott, "Spotty" Sorner, big Bannister, and the "loathsome Garrett twins." At the end of the story, Jill, Eustace, and Caspian rush *down* the same slope, weapons in hand, to chastise the gang. The modernism motif introduced in Chapter 1 recurs in Chapter 16, with a political twist. The head of the school goes into hysterics when she sees the broken wall and a lion. It is clear she'll no longer be effective as a head, so she is made "an Inspector to interfere with other Heads." When they discover she isn't much good even at that, they get her "into Parliament where she lived happily ever after."

The seemingly catastrophic events of Chapter 1 turn in Chapter 16 to eucatastrophe, as things change "for the better" at Experiment House, and it becomes "quite a good school." Themes that seem distant and fanciful in the world of Rilian and the underworld are brought close and made real in the frame events, for Aslan seems to know all about Experiment House "quite as well as they did." By logical extension, he knows all other things in our world as well and gives us, here, the same assurance he gave in Narnia: that all things are "under him." And that assurance extends into the next book to be published, through the theme of Providence that runs through *The Horse and His Boy*.

Chapter 8

Place and Personal Identity in
The Horse and His Boy

If we are made for heaven, the desire for our proper place will be already in us, but not yet attached to the true object. . . . And this, I think, is just what we find.

"**M**ost good 'fairy-stories,'" Tolkien asserts, are about a place and its effect on persons. They "are about the *aventures* of men in the Perilous Realm or upon its shadowy marches." *The Horse and His Boy* deals with *aventures*, of two children and two horses rather than "men," but not in the Perilous Realm or even its shadowy marches. In comparison to the other Chronicles, *The Horse and His Boy* has fewer fairy-tale qualities — it generates less sense of wonder and mystery, and its world conveys a smaller aura of enchantment. Nevertheless, it is effective as a well-written romantic adventure story drawing more on techniques of realistic fiction than those of high fantasy. Central to those adventures is the importance of place — of a homeland — in finding and regaining one's sense of personal identity.

This is the only Chronicle in which there is no movement of characters between our world and Narnia and in which the main characters are inhabitants of the Secondary World. The events of the story occur within the final chapter of *The Lion, the Witch and the Wardrobe,* during the years the Pevensies rule in Narnia after the death of the White Witch and before they stumble back into our world. Characters from our world provide the link to the Narnian world, but in this case they are already there when the book opens and are still there when it closes. The result lessens the sense that the action is in a Secondary World. The settings for the first eleven chapters are Calormen, the desert, and Archenland, all of them human societies. Except for the presence of two talking horses, the action could as well have occurred in a Middle Eastern area of our world.

In this book the Pevensies are not the central characters, though an action by Susan supplies the unifying point of the plot. In the last chapter of *The Lion, the Witch and the Wardrobe*, Susan has grown into a beautiful young woman. Kings ask for her hand in marriage. In a subplot that occupies only a chapter of this book, we find that Susan is visiting a suitor, Rabadash, crown prince of Calormen, a large, powerful country south of Narnia. Realizing that Rabadash will hold them as prisoners if Susan refuses him, Tumnus the Faun and Edmund plan their escape from Calormen. The rest of the book focuses on a boy, a girl, and two horses, all on the move together (like Susan and her party) to escape a repressive or enslaving situation. The plot is not a traditional quest story, like that of *The Voyage of the "Dawn Treader"* or *The Silver Chair*; but, along with escape, it does, like the three preceding books, involve a journey with a purpose — in this case, to warn the Archenlanders about a planned sneak attack by Rabadash's army. Through that journey, the four central characters come to a deeper understanding of themselves: each returns home or reaches a new homeland and finds a new identity.

In constructing the plot, Lewis uses several motifs that in legend and literature have long been associated with themes of identity. It opens with a "lost child" motif, in which a child is separated from his or her parents by being sold, kidnapped, or put away, then later reunited with them. As Shasta, the boy, eavesdrops on a stranger's conversation with the man he calls Father, he discovers, contrary to what he has always supposed, that he is not the son of Arsheesh, who admits that he discovered the boy as a baby years ago in a boat that washed ashore and that he has no idea who the boy's parents are.

This plot situation is one frequently used in literature. We recall such examples as the Greek myth of Oedipus, Shakespeare's *Cymbeline*, Henry Fielding's *Joseph Andrews* and *Tom Jones*, along with many other plays and novels, as well as the biblical account of Moses. The heroes do not know who they are — their sense of identity is incorrect — and the story concerns their efforts to discover, or regain, their true identity. Thus Shasta understandably responds to the discovery that Arsheesh is not his father by exclaiming, "Why, I might be anyone!"

Readers relate powerfully to this motif because of the natural and universal need, even for those whose parentage is known, to learn who they are, but also, for Christians, because of their need to know *whose* they are. It aligns well with the Christian belief that when separated from their heavenly Father, people are lost and at a loss as to their true identity. Lewis, however, would not want such a parallel imposed in a reductive way, implying this is "all" that the story is about.

The "lost child" motif blends very naturally into the quest for one's homeland, introduced by the talking horse, Bree, with whom Shasta escapes from his home and Calormen. Bree ran away from Narnia as a foal, was captured and forced to work like an ordinary horse, and has been longing to return home ever since. This too is something humans have desired and needed throughout the centuries. Poets of all times have written about people's concern with their origins, with the community in which they were born, with a place that gives them a sense of their beginning and thus helps give them a sense of identity. This urge was especially deep among the ancients. The greatest of the classical stories is about Odysseus's longing to return to Ithaca, a rocky island on which horses could not run, few crops could be grown, and life was demanding and difficult. But it was Odysseus's homeland, and the urge to return to it became his driving passion. The Hebrews felt similar longings during their exile, longings movingly expressed in the words of the Psalmist: "By the rivers of Babylon, there we sat down, yea, we wept when we remembered Zion."

For Lewis this natural longing for home reflects something more than a natural origin. It suggests, and *The Horse and His Boy* illustrates, the longing a soul has for its real heavenly home. In his sermon "The Weight of Glory," Lewis discusses this "desire for our own far-off country"; in *Mere Christianity* he calls it "the desire for my true country, which I shall not find till after death." This deeper dimension of the search for one's home and thus for one's identity is conveyed by the symbolism of the North. Shasta from the first is interested in the North and says that he has longed to go there all his life. Bree frequently cries out "Narnia and the North" and speaks of the North in paradisal terms. For Lewis himself, the North was a source of longing. When he first saw the title *Siegfried and the Twilight of the Gods* in a review of a new edition of Wagner's opera, "pure 'Northernness' engulfed me," he recalls in *Surprised by Joy,* and the longing he felt was like "returning at last from exile and desert lands to my own country."

The way Lewis develops this longing for the North is by associating it and Narnia with images of lushness and rural life, in contrast to images of a desert and a city. A desert, though it of course can be a place of rugged beauty, is usually associated in people's minds with barrenness and death. So it is in *The Horse and His Boy.* When Shasta reaches the desert, it feels like the end of the world: the grass stops suddenly, the sand begins. Later, when Shasta and his companions are in the middle of the desert at dawn and Shasta can see the vast grey flatness on every side, "it look[s] absolutely dead."

The city, Tashbaan, on the other hand, is full of life, but not the beauties of nature. Its narrow streets are crowded and stifling and full of unpleasant smells. It is on an island, an isolated space, covered by roads, buildings, and terraces. Only in its upscale neighborhoods, appropriately situated near the top of its pyramidal shape, does one find grass and trees. Worst of all, it is repressive, with but one traffic regulation: "that everyone who is less important has to get out of the way for everyone who is more important." In striking contrast, when Shasta and his fellow travelers reach the end of the desert and the beginning of the North, they find water and life: soft grass, a river, cool delicious smells, and the sound of a nightingale. The North, in contrast to the denseness in Tashbaan, is open country, with not a road or a house in sight. Most important, instead of Tashbaan's repression, the North is characterized by freedom.

Shasta and Bree, two "long-lost captive[s] returning to home and freedom," set off on a journey, a traditional image for growth in experience. In their journey they present contrasting but complementary patterns: Shasta must become more adult, Bree more childlike. Shasta's journey begins in the ignorance of childhood. He is unfamiliar with the world beyond the limited horizons of the fisherman's hut — he knows nothing of geography, he has not been taught manners, he is ignorant of customs among the wealthy, and he has no idea of what a large city is like. His awkwardness is all the more pronounced because it is placed in constant contrast to the adult confidence of Bree, which is born of broad knowledge of himself and the world.

As a free-born Narnian and a trained, experienced warhorse, Bree distinguishes himself from the simple, dumb creatures he has lived among. His superior opinion of himself is manifest in his patronizing attitude toward Shasta. For example, when the boy struggles to climb onto his back for the first time, he says, "Funny to think of me who has led cavalry charges and won races having a potato-sack like you in the saddle!" Bree's attitude is marked by pride in his class and status (later he hopes he has not unknowingly picked up any "low, bad habits" in the South). Shasta has no reason for such self-confidence. He has always assumed himself to be the son, and little better than the slave, of a humble fisherman, who in turn was little better than a slave to his social superiors. Unlike Bree, he has no reason to be proud of what he is and no basis for knowing who he is.

Bree and Shasta are joined in their journey by two female characters, also on a journey to find a homeland and a new identity. Hwin, the horse, and Aravis, her girl, contrast to each other and to their respective male counterparts. In this case the human possesses self-confidence and needs to learn humility, while the horse needs to develop self-esteem and assurance. As their journey together begins, Hwin feels shy in the presence of Bree, a great warhorse, and she says very little. Not so with Aravis, who is, after all, a Tarkheena — cultured, sophisticated, and intelligent — and converses with the assurance that her social positions and experience have given her. In contrast to both Shasta and Hwin, she is haughty and self-centered, as is seen especially in her indifferent attitude toward the punishment that the servant whom she drugged in order to slip away from home will receive. Her attitude is epitomized a bit later when Bree has to urge her to "try to look less like a princess," a problem Hwin and Shasta do not face at all.

On their journey, the four pass through testing grounds that lead to self-understanding and growth — Shasta and Aravis in the city (Chapters

3-8), Bree and Hwin in the desert (Chapters 9-11). In the city of Tashbaan, Shasta and Aravis encounter models instrumental in their development. Shasta's is a positive model of what he can and would like to be, a group of men from Archenland and Narnia who look and act very different from the people he has lived with all his life: "Instead of being grave and mysterious like most Calormenes, they walked with a swing and let their arms and shoulders go free, and chatted and laughed." When Shasta is mistaken for a prince of Archenland and taken to the palace where the Narnians are staying, he gets to know them as "the very nicest kind of grown-up[s]." Although he wants to make a good impression on them, he withdraws and stays silent, the way his life in Calormen has taught him; and because he is in the room as the Narnians discuss their strategy for escaping from Prince Rabadash, he assumes they will kill him if they discover who he is: "He had, you see, no idea of how noble and free-born people behave."

The model they provide him is a helpful one, as is that of Prince Corin of Archenland, for whom Shasta had been mistaken and whom he soon meets. The mistaken identity introduces another traditional literary motif, the "missing twin." Shakespeare borrowed this motif from classical literature to use in *The Comedy of Errors* and *Twelfth Night*. It also appears in the works of many other authors, including Mark Twain's *The Prince and the Pauper* and *Pudd'nhead Wilson*. The motif relates closely to the theme of personal identity. When he sees Shasta, Corin asks, "Who are you?" and Shasta replies, "I'm nobody, nobody in particular, I mean." But now he has met a boy "almost exactly like himself" who provides him an example of openness and honesty. Both his meeting nice people and caring what they think about him and his meeting Corin become major steps in learning to know who he is and the kind of person he wants to become.

The model Aravis finds, on the other hand, is a reminder of the kind of life she is fleeing from. While waiting on a street for a litter to pass, she is recognized by an old acquaintance, Lasaraleen Tarkheena, who takes her and the horses home. Lasaraleen exhibits the same haughtiness and self-concern as Aravis. Self-indulgent and empty-headed, she cares only about "clothes and parties and gossip." Running through Aravis's adventure is yet another motif, that of disguise — she is disguised as her brother when she runs away from home, as a peasant when she enters Tashbaan, and as a slave girl when she leaves. Disguise is another device often associated with the identity theme, symbolizing a confusion of identity for the person wearing the disguise. In this case it suggests that Aravis has not reached a comfortable level of self-acceptance — she seems to think the "common little boy" she is traveling with is "not good enough" for her, and she finds it painful to walk into Tashbaan as a peasant rather than ride in on a litter attended by slaves.

Aravis comes to a clearer understanding of who she is and what she values by spending time with Lasaraleen and particularly by hearing Lasaraleen rebuke her for having a peasant boy as companion: "It's not Nice." Aravis, by now so tired of listening to Lasaraleen that she would rather be with Shasta, replies, "You forget that I'll be a nobody, just like him, when we get to Narnia." The answer again brings in the identity theme, though this time with an ironic twist, for by now the reader has ample hints that Shasta will not be a mere nobody in Narnia. The fact that Aravis says it signals the direction her growth will take, with a humility and acceptance new to her character.

The testing ground for the horses is the desert. From their adventures in Tashbaan, Shasta learns the best route across the desert, and Aravis learns about Prince Rabadash's plan for a surprise attack on Archenland and Narnia. As the horses and children set out to warn King Lune of the danger, the grueling trip across the desert brings out the main attributes of the two horses. When the worst is over but the journey is not yet complete, Bree insists on a rest and a snack, but Hwin replies, "I feel just like Bree that I *can't* go on. But when Horses have humans (with spurs and things) on their backs, aren't they often made to go on when they're feeling like this? and then they find they can. I m-mean — oughtn't we to be able to do even more, now that we're free." But she says it modestly and shyly and allows Bree to overwhelm her with his forceful assertion that he knows more about what a horse can stand than she does. Hwin is "a very sensible mare" — she, after all, thought up the plan they used for getting past Tashbaan. She must gain more confidence and thoughtfully assert herself. And slowly she does, for Hwin, though the weaker and more tired of the two, sets the pace the rest of the way.

It takes the threat of a lion, as they approach Archenland, to force Bree to begin to know himself. The contrast in the responses of Bree and Shasta to this danger reminds us again of the different directions their growth must take. Shasta's cry to Bree, as he sees the lion snapping at Hwin's heels and clawing at Aravis's back — "Must go back! Must help!" — is a recognition that his sense of duty now overrides his personal desire. He discovers the meaning of courage as he turns back to help Aravis and Hwin with no weapon and little chance of saving himself or them. All his awkwardness and self-consciousness disappear when he responds to an as yet undefined desire to do the right thing, another indication of how he benefited from meeting the Narnians. In comparison with Shasta's bravery, Bree's desperate flight from the lion looks very much like cowardice. He says of it later, "[Shasta] ran in the right direction: ran *back*. And that is what shames me most of all. I, who called myself a war-horse and boasted of a hundred fights, to be beaten by a little human boy." In facing this shame, Bree learns a first and necessary — but not yet adequate — lesson in humility.

The separation of Shasta and Bree is a further step in their progress toward identity and maturation. Shasta moves on into Narnia and initiation into adulthood (Chapters 12-13); Bree remains at the hermitage until, by giving up his illusions about his own worth, he becomes like a little child (Chapter 14). Shasta discovers that his act of courage was only the beginning of doing good. He is sent running to warn King Lune about Rabadash's approach. After fulfilling that responsibility, he travels over the mountains and joins Corin and the Narnian army on its way to aid the Archenlanders. Now Shasta, rather than Bree, participates in battle, not arrogantly but with determination. And though "he knows nothing about this work, . . . hasn't the faintest idea what to do with his sword," he again does what he believes he should, taking another major step toward adulthood.

Rather than action, Bree needs rest, time to reflect upon the lessons he has been taught along the way. His host, the Hermit of the Southern March, tells him, "You're not quite the great horse you had come to think, from living among poor dumb horses. . . . But as long as you know you're nobody very special, you'll be a very decent sort of Horse." As Bree is discovering that he is no longer a great Calormene warhorse and that he must accept a new identity as an ordinary citizen of Narnia, Shasta is meeting King Lune and discovering his father and his true identity: he is no longer

Shasta, the common, self-conscious fisherman's child, but Cor, Crown Prince of Archenland.

For all four main characters in *The Horse and His Boy,* an encounter with Aslan is the final step in gaining their fullest sense of identity. Shasta meets Aslan on the road across the mountains into Narnia. Riding along in the fog, he senses the breathing of a creature beside him, but notices it only gradually and doesn't know how long it has been there. When told that the creature has been beside him all his life, comforting, protecting, and preparing for him, he asks, "Who *are* you?" Three times the voice answers, "Myself," first low and deep, then loud and clear, and then in a soft whisper, the reply alluding to the answer God gave Moses when he asked the same question beside the burning bush, "I am." It also catches up in three tonal images the Christian idea of a God in three persons. Gradually, as the light increases, Shasta sees his companion: "After one glance at the Lion's face he slipped out of the saddle and fell at its feet. He couldn't say anything but then he didn't want to say anything, and he knew he needn't say anything." This is a powerfully numinous moment, culminating in a description of the effect on Shasta of being in the divine presence: "A new and different sort of trembling came over him," not trembling from fear for his physical safety but trembling from awe out of his sense of insignificance compared to the greatness of the being beside him.

Shasta's encounter with and commitment to Aslan are not the only ways Christian themes are incorporated into the story. Unlike the other books, this one does not offer characters and events that invite readers to think of biblical parallels. Instead, the story uses repeated episodes to build an atmosphere of assurance. Out of this emerges a theme of Providence, appearing most explicitly in words spoken by the Hermit of the Southern March. Aravis arrives at the Hermit's compound with only some scratches from the lion that chased her and Hwin. "I say," she exclaims, "I *have* had luck." The Hermit replies, "Daughter, . . . I have now lived a hundred and nine winters in this world and have never yet met any such thing as Luck." The word appears several other times in the book, each time in a situation where it emphasizes that none of the occurrences has been accidental.

From the apparently fortuitous encounter of Shasta and Bree at a remote cottage along the sea, to the seeming coincidence of a look-alike being seen and brought where he would learn directions across the desert, to the seemingly trivial recognition of Aravis by Lasaraleen, which put her in a position to learn of the plans to attack Archenland and Narnia, all was shaped and guided by Aslan. Talking to Shasta later, Aslan adds other details to fill out the plan: it was he whose roaring forced Shasta and Aravis together and who chased them for the last mile so that Shasta could get to Archenland in time. It was he who, long ago, brought the boat in which the young prince lay to shore, where Arsheesh found him. Aslan allowed Shasta to spend years in a disagreeable situation and then triggered a series of interrelated events in order to put Shasta in a position to rescue Archenland from the greatest danger it ever faced. In the words of Joseph in the Bible, who, after undergoing a similar series of oppressive but important events, said to the brothers who sold him into slavery, "Ye thought evil against me; but God meant it unto good, to bring to pass, as it is this day, to save much people alive."

The other three characters also meet Aslan, though less dramatically, and in meeting him they too confront their inadequacies and begin to trust in him. Bree, in his desire to be self-sufficient, asserts disdainfully that it would be ridiculous to think Aslan is a real lion, one that can really help or hurt those who need it. When the lion's whiskers tickle his ear, however, he must face up to himself and the fact that he has been "rather a fool." His pretensions have been destroyed, his pride has been lost, and he enters his homeland like a child, lacking experience and a settled sense of his identity, but now with a firm basis for regaining them.

When Aravis meets Aslan, she learns that she has encountered him before. It was Aslan who scratched her back to teach her an essential lesson: "The scratches on your back, tear for tear, throb for throb, blood for blood, were equal to the stripes laid on the back of your stepmother's slave because of the drugged sleep you cast upon her. You needed to know what it felt like." On her journey, Aravis learns to understand more about herself and to care more about others. She learns the humility and openness she needs for further growth and maturity.

Hwin, from being pressed into the leadership role on the journey, gains assurance without losing her humility. When she sees the lion, she shakes with fear, but she has the strength to trot directly across to him and say, "I'd sooner be eaten by you than fed by anyone else." In handing herself over to Aslan, she finds confirmation and affirmation of her being: "Dearest daughter, . . . Joy shall be yours." Only after the four main characters encounter Aslan, then, can it truly be said, as they enter Archenland and the North, that they are "returning to home and freedom."

This central theme, the finding or regaining of identity, is summed up through Prince Rabadash in the final chapter. Like Shasta (now Prince Cor), Rabadash has met the Narnians in Tashbaan and been on a journey through the desert. He has, however, not profited from his experiences. In contrast to Cor, who humbly apologizes for the courtly clothes he now wears and the trumpeter who goes before him, Rabadash is arrogant and defiant. Of the major characters, only Rabadash claims to know Aslan's identity already when he meets him: "You are the foul fiend of Narnia." Obviously he does not know Aslan, however. He must learn that he also does not know himself, does not realize that he is being an ass.

He must learn the lessons of humility and submission that Cor and the others had to learn. "Forget your pride," Aslan urges him, "and accept the mercy of these good kings." Because he will not give up the traits and actions that he thinks make him what he is, he must lose his identity. He can face up to what he is only by being turned physically into the ass he has already become through his attitude and behavior. Only by submitting himself to his own god, Tash, will he regain his identity and be healed. At the great Autumn Feast that year, he stands before the altar of Tash and turns again into a man. Eventually he becomes "the most peaceable Tisroc Calormen had ever known" — not because this experience has transformed his personality, but because he will turn into an ass permanently if he travels more than ten miles from Tash's temple. The change in Rabadash could come only by the Calormene modes of compulsion and constraint, not in the joyful, fulfilling way by which Hwin, Bree, Aravis, and Shasta found themselves and freedom on their way to Narnia and Aslan.

In many cases journey plots conclude with a marriage, as *The Voyage of the "Dawn Treader"* ended with the marriage of Caspian to Ramandu's daughter, symbolizing harmony, order, and attainment of personal maturity. That is the case also in *The Horse and His Boy*. Shasta and Aravis, years later, get married, and Bree and Hwin get married, but not to each other, and in the end all three couples form homes within their homeland. The themes of home and harmony, of place and personal identity, carry over to the next book in order of publication. *The Magician's Nephew* begins with a boy displaced from home and lacking harmony in his life, and ends with him living in a new place with a deeper sense of his personhood. In between he witnesses a creation scene in which harmony, order, and place are attained on a much grander scale.

Chapter 9

Endings and Beginnings in
The Magician's Nephew

Either the stream of events had a beginning or it had not. If it had, then we are faced with something like creation.

"In O[xford] I wrote a cosmogonical myth," Tolkien wrote to a correspondent, describing the origins of the Other-world that was developing in his imagination. His fairy stories are deeply involved in issues of beginnings and endings, of eras and of worlds. Lewis also wrote a creation myth. The sixth of the Chronicles to be published, *The Magician's Nephew*, does not begin with the beginning of Narnia. Instead, first comes the account of the ending of another world. Structurally and thematically, the book suggests, beginnings and endings cannot be separated.

The story begins with the ordinary: in the back garden of a row house in London are two children, Polly Plummer and Digory Kirke. The opening occurs in a specific historical time, the early 1900s, when (for children reading the book in 1955), "your grandfather was a child." But that ordinary place and time turns out not to be ordinary at all: "In those days Mr. Sherlock Holmes was still living in Baker Street and the Bastables were looking for treasure in the Lewisham Road." This is a world in which people generally assumed to be characters in books turn out to be real, in which someone's godmother could have "fairy blood in her," and in which a magician can send guinea pigs and children off to an Other-world.

The Magician's Nephew is the story of two starkly contrasting magical worlds, Charn and Narnia, using strikingly different kinds of magic in profoundly different ways. The magic of the one world appears first in an ordinary attic room of the house shared by Digory's uncle and aunt. When Digory and Polly accidentally enter Uncle Andrew's study, they find a tray of brilliantly colored green and yellow rings emitting a faint humming sound, rings that turn out to be magical means of conveyance between different worlds.

The rings are an example of what Tolkien calls "the vulgar devices of the laborious, scientific magician." And Uncle Andrew is just such a practitioner of magic. He studied diligently to discover the source of the box his fairy godmother told him to destroy and learned about magic from "some devilish queer people." He carried out experiments to learn the magical properties of the dust contained in the box, succeeded at last in fashioning the magic rings, and then experimented with their powers, first on a guinea pig and finally on Polly. Such power, according to Tolkien, is "not an art but [only] a technique."

Uncle Andrew's only desire is power, domination over things and people. His total lack of concern for others is epitomized at a level children can understand by his earlier experiments on guinea pigs: "Some of them only died. Some exploded like little bombs." Young readers, many of whom, like Digory, have guinea pigs of their own, will understand. And they will see through the cruel thing he does to Polly and Digory: tricking Polly into taking a yellow ring, which makes her disappear from their world, and then forcing Digory to use a yellow ring to bring her the green ring that she will need to return. When Uncle Andrew admits he had planned out the entire thing, Digory reiterates the point for the readers: "You're simply a wicked, cruel magician like the ones in the stories."

The yellow rings take them to "the Wood Between the Worlds," as the title of Chapter 3 calls it, one of Lewis's most creative imaginative inventions. Digory describes this as an "in-between place" — not an Otherworld itself but a profoundly magical place from which one can go to any number of Other-worlds, the portals to which are magical pools of water. Digory and Polly experiment with them, first making sure that the pool from which they emerged will take them back to Uncle Andrew's attic. Then they set out to explore other worlds by jumping into another pool:

"Any pool will do," Digory says. "Let's try that one." Earlier books in the series (for those who do not read this one first) would suggest that Digory's apparently casual choice was not in the larger scheme of things a random one.

The children arrive in an Other-world that is full of enchantment but is not a Faërie world. They begin exploring it and discover that they are in the ruins of a very ancient world, dead, cold, and empty. There are not, and apparently never were, any talking animals or fairies, dryads, or dwarfs in it. It had been inhabited by apparently ordinary humans, "taller than the people of our world" but not otherwise different. When the children discover a Hall of Images, with hundreds of lifelike effigies tracing the history of the royal family, the figures are referred to and described as "people." Except for the fact that the whole room is "stiff with enchantments," the city Digory and Polly are in could as well be the ruins of an ancient city in our world.

In the Hall of Images they find a little golden bell and hammer on a stone pillar engraved with enchanted letters:

> Make your choice, adventurous Stranger;
> Strike the bell and bide the danger,
> Or wonder, till it drives you mad,
> What would have followed if you had.

Digory here, as earlier in his first visit to the Wood between the Worlds, shares with Reepicheep and Caspian a sense of honor and daring. Like Reepicheep throughout *The Voyage of the "Dawn Treader,"* and like Caspian as he looks longingly into Aslan's country in that book and Rilian as he looks longingly into Bism in *The Silver Chair,* Digory wants to leave no adventure untried. He is willing always, heroically, to "bide the danger." He strikes the bell and thus awakens from a magic spell the last effigy in the line, a very tall, beautiful woman, richly dressed, with a look of fierceness and pride.

The woman, who identifies herself as Jadis, the last queen of Charn, is a magician. Like Uncle Andrew, she is interested only in power and in magic solely as a technique that will give her domination over others. Uncle Andrew's evil, in one sense, is only a pale reflection of the wickedness of Queen Jadis, to whom he is compared explicitly. Both Uncle Andrew and Jadis, for example, break promises, believing that they are above conventional moral rules. And both end their claims to moral freedom with the words "Ours . . . is a high and lonely destiny," although, as Digory notices, the words sound more impressive when Queen Jadis says them. Both have a greedy look on their faces, produced by their self-centeredness. As Uncle Andrew asserts his freedom to do as he pleased with his guinea pigs ("That's what the creatures were there for. I'd bought them myself"), so Jadis claims that the common people of Charn were hers to do with as she pleased: "They were all *my* people. What else were they there for but to do my will." And both admit that they have "paid a terrible price" to attain the evil knowledge and power they possess. Uncle Andrew may not be as evil as Queen Jadis: he is only a dabbler in black magic, lacking "the Mark" of those who have sold their souls to the art. But the parallels between them point out a continuity in corruption. The difference between slight evils and greater ones, between the "pantomime demon" and the supremely evil temptress, is a matter of degree, not of kind.

Jadis's greed for power was so great that she would rather destroy her world than lose it to her sister. Thus, at the end of a great battle, when the last of Jadis's soldiers had fallen, she used her ultimate weapon: she "spoke the Deplorable Word." This was a magical word which, uttered with proper rituals, would destroy all life in that world except that of the one who spoke it. "A moment later," she continues, "I was the only living thing beneath the sun." She then put a spell on herself to cause herself to sleep until someone rang the enchanted bell. Now she has returned as her world is about to end.

Thus *The Magician's Nephew* begins with a world that is dying. The children see a great, red sun over Charn, one "near the end of its life." The book continues, however, with the beginning of another world. After the children unintentionally take Jadis to London, occasioning the delightful account of her madcap adventures in that staid, sedate city, they manage to get her — along with Uncle Andrew, a cabby, and his horse — back to the Wood between the Worlds, and from there they pass through another portal into another world, the as yet "empty world" of Narnia.

This too is a world of enchantment, but its magic is of a different kind from that of Uncle Andrew and Jadis. Closer to it is Tolkien's "elvish craft," creative power, "artistic in desire and purpose." But what we see here is even higher: divine creativity. At first this world is dark and, like Charn, seems cold and lifeless. Soon differences become evident, however. A voice that seems to come from the depths of the earth, even to be the deep voice of the earth, begins to sing, the voice of Aslan, marvelously bringing into that world the light and warmth needed for life. The sky turns from black to gray, then to white, pink, and gold. As the voice rises and reaches its mightiest note, the sun comes up. It is explicitly contrasted to the dying sun in Charn. That one had looked older than ours. This one looks younger, and even seems to be laughing and full of joy as it comes up. As the song continues, Narnia becomes clothed with grass and flowers, decorated with shrubs and trees, and populated with animals and insects. The creation reaches its climax when Aslan, having selected two of many kinds of animals to be talking animals, says, in the deepest, wildest voice the children had ever heard, "Narnia, Narnia, Narnia, awake."

Lewis's creation account is one that children can respond to more easily than the biblical version, first because they identify with the two children who are present at it and through whose eyes readers see what takes place, and second, because of Lewis's use of detail. One can readily imagine the grass spreading out from the lion like a pool and running up the sides of little hills like a wave, or visualize animals slowly, with some difficulty, emerging from the soil. In all directions the grassy land swells into humps, and the humps vibrate and expand until they burst open, sending dirt flying in all directions. From each an animal emerges slowly and begins to shake itself off.

Vivid as the details, drawn from several creation stories, are, they are less important than the total effect of the story. Parallel to the natural and deep-seated human need to know individual origins (the identity theme discussed in Chapter 8) is the need, equally natural and deep-seated, to know the origin of the world. The desire is not so much to know the methods and details as to know the meaning and purpose behind it all. Lewis, therefore, is less concerned with the how than the who. God the Son, who was the creator of our world, in his incarnation as Aslan is creator of

Narnia. Aslan is the focal point of the scene, always present, always at the center of the important events. There is purposefulness, even an inexorability about his actions as he walks forward, always at the same steady pace. His impact on the scene and on the children is suggested by the narrator's comment about how exciting and intense the colors of Narnia were, "until you saw the Singer himself," which made you forget everything else. The character of the creator tells a great deal about the purpose of his creation: "Creatures, I give you yourselves," he says, and "this land of Narnia . . . and . . . myself."

Aslan's importance is brought home decisively when Polly concludes, with an unspeakable thrill, "that all the things were coming (as she said) 'out of the Lion's head.'" Polly's phrase is very close to words Lewis used in talking about the creation in *Mere Christianity*: "Christianity . . . thinks God made the world — that space and time, heat and cold, and all the colours and tastes, and all the animals and vegetables, are things that God 'made up out of His head' as a man makes up a story."

The *Mere Christianity* passage goes on to state that Christianity "also thinks that a great many things have gone wrong with the world that God made and that God insists, and insists very loudly, on our putting them right again." Those passages, linking creation and moral choice, clarify the structure and unity of *The Magician's Nephew*. The dominant quality of the book is the newness, vitality, and fecundity of the creation scene: that sense of life and growth lingers on as the principal flavor of the story. But one can never disassociate it completely from the sense of defeat and death that preceded it, in the story of Charn.

And Lewis's point is that the two can never be separated. Life leads, inevitably, to choice, and choice, just as inevitably, makes wrong decisions possible. There is a tinge of death, then, mixed in with the dominant theme of life in *The Magician's Nephew*. At Narnia's birth, corruption entered the land, and "evil will come of that evil," but Aslan makes provision to delay its full effects as long as possible. Digory, who brought evil from the wasteland of Charn, is sent to a garden — the contrasting images are important — for the means to contain that evil. The journey to the garden to fetch a silver apple that can protect Narnia is another traditional journey of testing and growth.

Digory is tempted first to take an apple for himself, but he resists the temptation in part through his early moral training and in part through the glance of a Phoenix (a symbol of resurrection and here an incarnation of Aslan, who had briefly taken the form of a lamb in *The Voyage of the "Dawn Treader"*), which is roosting in a tree above him. Digory is tempted next with the kind of power Uncle Andrew and Jadis craved early in the story — he can eat the fruit, live forever, and be king of this world. But this temptation Digory can shrug off easily, for he has no desire for power and glory.

Finally, he is tempted to substitute his own personal desire — bringing health to his mother, who has been near death throughout the story — for the broader purpose Aslan has in mind, of making Narnia the benevolent land he intends it to be. Jadis, whom he encounters there, urges him to take an apple to his mother to heal her: "Soon she will be quite well again." This temptation, with its mixture of unselfishness, is the great test. The language used in describing Digory's dilemma reminds us of the "terrible price" Uncle Andrew and Jadis paid to gain their ends, as "the most terrible choice" confronts him.

He is able to resist the temptation, however, when Jadis suggests that he leave Polly behind, which makes all that Jadis has been saying sound "false and hollow." Through his adventure, Digory has grown in strength and spirit: he has achieved an inner harmony that allows him to face and resist the most powerful of temptations to evil. Upon his return to Aslan with the apple, he receives the accolade "Well done." Lewis's allusion here to Matthew 25:21 suggests that Digory, like the servant in Jesus' parable who used his talents wisely, is a good and faithful servant, preparing himself to enter into the joys of his Lord.

The importance of choice goes beyond individuals to nations, a motif introduced by the story of Charn in the first half of the book and extended through the story of Narnia to our world. Charn, though its actual life had ended long before through violence and cruelty, reached the time of its dissolution late in the book: "That world is ended, as if it had never been." Narnia did have, and continues to have, the potential to become a "strong and cruel empire" similar to Charn if its people also become selfish and cruel. But that danger is even greater for our world, and Aslan issues a warning that some wicked person of our race may discover "a secret as evil as the Deplorable Word and use it to destroy all living things." Before Polly and Digory grow to be an old man and an old woman, he adds, great nations in our world will be governed by tyrants "who care no more for joy and justice and mercy than the Empress Jadis."

The passage contains one of the most direct contemporary social comments to be found in the Chronicles. According to the "Outline of Narnian History So Far As It Is Known," Digory and Polly were born in 1888 and 1889, respectively, and were carried into Narnia by the rings in 1900. Long before they were old, their world had seen a Hitler and a Stalin and had learned to live with the fear of an evil secret — the atomic bomb. But the impact of the passage goes deeper as well: the fate of our world, too, will be determined by its choices. The people of our world must decide if they will resist the temptation to become selfish, cruel, and tyrannical, and live instead in the joy and justice, mercy and peace that were intended for them.

The contrasting possibilities of joy and oppression are reflected in the book's images of country and city, which traditionally have been used to symbolize good and evil, the idyllic and the undesirable. Although Charn is, of course, the prime example of evil associated with a city, it is not the only one. There is also the oppressiveness of London, noted first in the opening chapter: Digory tells Polly she would cry too, if she'd always lived "in the country and had a pony, . . . and then been brought to live in a beastly Hole like this." Later, the horse Strawberry complains about London: "It was a hard, cruel country. . . . There was no grass. All hard stones." And the cabby agrees, "You were a country 'oss, and I was a country man. . . . But there wasn't a living for me there."

Narnia, on the other hand, is rural, a country setting where a king is expected to be able to "use a spade and a plough and raise food out of the earth." Its goodness is manifest in the effect it has on those who have been corrupted by the city, especially the cabby — his voice becomes "more like the country voice he must have had as a boy and less like the sharp, quick voice of a cockney," and his behavior becomes more gentle, less sharp and quarrelsome. It is almost inevitable, then, that the story should end with Digory and his family moving to a "great big house in the country" where things will "go on getting better and better" for them all.

The potentially tragic ending of having the hero's mother die turns to eucatastrophe. Digory's mother is restored to health — it was "like a miracle." And other happy events occur. His father receives a large inheritance and can retire and come home from India permanently. Polly comes to visit Digory in the country nearly every holiday, where they ride, swim, and climb together. In Narnia the animals live in peace for hundreds of years. It is indeed an ending that could lead one to think they all will "live happily ever after." But the happy ending is not assured yet, for this is only the beginning of the story of Narnia. Much hardship, sorrow, and pain must occur before the truly happy ending is reached, some twenty-five-hundred Narnian years later, at the conclusion of *The Last Battle*.

Chapter 10

Endings and Transcendings in *The Last Battle*

Our lifelong nostalgia, our longing to be reunited with something in the universe from which we now feel cut off, to be on the inside of some door which we have always seen from the outside, is no mere neurotic fancy, but the truest index of our real situation.

"**P**robably every writer making a secondary world," Tolkien writes, "every sub-creator, wishes in some measure to be a real maker, or hopes that he is drawing on reality: hopes that the peculiar quality of this secondary world . . . [is] derived from Reality, or [is] flowing into it." In the epilogue to "On Fairy-Stories," he indicates that "Reality" includes the *evangelium*, or Good News of Christianity. He describes the birth of Christ and his resurrection as eucatastrophes anticipating "the Great Eucatastrophe," the joy, the *Gloria*, to be found transcending the end of our world. The final book in the Chronicles of Narnia, about the end of Narnia and what transcends that ending, puts into story form the ideas Tolkien expresses here. It gives readers a "sudden glimpse" of Reality or Truth. The "peculiar quality of 'joy'" in it affords readers a gleam or echo of *evangelium*, not just "in the real world" but in the Real World.

The story, like *The Horse and His Boy*, opens in Fairy-land, Lewis assuming that his readers know the earlier stories and that the name *Narnia* identifies the setting as Other-world. However, even for readers new to the series, encountering an ape named Shift and a donkey named Puzzle as the opening characters clarifies that this is a fairy tale, as do references to talking animals and dwarfs. Tolkien writes that a fairy story is one that touches on or uses Faërie, "whatever its own main purpose may be: satire, adventure, morality, fantasy." Other Chronicles pursue adventure, morality, and fantasy as main purposes; the early chapters of The Last Battle emphasize satire.

The Last Battle is the only Chronicle to rely heavily on irony. From its opening scene, the story requires readers to discern the discrepancy between reality and appearance. As Shift explains why Puzzle, rather than he himself, should plunge into the pool for the lion skin, the expressed reasons — what weak chests apes have and "how easily they catch cold!" — are not the actual ones. In a noble tone he declares he would jump in, though he's feeling very cold already, and "I shall probably die. Then you'll be sorry."

Early in the book that tone appears again and again, as, for example, when Puzzle has refused to try on the coat Shift fashioned out of the lion skin while Puzzle was trudging to Chippingford for oranges and bananas: "'You are unkind, Puzzle,' said Shift. 'If you're tired, what do you think I am?'" All day while Puzzle was having "a lovely refreshing walk," Shift goes on, he was slaving away, and now Puzzle won't say thank you and "won't even look at the coat." The irony here is not very sophisticated — a child has no trouble seeing through the deception. But that is just the point, for the irony becomes a key indicator that the ape and his allies are not to be trusted.

The extent of Shift's untrustworthiness is revealed only later, as it becomes evident that he has deceived the Narnians by using the lion skin to make Puzzle appear to be Aslan and has betrayed them by inviting the Calormenes to begin infiltrating Narnia. The theme of treachery, introduced through Edmund in the first of the Chronicles to be published, reappears in the one published last. The Calormenes take over the western area of Narnia, cutting down the old forests, using talking horses as beasts of burden, and establishing Shift as spokesperson for "Aslan" and a figurehead governor for that area.

Verbal irony continues in the fourth chapter, as Shift informs the Narnian citizenry about conditions under the new regime, and develops into a vein of satire on political and religious tendencies in Lewis's day.

Shift, in a passage touching on politics, tells the other animals to get ideas of freedom out of their heads. Everyone who can work will be forced to work, he says, pulling, carrying, digging, the way animals do in other countries. This, he assures them, will not be slavery: they'll be paid — that is, their wages will go into Aslan's treasury, and Aslan will use them for the good of the whole, "to make Narnia a country worth living in."

These lines surely reflect Lewis's concern over the increasing tendency, in his day, toward collectivism and governmental intrusiveness. He disagreed with policies of the liberal government that was voted into office in Britain after World War II, and he pointed out in 1958 that government was no longer looked upon as existing to protect our rights, but "to do us good or make us good — anyway, to do something to us or make us something. Hence the new name 'leaders' for those who were once 'rulers.' We are less their subjects than their wards, pupils, or domestic animals. There is nothing left of which we can say to them, 'Mind your own business.' Our whole lives *are* their business."

This tendency came at the same time as a loss of personal freedom: "Two wars necessitated vast curtailments of liberty, and we have grown, though grumblingly, accustomed to our chains. The increasing complexity and precariousness of our economic life have forced Government to take over many spheres of activity once left to choice or chance." In *The Last Battle* Lewis points toward the dangers in that trend. In reply to the bear's assertion that "we want to be free," Shift says that true freedom isn't doing what you like. "True freedom means doing what I tell you."

The religious equivalent to this political tyranny is Shift's insidious attack on belief in Aslan. It begins with the argument that everyone actually believes in the same thing: "Tash and Aslan are only two different names for you know Who." In forming that argument, Shift twists Puzzle's reverent, awe-filled reluctance even to speak Aslan's name ("you know Who") into an irreverent, meaningless generality. Here clearly is a return to the critique of modernism in earlier books. Shift's equivocation turns into a Narnian version of the accommodation and whittling down of the truth of the Gospel that Lewis complained about in our world: "I have some definite views about the de-Christianizing of the church," he commented in an interview in 1963. "I believe that there are many accommodating preachers, and too many practitioners in the church who are not believ-ers. Jesus Christ did not say 'Go into all the world and tell the world that it is quite right.' The Gospel is something completely different. In fact, it is directly opposed to the world."

From accommodation of modern ideas it is an easy step, or slip, to re-jection of the fundamental ideas of the faith: Lewis often heard, from churchmen in his day, doctrine that was "so 'broad' or 'liberal' or 'modern' that it in fact excludes any real Supernaturalism and thus ceases to be Christian at all." The Narnian world experiences a somewhat similar situa-tion, as Poggin the Dwarf's report of a conversation between Ginger the Cat and Rishda Tarkaan, the Calormene commander, illustrates: "'I just wanted to know exactly what we both meant to-day about Aslan meaning *no more* than Tash.' . . . 'You mean,' says Ginger, 'that there's no such person as either.' 'All who are enlightened know that,' said the Tarkaan."

In an act of honor that contrasts strikingly to the deceit of Shift and the Calormenes, King Tirian turns himself over to the false Aslan for igno-bly killing a Calormene soldier without warning. Held prisoner, tied to a tree, he in his despair asks Aslan for help and then calls to the children from our world to come and help Narnia. As he does so, the worlds of the story intersect momentarily, as Tirian finds himself present in a room in our world, with seven people he doesn't recognize but whom readers of the earlier Chronicles will know: Digory and Polly, Peter and Edmund, Lucy, Eustace, and Jill. Though he can see and hear them, he cannot speak to them, and they can see him but only as a ghostly figure who soon fades away. This initiates the most unusual entry to the Secondary World, quite different from the earlier portals. Tirian's prayer conveys to those in our world that they are needed in Narnia, and they decide to use the magic rings, which Digory and Polly had buried years before, to convey them there. However, before Jill and Eustace can do so, the force of a train crash in Britain pitches them into Narnia.

Despite the arrival of the children, the situation continues to deterio-rate. Narnia remains endangered by those from without who care only about their own profit, not about either Tash or Aslan, and by those from within who begin accepting the same premise: "The Dwarfs are for the Dwarfs." The extent of Shift's treachery becomes clear only after the faithful few learn that Cair Paravel has been attacked and taken. The situation as a whole appears hopeless.

The sense of danger and foreboding in the early part of the story stands in contrast with the beauty all around the main characters. As Jill and Eustace walk with Tirian after freeing him from the Calormenes, the sun is up, drops of dew sparkle on the branches, and everywhere birds are singing. Later, on the first warm day of spring, the king with his now larger group of followers sets out toward Cair Paravel to organize the army and attack the invaders in a unified way: "The snowdrops were over, but they saw several primroses." Because of what they see, Jill hopes Narnia can go on forever, and Tirian's heart grows lighter as he leads the way, "humming an old Narnian marching song."

But there are constant reminders that the optimism is only false hope, that Narnia will not go on and on. The opening words of the book are "In the last days of Narnia," and the first reference to Tirian describes him as the last king of Narnia. The foreboding tone continues when Roonwit the Centaur, who comes to warn Tirian, reports that he finds, as he studies the stars, "terrible things written in the skies." Shortly thereafter, when Tirian and his dearest friend, Jewel the Unicorn, go alone and in haste to stop the murder of the trees, Tirian feels "horrible thoughts aris[ing] in [his] heart," and the narrator comments that "much evil came of their rashness." And as the children and Tirian walk through the woods on their way to Stable Hill, the silence all around them evokes the mood of the whole country: "Gloom and fear reigned over Narnia."

Nowhere is the effect of the contrasting tones, of optimism and fear, of hope and doom, more striking than at the end of the scene of beauty and lifted spirits described above. Immediately after Tirian feels his heart grow lighter and Jill expresses her hope that Narnia would go on and on, Jewel warns that all worlds will come to an end, "except Aslan's own country," and Farsight the Eagle arrives to report that Cair Paravel has been captured and Roonwit their messenger has been killed. There will be no help, and there is no more reason for hope: as the king says after a long silence, "Narnia is no more." True, the springtime setting and the beauty of the countryside have increased the children's desires for Narnia, but only in order to intensify by contrast their growing despair at its approaching defeat.

The despairing tone in *The Last Battle* is intensified all the more by imagery of darkness, death, and dissolution. Shift figures, for example, that if
they didn't get too close and if the light wasn't very good, those who saw
Puzzle in his lion skin "might mistake him for a lion." The false Aslan,
partly for that reason, is shown only during the night, at "dreadful midnight meetings," and consultations among the enemy forces generally are
held at times and places "black as pitch." The evil god Tash passing
through Narnia evokes the feeling that a previously sunny day was "clouding over." The last battle is fought at night, with firelight outlining objects,
and the inside of the stable, especially to the dwarfs, is "pitch-black." All of
the darkness, all of the blackness creates an atmosphere of doubt and
dread and reinforces the despair already growing out of early events.

Death is first mentioned in *The Last Battle* as the seven loyal Narnians
are on their way toward Stable Hill and Eustace wonders what would happen if they were killed in Narnia — would they still be alive in England, or
would they vanish and never be heard of again? Jill replies that she would
rather die "fighting for Narnia" than grow old and decrepit back home,
and Eustace adds, "Or be smashed up by British Railways!" Later the children discover that there was indeed a railway accident in which the other
friends of Narnia and the Pevensie children's parents were killed. Lewis re-
solves the dilemma about the effect of death in one world on the other
world by setting up a death situation in both: Jill and Eustace are drawn
into Narnia in the split second before their deaths in our world, and that,
because of the different time sequences, makes it possible for them to die
simultaneously in both worlds.

There have been deaths, of course, in earlier Chronicles, viewed as
something children should be introduced to as a natural part of life. At the
conclusion of *The Silver Chair*, Lewis made a special effort to take the fearfulness out of death by depicting it as a transition to a new and more glorious existence. But death in the earlier books involves characters with
whom the readers do not closely identify, at least not at the time of their
deaths. However, in *The Last Battle*, Jill and Eustace are the characters facing
imminent death, characters with whom readers have identified in earlier
books as well as this one, along with Tirian, the character from whose
viewpoint most of this story is being told. Bringing death so close without

imposing an impossible emotional burden on young readers demanded careful, sensitive handling. Lewis solved the problem by use of the stable door.

The stable door becomes, throughout the battle, a representation of death. Lewis achieves the authenticity of having his characters die in a losing battle, without the naturalistic detail inappropriate in a fairy tale, by having his characters pass through the stable door into eternity. The Calormene leader, Rishda Tarkaan, orders that the Narnians be taken alive and thrown into the stable, which will then be set on fire as an offering to Tash. The symbolism of death is clear. As Poggin the Dwarf looks at the stable, he predicts that each of them, one by one, will "pass through that dark door before morning," and Tirian replies, "It is indeed a grim door." And indeed, when the children have passed through it, they meet the others who died in the train crash. Death and the door are, in effect and meaning, the same, the important thing being that neither represents an end but a beginning, not an exit but an entrance.

As one catastrophe follows another, as the children are thrown through the stable door and the fall of Narnia is imminent, the story seems destined to have a tragic ending. But *The Last Battle* is not tragedy. It is fairy tale. Eucatastrophe overwhelms catastrophe, and therefore the end of Narnian history is not the end of the story. As Tirian is thrown through the stable door, the imagery shifts abruptly: he finds not darkness, as he had expected, but light. He and Jill and Eustace, along with Peter, Edmund, Lucy, Aunt Polly, and the Professor, in whose company he finds himself, are not in the stable at all, but standing on fresh grass, under a deep blue sky, with an early summer breeze blowing gently against their faces.

The door of the stable has become the portal to that most otherly of Other-worlds, the same one Jill and Eustace visited briefly in *The Silver Chair*: Aslan's country. There it was only sketched broadly, as extremely high up and surpassingly beautiful, filled with blazing sunlight, riotous birds, huge trees, and rippling streams. Now Lewis gives his imagination freedom to develop that world in detail. It is a country of youth: as Jill puts it, the Professor and Aunt Polly aren't "much older than we are here." It is a place of health (Edmund's knee ceases to be sore, and the Professor suddenly feels "unstiffened"), of abundance (they have "crowns on their heads" and are in "glittering clothes"), and of freedom (it feels like "the country where every-thing is allowed"). And it is a place of beauty and of bounty: they see groves of trees, thick with leaves, and under every leaf there peeps out the rich col-ors of fruits more colorful and appealing than anything in our world, fruits compared with which "the freshest grapefruit you've ever eaten was dull, and the juiciest orange was dry." After doing his best to say what it was like, the narrator confesses he can't describe it: you can't grasp fully what it is like without going to that country and experiencing it yourself.

Most of all, it is a place where those who love and long for Aslan find fulfillment. Soon after passing through the stable door, Tirian sees a brightness and turns around: "There stood his heart's desire, huge and real, the golden Lion, Aslan himself." At the heart of Faërie is desire, and here is the real object of all the unsatisfied and unsatisfiable longings expe-rienced on earth. A passage from *Mere Christianity* quoted earlier deserves repetition here: "If I find in myself a desire which no experience in this world can satisfy, the most probable explanation is that I was made for an-other world. . . . I must [therefore] keep alive in myself the desire for my true country, which I shall not find till after death." Jewel the Unicorn's words echo those sentiments closely: "This is my real country! I belong here. This is the land I have been looking for all my life, though I never knew it till now."

This is also the land that Emeth, the Calormene officer, has been look-ing for all his life, though he didn't know it until now. Because of his great desire for God and goodness, for wisdom and understanding — which he thought were embodied in Tash, harsh and cruel though he might seem to be — he is admitted to the new Narnia. In desiring and doing good, he was actually serving Aslan, not Tash, and the God of truth and love accepts his service as unto himself. Even his name, a transliteration of the Hebrew word for *truth*, identifies him as a seeker of the Truth (and thus of Aslan), and one who rejects falsehood (therefore, Tash).

Because Emeth believes, he can see. The Dwarfs, on the other hand, even though they say "Seeing is believing," do not believe and cannot see, reprising a prominent theme of *Prince Caspian*. They find only a small, dark stable on the other side of the door. Even Aslan can do little for them: the rich feast he provides tastes to them like stable litter. "They will not let us help them," he explains. "They have chosen cunning instead of belief. Their prison is only in their own minds, yet they are in that prison." And presumably they are in it still. Dante, in the third canto of the *Inferno*, left those who were unwilling to commit themselves to goodness or evil outside heaven and hell — neither place would accept them. Perhaps it is similar in the Narnian situation. The Dwarfs, after all, are for the Dwarfs: they shot arrows at both talking horses and Calormenes. Thus they neither disappear into Aslan's shadow nor enter the new Narnia. Because Aslan was not their heart's desire, because they did not long for his country, they apparently remain forever in that "pitch-black, poky, smelly little hole of a stable."

The others, those who have a deep desire for Narnia and for Aslan, discover that they now have both. Farsight the Eagle sums it up for the others. From far above he sees Ettinsmuir, Beaversdam, the Great River, and Cair Paravel, and concludes, "Narnia is not dead. This is Narnia." As Lewis smuggled theology into several of the Chronicles, here he smuggles in Plato's theory of ideas. First the Professor explains that the Narnia to which the Pevensie children could not return was not the real Narnia: "That had a beginning and an end. It was only a shadow or a copy of the real Narnia," which is eternal and unchanging. Such idealistic philosophy is, of course, difficult to get across successfully, and Lewis tries to clarify it by an analogy, the difference between looking at a beautiful natural scene through a window and then turning around and seeing a reflection of the scene in a mirror, which makes it look deeper and more wonderful, "like places in a story: in a story you have never heard but very much want to know."

Lewis's comparison captures once again, through the distancing effect of a mirror's reflection, a fairy-tale quality, a sense of wonder and ineffability, and reinforces his point that the "reality" of the physical world out the window is not the ultimate reality. Heaven is, as Lucy says, something new and different and yet familiar: "This is still Narnia, and, more real and more beautiful than the Narnia down below." Once more Lewis holds the prospect out before the reader enticingly: "I can't describe it any better than that: if you ever get there, you will know what I mean."

After death comes dissolution. Aslan summons Father Time, of whom it was foretold in *The Silver Chair* that he would wake "at the end of the world." Although his name while he was sleeping was Time, now that he is awake, Aslan says, "He will have a new one," presumably Eternity. Aslan then summons the creatures of the Narnian world — those who have been dead, like the boar, the bear, and the horses, and those who have not died: some were living in distant parts of Narnia or in foreign countries, while others were at Stable Hill but "just crept quietly away during the fighting." The door now becomes a portal to paradise, the way of acceptance. Aslan stands at the doorway, on its left side, and the creatures approach him. In a scene drawing upon the separation of the sheep from the goats in Matthew 25, those who do not love Aslan veer away to his left, into his shadow, and are never seen or heard of again, while those who love Aslan come through the door to Aslan's right, to live with him in his country forever.

Aslan has already called the stars home, leaving "spreading blackness, . . . emptiness" behind. Images of water and then ice reinforce the image of darkness. After dragons and lizards reduce Narnia to a desert, "a foaming wall of water" roars across it, covering it completely. The dying sun — similar to the one Digory and Polly saw in Charn — then licks up the moon and is squeezed to death by Father Time, "and instantly there [is] total darkness." Finally comes the cold: all but Aslan jump back from "the ice-cold air" now blowing through the doorway, which quickly is "covered with icicles." Lewis's choice of ending was probably influenced by the Icelandic myths he loved throughout his life. But the question of a specific source is not important: contrasting starkly with the description of Aslan's country that follows, it was the "right" conclusion.

As in *The Magician's Nephew*, where the story of an ending is followed by a story of "beginning," of new life, so it is here — the beginning of a new Life in Aslan's country. The Other-worldliness of heaven is conveyed now by youthfulness (Tirian's father is "young and merry" again), brightness (the light grows stronger and stronger), and beauty (forests, green slopes, sweet orchards, and flashing waterfalls), and by the mountains that Lewis used frequently to image the source of the longing for heaven he called Joy. All the creatures who love and long for Aslan enter the golden gates of a garden that, like the stable in our world that Lucy referred to earlier, is "far bigger inside than it was outside." Here they encounter delicious odors from the garden and a "cool mixture of sunlight and shadow" as they walk among the trees on springy turf "dotted with white flowers."

For the characters in the book, their longings are satisfied: they have reached their true country and will never be sent away to our world again. They are united with him they have longed for, no longer looking like a lion, but seen now in the human form of his earthly incarnation. And then things begin to happen that are so glorious the narrator can't find words to express them. Digory felt sure at the end of *The Magician's Nephew* that everyone would "live happily ever after." But his expectation was premature: that was only the beginning of the story. Much unhappiness was still to come. Now the end of their story has arrived and the narrator can say truly that "they all lived happily ever after." This is the way fairy tales often end, but never so justifiably.

For readers, however, the sense of longing is not satisfied but increased by the descriptions of the new Narnia, by the reappearance of characters from the previous books, and by the knowledge that although this is the last of the books, it is not the end of the real story. Perhaps the chief glory of the Chronicles is that they create in many readers longings that cannot be satisfied in this world and point them toward the Great Story in which such longings will be satisfied at last.

Chapter 11

The Stories Told:
Fairy-land and Its Effects

Supposing that by casting [familiar Bible stories] into an imaginary world, stripping them of their stained-glass and Sunday school associations, one could make them for the first time appear in their real potency? Could one not thus steal past those watchful dragons? I thought one could.

If Lewis is correct that understanding any work from a corkscrew to a Chronicle begins with knowing what it is, then a consideration of the Narnian books must begin with their literary form. The Chronicles of Narnia, as chapters 3-10 have shown, are best understood as fairy tales. That is, they recount events that take place in Fairy-land, a magically mysterious realm inhabited by such creatures as fairies, dwarves, witches, giants, and dragons, a realm that creates a sense of mystery and wonder in all who come there, whether children who enter it through magic portals or readers carried there by the magic of well-crafted words.

The Chronicles use what Tolkien calls the "elvish craft" of fantasy to bring into existence a unique and appealing Secondary World, a sub-region of Fairy-land called Narnia, which readers can enter and explore by the power of Secondary Belief. That region is populated mainly by talking animals, but includes also figures from differing mythological backgrounds in our world: Father Christmas from the Christian tradition; fauns, nymphs, satyrs, dryads, Bacchus, and Silenus from the Greek tradition; dwarfs and giants from the Norse tradition. For some readers — including Tolkien — such eclecticism is a flaw. For them, encountering figures from different traditions breaks the spell of the fairy tale, forces a return to the Primary World and makes Secondary Belief impossible; they can re-enter Narnia only by suspending their disbelief.

Tolkien expressed his frustration with the Chronicles to Roger Lancelyn Green shortly after Lewis completed *The Lion, the Witch and the Wardrobe:* "I hear you've been reading Jack's children's story. It really won't do, you know! I mean to say: '*Nymphs and their Ways, The Love-Life of a Faun.*' Doesn't he know what he's talking about?" In a letter written the year after Lewis's death, Tolkien remarks, "It is sad that 'Narnia' and all that part of C.S.L.'s work should remain outside the range of my sympathy."

For fantasy purists like Tolkien, the eclecticism of the Narnian world is a serious hindrance. But for general readers, it is one of the primary attractions of the series. The sense of strangeness and wonder such readers experience as they read the Chronicles derives precisely from the magical reality in that world of figures they know to be only mythical in our world. And that magical effect is heightened, not diminished, by the mixing of figures from different traditions — dwarfs and dryads, Bacchus and Father Christmas. Eclecticism is a distinctive feature of Lewis's fantasy world, and it is crucial to the success of the Chronicles. The stories are effective in part because they enable readers of varied backgrounds and differing interests to find things to connect with.

Lewis was among the most widely read people of his time and had, as George Sayer notes, "an astonishing verbatim memory." He could "repeat whole passages of prose to illustrate a point arising in discussion. Given any line in *Paradise Lost*, he could continue with the following lines." So it comes as no surprise that in writing fantasy, he drew details from everywhere in his reading. Not that he set out to make his stories a compendium of allusions. It was simply that his mind was full of material that came out naturally in the imaginative process, and the richness of background detail, stored and blended in his memory, makes his world a unique and fascinating mixture of England and Other-world, paradise and imperfection, animal and human, adult and childlike. Becoming absorbed in the atmosphere of the Narnian world — being able to live imaginatively in that world for as long as the book lasts — is one of the powerful appeals of Lewis's stories.

The line "Always winter but never Christmas" illustrates this quality. Looked at in terms of the Secondary World, the line should not be in the book. We find out later that the Narnian name for Christ is *Aslan*. If his birthday is celebrated in Narnia, it should be called *Aslan-mass*, not *Christmass*. (Of course, the reference to Mass also is unknown in Narnia, which has no formal religious services or liturgies.) Although the reference to "never Christmas" should *not* work, it *does* work. It takes us back to the Primary World and should break the imaginative spell, but for most readers it does the opposite and helps sustain the spell.

This is, in fact, a vital sentence, one on which the book — even the series — turns, one that was crucial in making the book and the series successful. In addition to helping young readers grasp the evil nature of the White Witch and the horror of living under her tyrannical, repressive regime, it's memorable, with perfect rhythm and balance. It's humorous, for adults if not for children. The line simply "works." It lets readers know this is a book they want to go on reading. That it doesn't "belong" in Narnia doesn't even occur to most readers, because it is so effective in making Narnia belong to them.

One effect of the line is to "recover" Christmas for many readers. After being taken to a cold, bleak world, a place of bondage and without joy, readers may return to our world with a new appreciation of what Christmas is and how important it is to their lives. Recovery, in Tolkien's sense of the term, is a key to the Chronicles as fairy tales. The stories take readers out of the Primary World and allow them to experience a Secondary World that changes their outlook, so that as they re-enter the Primary World, they see new things in it and see old things in fresh ways. Visiting Narnia gives readers a revitalized awareness and appreciation of things that to us may have come to be mundane, things like lions, mice, ships, or even castles and royalty.

Recovery in the Chronicles functions most significantly as it enables readers to renew their sense of the spiritual in places where that sense had become dulled or overly familiar, or to see spiritual dimensions where they hadn't seen them before. Reading the Narnian creation story and the account of the end of the Narnian world refreshes the way readers imagine and feel about biblical texts many of them have long known. Similarly, the descriptions of Aslan's country expand the way readers think about heaven.

The Chronicles also lead readers to sense a spiritual presence in nature. Having encountered the spirits of trees — and stars! — in Narnia, readers will never again see a tree or a star in our world as just a physical object.

The most important effect of the series as a whole is to make room for the spiritual. Lewis, deeply aware that many of those around him deny the reality or importance of anything except the physical, urges us to consider that there might be more. When Peter asks the Professor, in *The Lion, the Witch and the Wardrobe*, "Do you really mean, Sir, . . . that there could be other worlds — all over the place, just round the corner," Peter raises an issue of deepest significance. The Professor's answer, "Nothing is more probable," invites readers to take a new look at the narrowness of modernist, materialistic certainty and recover a sense of the openness of Platonic and Christian possibility.

Lewis uses his alternative universes to recover the old belief in Moral Law, not, as in some contemporary fantasy works, to advance the acceptance of relativism. Lewis always insisted that the same moral laws hold throughout his Other-worlds. As the guardian angel of Malacandra (Lewis's name for Mars in *Out of the Silent Planet*) says, "There are laws that all *hnau* know, of pity and straight dealing and shame and the like" — that is, all rational creatures *(hnau)*, whatever their form and whatever universe they inhabit, know and should strive to adhere to the same moral principles. The Chronicles have been unfairly criticized for alleged didacticism. The stories do not talk down to readers, do not preach about correct behavior and values. Rather, the stories present proper behavior and values objectively, as something readers already know perfectly well. They do not instruct, they remind, thus following a maxim of Samuel Johnson, the eighteenth-century moralist whom Lewis admired greatly: "Men more frequently require to be reminded than informed."

The recovery of Moral Law achieves in the stories a moral perspective common to both younger and older readers, created partly by the blending of childhood and adult experiences through the use of talking animals and children. Lewis's animal characters are supposed to be adults but seem in many respects like children. Humanized animals, even old ones, invariably do not seem to be as old as their human counterparts would be. Although Mr. and Mrs. Beaver seem to have the experience and moral authority of grandparents, they also convey the aura of children, of children fortunate enough to have potatoes and tea and hams and marmalade in a larder without wondering how they got there.

At the same time, the children in the stories seem in many respects like adults. Actual human adults in Narnia (with the few exceptions of Professor Kirke, Frank and Helen, King Lune, and the later kings of Narnia) are the enemy. Children achieve victories over evil or misguided adults, achieve them notably without the help of parents, who are referred to but do not appear in the action. The stories point out how spending time in Narnia makes the children physically stronger and more mature in outlook. They are independent and self-sufficient, adult-like without having passed into the distant and undesirable state of adulthood.

Maturity, especially maturing spiritually, is a central theme throughout the Chronicles. They depict a series of young people — Edmund, Lucy, Peter, Caspian, Eustace, Shasta, Aravis, and Digory notable among them — who, through encountering Aslan and coming to love him, turn their lives around and experience significant growth in character and maturity. That said, the Chronicles are not theological or evangelical books. They are fairy tales, taking to a higher level Tolkien's point that fairy stories are primarily concerned with what we desire. The Chronicles implant in readers (or hearers) a sense of longing for Aslan and for goodness that can grow, as younger readers mature, into love for and acceptance of Christ, though it may be only later that it's identified as such. In that case, younger readers may "recover" Aslan by coming to know Christ, just as older readers recover Christ by coming to know Aslan.

It has often been said it was Lewis's inclusion and handling of Christian themes that made the Chronicles so popular and effective. But other writers, before and after Lewis, have used Christian materials without achieving his appeal; and the Chronicles have proved popular with many readers who had no inkling of their Christian themes. The appeal of the Chronicles derives to a significant extent from the magic of Faërie evident everywhere in them: the "elvish craft" of stories well told. Lewis as storymaker proved to be a highly successful subcreator, bringing to life a series of fairy tales that relate exciting adventures in an enchantingly real world but also, through their mythical dimensions, offer readers a taste of Reality.

The Chronicles:
Annotations

There would be value in having an edition of the Chronicles of Narnia with marginal notes clarifying unfamiliar or archaic words, identifying allusions, indicating parallels to other works of Lewis, and offering interpretive comments for problematic passages. In the absence of such an edition, this section selectively provides such annotations as a guide to consult while reading the books, or as a reference later to answer questions that arise. Because the Chronicles now exist in many editions, it identifies items by chapter and paragraph instead of page number.

One effect of giving attention to Lewis's vocabulary in the Chronicles is to notice how he varies the register — the variety of language used in specific communication situations — as an element of characterization and setting. For example, he uses a good many words that dictionaries label "archaic" to establish the premodern setting of the Chronicles' world. He also gives aristocratic diction to characters such as kings and centaurs, to fit their noble status, in contrast to the "common" language of "working class" characters such as dwarfs and lesser animals like hedgehogs.

The books are annotated separately. Thus, an unfamiliar word used in more than one book will be annotated for all the books in which it appears, but for only the first appearance in each book. The majority of the definitions are taken or adapted from the *Oxford English Dictionary*. Sources are found on pages 163-91.

I have noted some allusions, ones that are functional and in some way enrich the work. I have not tried to point out every passing verbal echoing of the Bible and other works, ones that may or may not be actual allusions or, if they are, are merely interesting curiosities.

In referring to the Chronicles, "British edition" means copies sold worldwide except in the United States from publication through 1993; "U.S. edition" means copies sold in the United States through 1993; "1994 edition" means the HarperCollins editions sold worldwide since 1994. For discussion of the different editions, see pages 13-15.

The Lion, the Witch and the Wardrobe

This was the first of the Chronicles to be written and published. Lewis probably began working on the story as we have it during the spring or summer of 1948, for he told Chad Walsh in August of that year that he was working on a children's book. He read two chapters of it to Roger Lancelyn Green on 10 March 1949 and finished the book by the end of the month. It was published in Britain by Geoffrey Bles on 16 October 1950 and in the United States by Macmillan on 7 November 1950.

Ch. 1, par. 1, they were sent away from London during the war because of the air-raids: Thousands of children were evacuated from London in the first four days of September 1939 and many more during the Blitz carried out by German bombers mostly from late August 1940 through early May 1941. Lewis and Mrs. Moore served as hosts for several groups of children, always girls, usually in groups of three. Their first group arrived on or just before 2 September 1939. In the "Outline of Narnian History So Far As It Is Known," Lewis gives 1940 as the year in which the Pevensie children first reach Narnia through the wardrobe.

Ch. 1, par. 14-15, "Foxes!" said Edmund and **"Rabbits!" said Susan,** in the first British edition, was changed to **"Snakes!" said Edmund** and **"Foxes!" said Susan** in the U.S. edition. Paul Ford suggests that Lewis's afterthought better fits their characters in this and later books and improves the imaginative experience of reading the books. "Snakes" conveys associations (including biblical ones) that suit the deceptive traitor Edmund is to become. "Rabbits" gives a warm, cuddly feel that ultimately doesn't fit Susan, but "foxes" suggests a wiliness that does fit and may also convey, as Ford indicates, "a veiled reference to her desire for a high social life, riding to the hounds, and the like."

Ch. 1, par. 18, wireless: Early term for *radio*.

Ch. 1, par. 20, wardrobe: One of the children staying with Lewis and Mrs. Moore during the air raids in 1939 may have triggered the idea of using a wardrobe as a door to another world when she saw an old wardrobe at the Kilns, asked if she could enter it, and wondered if there was anything behind it. Her questions may have reminded Lewis of a short story by Edith Nesbit that he probably read when he was ten, "The Aunt and

Amabel," in which a child enters another world through a wardrobe in a spare bedroom.

Ch. 1, par. 20, blue-bottle: A variety of blowfly (genus *Calliphora*) with a large, bluish body.

Ch. 1, par. 27, Faun: One of a class of rural gods in Roman mythology, at first represented like men with horns and the tail of a goat, and later with goats' legs like the satyrs, with whom they came to be assimilated. Traditionally they were regarded as lustful, but Lewis eliminates that element.

Ch. 2, par. 2, Daughter of Eve: A human, a descendant of Eve, the mother of the race in Genesis 3. Both "Daughter of Eve" and "Son of Adam" (par. 8) are examples of the eclecticism of Lewis's Secondary World (see above, pages 114-16); the biblical references should break the imaginative spell by taking the reader back to the Primary World. But they don't seem to — they instead seem to increase the enchantment of a world where references to Adam and Eve seem remote and mysterious.

Ch. 2, par. 10, Narnia: The name is that of a small medieval town in Italy, halfway between Rome and Assisi, and was chosen probably because Lewis liked the sound of the word.

Ch. 2, par. 25, tea: In Britain, a light meal, usually including tea, sandwiches, and cakes, eaten in the late afternoon. Meals and the delights of eating are a recurrent motif in the Chronicles. In addition to Lucy's tea with Mr. Tumnus, there is the children's supper with the Beavers in *The Lion, the Witch and the Wardrobe*; there is the movement from subsistence on apples at the beginning of *Prince Caspian* to the feast that Bacchus, Silenus, and the Maenads evoke magically at the end; there is the feast on Ramandu's island in *The Voyage of the "Dawn Treader"*; there are the contrasting meals when Jill and Eustace in *The Silver Chair* arrive at Cair Paravel and when they arrive at the House of Harfang; and many more. Usually the food is traditional British fare, described in considerable detail. Perhaps writing about food is always a good strategy for children, but it may have been especially appropriate when Lewis was writing. Food was rationed in Britain during the war and remained in short supply in the bleak years immediately following. One of the best ways to make Narnia a positive and desirable place for his initial readers was to make it a place in which there was tasty, wholesome food in abundance.

Ch. 2, par. 25, Nymphs: Minor deities in classical mythology conceived as beautiful maidens inhabiting the sea, rivers, mountains, woods, trees, or other natural locations.

Ch. 2, par. 25, Dryads: Nymphs supposed to inhabit trees; woodnymphs.

Ch. 2, par. 25, Silenus: In Greek mythology, a forest spirit often depicted as a bearded, elderly man and sometimes as the foster father and teacher of Dionysus and leader of the satyrs.

Ch. 2, par. 25, Bacchus: Another name for Dionysus, who in Greek and Roman mythology was god of wine and vegetation (a fertility god), who loosens inhibitions and inspires creativity in music and poetry.

Ch. 3, par. 30, Make it Pax: Let's make peace.

Ch. 3, par. 33, icing sugar: Also known in the United States as "powdered sugar."

Ch. 3, par. 40, the Queen of Narnia: Some readers interpret the White Witch as a representation of Satan. I think a good case can be made that Lewis in this book was thinking of her simply as the evil witch in a fairy tale, thus remaining within his Secondary World, not moving outside it in allegorical fashion. She is a magician with power great enough to turn living beings into stone and to create perpetual winter, and like other fairy-tale witches, she is a temptress. But the fact that she is said to be dead in Chapter 17 indicates that Lewis was not equating her with the Devil.

Ch. 4, par. 18, Turkish Delight: A sweet consisting of firm citrus gelatin, cubed, and dusted with powdered sugar (or, today, chocolate-coated). Lewis probably chose it partly for its name.

Ch. 4, par. 32, Do you see that lamp? . . . way to the World of Men: For the Witch to know where to find the door from our world to Narnia would seem to be a minor slip in the narrative. In that case, she wouldn't need to rely on Edmund to bring his brother and sisters to her. She could post sentinels in the area and kill or capture humans as they enter Narnia.

Ch. 5, par. 4, And now we come . . . in this story: This is the first time the narrator steps forward in the story as a distinct personality, ren-

dering a judgment upon a character or an action. For a discussion of the
"story-teller" as one of the most important characters in the series, see
Schakel, *Imagination and the Arts in C. S. Lewis* (Columbia: University of Missouri Press, 2002), chapter 5.

Ch. 6, par. 36, Chatelaine: The mistress of a castle.

Ch. 6, par. 36, and **chap. 13, par. 15: Maugrim,** in the first British edition, was changed to **Fenris Ulf** in the U.S. edition. As Paul Ford notes, Fenris, the great wolf of Scandinavian mythology, was spawned by Loki, god of strife and spirit of evil, and was killed by the fearless Vidar, son of Odin. For readers who recognize the allusion, "Fenris" creates a much richer imaginative experience than "Maugrim" (meaning perhaps "savage jaws" or "ill will"), carrying multiple ripples of meaning.

Ch. 7, par. 35, Aslan: *Aslan* is the Turkish word for *lion*. In a letter in 1952, Lewis wrote, "I pronounce it Ass-lan." The British pronunciation of the *a* in both syllables is closer to that (in American speech) of the *a* in *father* than in *cat*.

Ch. 8, par. 21, the great Lion: The choice of a lion as the embodiment of God the Son in Narnia is appropriate because of the lion's fairy-tale status as King of the Jungle on the one hand and biblical allusion on the other (Christ being referred to as "the Lion of the tribe of Judah" in Revelation 5:5).

Ch. 8, par. 33, Lilith: A female demon in Jewish mythology (the Hebrew word occurs in Isaiah 34:14), perhaps having roots in Babylonian demonology. According to medieval folklore, Lilith was Adam's first wife, created together with him (some sources interpret Genesis 1:27 as indicating that Adam had a wife before Eve) and thus seemingly equal to him in status. She refused to accept the subordinate role Adam expected of a woman, ran away from him, and became the enemy and oppressor of men, children, and women who accept their "proper" role, as epitomized by Eve (created as Adam's inferior in Genesis 2:21-23). Lewis's claim that she lacks even a drop of human blood would not be congruent with the legends holding that she was created with Adam as his first wife. Some legends hold that she was changed to a demon (or jinn) as punishment for leaving Adam, or that she became Satan's wife and through him gave birth to the jinni.

Ch. 8, par. 33, Jinn: In Middle Eastern demonology, one of a class of intelligent spirits, lower than the angels, capable of appearing in human and animal forms and influencing humankind for good or evil (comparable to a *genie*).

Ch. 8, par. 39, Cair: Lewis's adaptation of the Welsh *caer*, "castle" (cf. Welsh Caernarvon, Caerphilly).

Ch. 10, par. 35, Father Christmas: Some readers of the Chronicles have objected to the inclusion of Father Christmas in the story. Roger Lancelyn Green, for example, urged Lewis to omit him as somehow "breaking the magic for a moment: he still does not seem to fit quite comfortably into his place." But see above, pages 115-16.

Ch. 10, par. 46, cordial: Medicine that stimulates or invigorates the heart (the Latin word for *heart* is *cor*) or, more generally, is restorative, reviving, cheering. Magic potions with healing powers are staples of the romance tradition. Lewis's details here were surely influenced by *The Faerie Queene* (1.9.19), where Prince Arthur gives to the Redcrosse Knight "a boxe of Diamond sure/ . . . /Wherein were closed few drops of liquor pure,/That any wound could heale incontinent [immediately]."

Ch. 12, par. 6, pavilion: In this case, a large, stately tent, probably with a pointed roof.

Ch. 12, par. 7, centaurs: Creatures from Greek mythology having the head, upper torso, and arms of a man, and the body and legs of a horse.

Ch. 12, par. 7, standard: A flag indicating the presence of a sovereign or public official.

Ch. 12, par. 37, never forget to wipe your sword: Some readers try to find an allegorical meaning for this injunction; but it is probably a bit of realistic detail, as Lewis pays attention to the messy details other stories frequently leave out. (Thus, similarly, after Trumpkin in *Prince Caspian* kills a bear and prepares to dress it, Susan knows "what a horrid messy business *that* will be." Also, in *The Last Battle*, Tirian dries his sword after wading through a river, and later scolds Eustace for putting his sword "back in the sheath all messy" from killing a Calormene and makes him "clean and polish it.")

Ch. 13, par. 16, all our people: Ghouls: Evil spirits supposed to rob graves and prey on human corpses. **Boggles:** *Bogles* are goblins, bogies, or spectres that cause fright. **Ogres:** In folklore, man-eating monsters, usually represented as hideous giants. **Minotaurs:** In Greek mythology, monsters with the bodies of men and the heads of bulls. **Cruels:** Lewis's invention. **Hags:** Witches or sorceresses, especially ones who are ugly or repulsive. **Spectres:** Ghosts, phantoms, or apparitions of a terrifying nature. **The people of the Toadstools:** Lewis's invention.

Ch. 13, par. 42, the trunk of the World Ash Tree: This wording in the U.S. edition represents a change from **the fire-stones of the Secret Hill** in the British and now the 1994 editions. Paul Ford thinks that Lewis may have used "the fire-stones of the Secret Hill" to evoke in the imaginations of his readers "pictures of annual druidical rites throughout the British Isles in which the old year's fires were extinguished and the new fire was kindled at a sacred place, usually a low, round hill." The associations are vague, but properly sinister. The World Ash Tree alludes to Yggdrasil, the great tree of Scandinavian mythology, whose branches tower into the heavens, whose trunk upholds the earth, and whose three roots reach into the realm of the dead, the land of the giants, and the abode of the gods. For those recognizing the allusion, the tree reinforces the truth that Deep Magic, or Natural Law, is universal, embedded in the created universe from the dawn of time, and the foundation upon which social order rests. Opinion on whether this was a desirable change varies, but the later version, like the change from "Maugrim" to "Fenris Ulf," offers the potential for a richer imaginative experience to readers aware of the mythic background.

Ch. 13, par. 42, Emperor-Beyond-the-Sea: The British and 1994 editions have **Emperor-Over-Sea.** These two names for Aslan's father (God the Father), with or without hyphens, are used interchangeably throughout the Chronicles in all editions.

Ch. 13, par. 57, "Wow!" roared Aslan: An instance in which Lewis's revision in the U.S. edition does not seem an improvement. The British and 1994 editions have **"Haa-a-arrh!" roared Aslan,** which seems much closer to the sound of an angry lion. Lewis undoubtedly was not familiar with the U.S. slang word "Wow."

Ch. 14, par. 39, But such people!: See the note on Ch. 13, par. 16, above. Also, **Incubuses:** Evil spirits or demons supposed to descend upon persons in their sleep, especially to have sexual intercourse with women. **Wraiths:** Phantoms or ghosts of persons already dead or of persons soon to die. **Horrors:** Lewis's coinage for a terrifying or revolting creature. **Efreets** (or Afreets): Evil demons or monsters of Muslim mythology. **Sprites:** Spirits. **Orknies:** Probably from the Old English *orcneas*, walking corpses (also a source for Tolkien's Orcs). **Wooses:** In Old English folklore, forest savages such as the Green Man; the word was probably influenced by Tolkien's *Woses*. **Ettins:** From the Old English term for *giant*.

Ch. 15, par. 3, **skirling pipes:** Bagpipes, noted for their shrill sound.

Ch. 17, par. 27, **Marry:** A mild oath invoking the name of Mary. Inserted in the U.S. editions; the British edition and 1994 editions read **By the Lion's Mane.**

Ch. 17, par. 39, **It was the same . . . hour of the day:** The handling of time — the fact that no time passes in our world while the children are in Narnia — establishes the fact that this Secondary World is an alternative universe, not a distant part of our universe, and reinforces the sense of strangeness and wonder of being in that world. Readers, on the other hand, no matter how much time passes in our world, can return to Narnia the same day and the same hour they left it. Readers thus have a sense of discovery and nostalgia similar to that of the characters.

Prince Caspian

Prince Caspian was the second of the Chronicles to be written. After completing *The Lion, the Witch and the Wardrobe,* Lewis's immediate impulse was to write the book that eventually emerged as *The Magician's Nephew,* explaining the origin of Narnia and how the lamppost came to be there. Lewis abandoned that effort because he wasn't satisfied with it, and because a new idea came to him. In many stories, he pointed out to Roger Lancelyn Green, people are summoned by magic across space or time, but the stories are always told from the viewpoint of the magician. What, he asked, would it be like to be on the other end, to be pulled suddenly by magic into a different land or time, or both? He began writing the new story in the summer of 1949 and finished it by early December. The original title, *Drawn into Narnia*, was rejected by the publisher, as was a second choice, *A Horn in Narnia*. It was published with the title *Prince Caspian* in Britain by Geoffrey Bles on 15 October 1951, and in the United States by Macmillan the following day.

Ch. 1, par. 2, playboxes: Boxes in which a child, especially at a boarding school, keeps toys, books, and other personal possessions.

Ch. 2, par. 21, fauns: See note on *LWW* Ch. 1, par. 27.

Ch. 2, par. 21, mer-people: Mermen and mermaids (from the French *mer*, "sea").

Ch. 2, par. 30, No one said anything: The British and 1994 editions have a paragraph break after this phrase; the U.S. edition does not. As a result, paragraph numbering differs for the rest of the chapter.

Ch. 2, par. 34 (British and 1994 editions, 35), Pomona: The Roman goddess of fruit.

Ch. 2, par. 66 (British and 1994 editions, 67), cordial: See note on *LWW* Ch. 10, par. 46. (Lucy was given the cordial by Father Christmas, *LWW* Ch. 10, par. 46.)

Ch. 4, par. 11, Naiads: Fresh water nymphs, spirits inhabiting a river or spring.

Ch. 4, par. 11, dryads: See note on *LWW* Ch. 2, par. 25.

Ch. 4, par. 36, Pulverulentus Siccus: Lewis derived the author of Caspian's grammar textbook (with its mock-Elizabethan title) by Latinizing *Dryasdust*, the name Sir Walter Scott gave to "the fictitious . . . learned pundit to whom he addressed some of his prefaces," in the words of *Brewer's Dictionary of Phrase and Fable;* "hence a heavy, plodding author, . . . very dull, and very learned; an antiquary without imagination."

Ch. 4, par. 40, buskins: High boots, reaching to the calf or knee.

Ch. 4, par. 41, leads: The sheets or strips of lead used to cover a roof.

Ch. 4, par. 44, the steps of their dance: For a discussion of the importance of dance as a symbol in Lewis's works, see Schakel, *Imagination and the Arts in C. S. Lewis* (Columbia: University of Missouri Press, 2002), chapter 7.

Ch. 4, par. 53, Satyrs: Rural gods in Roman mythology represented like men with horns and the legs and tail of a goat.

Ch. 4, par. 53, Centaurs: See note on *LWW* Ch. 12, par. 7.

Ch. 5, par. 1, theorbo: A large kind of lute popular in the seventeenth century, with a double neck and two sets of strings, the lower for melody and the upper for bass.

Ch. 5, par. 1, Heraldry: The study of armorial bearings and the right of persons to carry arms or such bearings.

Ch. 5, par. 6, wallet: A bag for holding provisions and clothing, especially on a journey on foot or on horseback.

Ch. 5, par. 18, seven noble lords: Lewis anticipates here the subject of the following story, *The Voyage of the "Dawn Treader."*

Ch. 5, par. 35, Destrier: Fourteenth-century word for a knight's warhorse.

Ch. 5, par. 38, heaths: Areas of elevated, open, uncultivated ground.

Ch. 6, par. 1, saddle: A long elevation of land with sloping sides, or a ridge, especially one connecting two hills.

Ch. 6, par. 5, water-butt: A large, open-headed cask set on end to receive rain-water from a roof.

Ch. 6, par. 6, Ogre: See note on *LWW* Ch. 13, par. 16.

Ch. 6, par. 6, Hag: See note on *LWW* Ch. 13, par. 16.

Ch. 6, par. 24, Clodsley Shovel: Lewis playfully adapts the name of a famous English admiral, Cloudesley Shovel (1650-1707), to make it the perfect name for a mole.

Ch. 7, par. 24, I desire your better acquaintance: Here Lewis humorously echoes a line Bottom (wearing an ass's head) says to a tiny fairy, Cobweb, in Shakespeare's *A Midsummer Night's Dream:* "I shall desire you of more acquaintance" (3.1.177).

Ch. 7, par. 34, Aslan's How: A *how* is an artificial mound, cairn, or barrow.

Ch. 7, par. 47, eggs in moonshine: Literally, a dish consisting of egg yolks on a sweet base that was popular in the sixteenth and seventeenth centuries; used metaphorically to mean appearance without substance, foolish or fanciful talk, ideas, plans.

Ch. 7, par. 62, White Magic: Lewis's use of magic in the Chronicles reflects the traditional division of magic into "white" magic and "black" magic (for the latter, see the note on Ch. 12, par. 63). White magic involves superhuman control over the processes of nature. Coriakin, the disobedient star assigned as punishment to oversee the Dufflepuds on the Island of Voices in *The Voyage of the "Dawn Treader,"* has magical powers. He owns a magical book and can make food appear on a table, transform Duffers into Monopods, turn descriptions of places into maps, and mend a damaged ship. White magic has traditionally been regarded as benign and fairly harmless, conveying a sense that there are mysteries in our world that go beyond the materialistic forms the everyday world presents to the senses. (For a fuller discussion of magic in the Chronicles, see Peter Schakel, *Imagination and the Arts in C. S. Lewis* 173-78.)

Ch. 8, par. 6, seneschal: An official in the household of a sovereign or great noble in charge of domestic arrangements and the administration of justice.

Ch. 8, par. 8, *The Arabian Nights*: Also known as *Thousand and One Nights*, a series of anonymous stories in Arabic, ca. 1000, supposedly told by Scheherazade to her husband for 1001 nights to entertain him and distract him from killing her. The boy Aladdin could summon two jinn (or genies) by rubbing a magic lamp.

Ch. 8, par. 8, Jinn: See note on *LWW* Ch. 8, par. 33.

Ch. 8, par. 24, a sucks: Disappointment, embarrassment.

Ch. 8, par. 47, hauberk: A coat of flexible ring mail or chain mail, covering the neck and shoulders and, in later uses, extending below the waist.

Ch. 9, par. 8, Hamadryad: A dryad (wood-nymph) who was the spirit of a particular tree and died when her tree died.

Ch. 9, par. 57, brick: A good person, one approved of for genuine good qualities.

Ch. 10, par. 7, knocked up: Exhausted or tired out.

Ch. 10, par. 19, battledores: Trumpkin could mean either a wooden bat used in washing clothes or a small racket used for hitting a shuttlecock.

Ch. 11, par. 8, bilge: The bottom of a ship's hull, or a contraction for *bilgewater*, the seepage that collects in the bottom of the hull.

Ch. 11, par. 23, rum: Odd, strange, outside ordinary experience.

Ch. 11, par. 43, Well done: See the note on *MN* Ch. 14, par. 1.

Ch. 11, par. 49, Son of Earth: Descriptive name for a dwarf. In Norse myth dwarfs live "in the bowels of the earth" and are "kings of metals and mines."

Ch. 11, par. 55, woods on the move: Lewis's image here could have been influenced by Tolkien's Ents, especially as they march off to attack Isengard in *The Lord of the Rings* 3.4. An earlier famous "moving wood" occurs in Shakespeare's *Macbeth* (5.4 and 5.5), though in that case soldiers carry branches in front of them to disguise their numbers.

Ch. 11, par. 56, youth, dressed only in a fawn-skin: Bacchus (Dionysus) is traditionally described as having his shoulders draped with a fawn skin.

Ch. 11, par. 56, Bromios, Bassareus, and the Ram: Alternate names for Bacchus (Dionysus), whom Hermes temporarily turned into a ram to protect him from Hera.

Ch. 11, par. 56, Euan, euan, eu-oi-oi-oi: A cry of ecstasy associated with Bacchic rites in Greek drama.

Ch. 11, par. 56, 62, someone on a donkey: Silenus, the companion of Bacchus (Dionysus) in Greek mythology, is usually drunk and carried by a donkey.

Ch. 11, par. 57, Tig: British term for the children's game known in America as *tag*.

Ch. 11, par. 57, Hunt the Slipper: A parlor game in which all the players but one sit in a ring and pass a slipper covertly from one to another, the remaining player standing in the middle and seeking to get hold of it.

Ch. 12, par. 18, till the sky falls and we can all catch larks: Echoing an old Irish proverb, "When the sky falls we'll all catch larks" (about foolish hopes).

Ch. 12, par. 26, cantrips: Spells or charms of necromancy or witchcraft, especially a witch's mischievous device. (The hag uses the term here as understatement; the following paragraphs clarify that she is able and ready to use the deepest kinds of magical spells.)

Ch. 12, par. 28, I'm hunger, I'm thirst . . . : The dull, grey voice uses the idiom of literary riddling which Lewis would have known from riddles included in the Old English *Exeter Book*. Riddling is important in Tolkien's *The Hobbit*, of course. The style in this paragraph is quite similar to Bilbo's riddling answers to Smaug's question in Chapter 12, "Who are you and where do you come from?"

Ch. 12, par. 58, 60, The Witch is dead . . . can always get them back: Since the Witch died in *The Lion, the Witch and the Wardrobe,* the hag here is proposing the deepest kind of black magic: calling up a spirit from the world of the dead.

Ch. 12, par. 63, Black sorcery: Lewis's use of magic in the Chronicles reflects the traditional division of magic into "white" magic and "black" magic (for the former, see above, the note on Ch. 7, par. 62). Black magic is the use of diabolical power to gain control over the forces of nature. The magician yields himself or herself to the devil and accepts damnation ("sells his or her soul") to obtain not just superhuman but supernatural powers. Black magic does appear in the Chronicles, but it is always and clearly depicted as an evil of the deepest kind, as in this episode in *Prince Caspian.* The evil Queen in *The Silver Chair* has black magic powers and uses them to enchant Prince Rilian and all the creatures of Underland. Uncle Andrew in *The Magician's Nephew* studies for years and gets to know "devilish queer people" (he's unconscious that his Victorian slang here is ironic) in order to learn how to use some dust from the lost world of Atlantis to gain control over this world and other worlds. While Uncle Andrew is only a "little, peddling Magician" who is "working with things he did not really understand," Jadis has "real Magic in [her] blood." Although she is called a Witch in *The Lion, the Witch and the Wardrobe,* in *The Magician's Nephew* she is termed a magician, dealing in the darkest of black magic. To defeat her sister in a civil war, she had used the Deplorable Word, which "if spoken with the proper ceremonies, would destroy all living things except the one who spoke it," and she cast strong spells so she could be preserved among the statues of her ancestors until someone came and struck the bell to wake her.

Ch. 12, par. 63, Wer-Wolf: Literally man-wolf (from Old English); a person who, according to medieval folklore, was transformed or was capable of transforming himself at times into a wolf.

Ch. 12, par. 87, pastries: A misprint in the U.S. edition. It should be **pasties**, as in the British and 1994 editions — small pastry turnovers of meat and vegetables enclosed and baked in a crust (rhymes with *nasties*).

Ch. 13, par. 14, *abhominable*: An Elizabethan "learned" spelling of *abominable*, based on false etymology and made fun of by Shakespeare (see, for example, *Love's Labor's Lost* 5.1.24).

Ch. 13, par. 14, monomachy: A duel, a fight involving single combat.

Ch. 13, par. 40, jackanapes: A tame ape or monkey, here referring to Caspian as a pert, forward child, an upstart, one behaving like a monkey in tricks or airs.

Ch. 13, par. 58, dotard: An imbecile, a silly or stupid person; especially one whose intellect is impaired by age, who is in dotage or second childhood.

Ch. 13, par. 58, dastard: A despicable coward; one who does malicious acts in a skulking way so as to avoid risk.

Ch. 13, par. 62, Marshals of the Lists: Persons (originally in a royal or noble house) responsible for arranging the order of a procession or supervising ceremonies, in this case the place and terms of a tournament.

Ch. 14, par. 5, Silvans: Deities or spirits of the woods or forests.

Ch. 14, par. 72, now was not water but the richest wine: Bacchus turning the water into wine is the Narnian counterpart to what Jesus did at the marriage in Cana (John 2:1-11). Lewis, in *Miracles*, calls that a Miracle of the Old Creation, a sudden and local instance of something that happens every year, more slowly, "as part of the Natural order." God "is the reality behind the false god Bacchus." At Cana, "God, now incarnate, short circuits the process: makes wine in a moment."

Ch. 15, par. 24, Bacchus and Silenus and the Maenads: For Bacchus and Silenus, see notes on *LWW* Ch. 2, par. 25. Maenads are the Bacchantes, the women who accompany Bacchus, dancing wildly around him.

Ch. 15, par. 24, mazers: Bowls, drinking cups, or goblets, usually without a foot, made from a burl or knot of a maple tree.

The Voyage of the "Dawn Treader"

In contrast to Lewis's struggles with the sequel to *The Lion, the Witch and the Wardrobe*, both settling on a topic and getting it written, the third book in the series emerged without difficulty. Lewis began *The Voyage of the "Dawn Treader"* in December 1949 and completed a draft within about two months. Roger Lancelyn Green read the manuscript in late February 1950 and suggested few revisions. It "was written obviously in the heat of inspiration with hardly a correction" made in the handwriting. It was published by Geoffrey Bles in Britain on 15 September 1952 and by Macmillan in the United States on 30 September 1952.

Ch. 1, par. 6, looking at a picture: For a discussion of the importance of art, architecture, and clothing in Lewis's life and works, see Peter Schakel, *Imagination and the Arts in C. S. Lewis,* chapter 8.

Ch. 1, par. 10, quite incapable of making anything up himself: The wording of the original British edition, which stated that Eustace was "far too stupid" to make things up himself, was changed in the U.S. edition to say that he was "quite incapable" of doing so. Paul Ford suggests that Lewis may have felt he should tone the line down for American readers or was beginning to like Eustace better as he wrote about him. It was a line that should have been changed in any case: calling a character "stupid" in a children's book is insensitive and unwise; it does not offer young readers a good behavioral model. Beyond that, and more importantly, "stupid" — as Ford says — is inaccurate; it does not fit Eustace's character. Details throughout the chapter indicate that Eustace has a high degree of intelligence, though he applies it in ways and to subjects for which Lewis did not have great respect.

Ch. 1, par. 12, balmier: More and more crazy or foolish.

Ch. 1, par. 23, Isle of Wight: An island two miles off the southern coast of England.

Ch. 1, par. 34, King Arthur: Legendary king of England who supposedly lived in the late fifth or early sixth century, thus about fourteen to fifteen hundred years before the events in this story.

Ch. 1, par. 35, Plumptree's Vitaminised Nerve Food: Satire on the kind of health-food product the Scrubb family would consume.

Ch. 2, par. 13, seven friends of my father's: Lewis planted the plot idea for this book in *Prince Caspian* Ch. 5, par. 18.

Ch. 2, par. 41, galley: Here it refers to a low, flat-built seagoing vessel with one deck, propelled by sails and oars, formerly in common use in the Mediterranean. The rowers were mostly slaves or condemned criminals.

Ch. 2, par. 49, lodge a disposition: To *lodge* is to deposit a formal statement with a court or an official. A *disposition* is a "characteristic attitude" or "state of mind" — here Eustace, in a desire to impress his hearers, seems to have used a big word that doesn't fit his intended meaning. He may have meant a *deposition*.

Ch. 2, par. 50, forecastle (pronounced *fok-s'l*): The short, raised deck at the fore end of a vessel.

Ch. 2, par. 50, boatswain: The officer in a ship in charge of the sails and rigging, whose duty it is to summon the crew to their duties with a whistle.

Ch. 2, par. 50, galley: Here it refers to the kitchen area of a ship.

Ch. 2, par. 50, cogs: Broad ships with rounded prow and stern, used before the fifteenth century primarily for cargo or transport.

Ch. 2, par. 50, dromonds: Very large medieval ships used both in war and commerce.

Ch. 2, par. 50, carracks: Large cargo ships also fitted for warfare.

Ch. 2, par. 50, galleons: Ships of war, shorter but higher than a galley.

Ch. 2, par. 52, swank: Pretentious attitude.

Ch. 2, par. 52, Queen Mary: The R.M.S. *Queen Mary*, at the time of its launching in 1934, was the largest and fastest ocean liner ever built. In the summer of 1942, when — according to the "Outline of Narnian History So Far As It Is Known" — Edmund and Lucy were staying with the Scrubb family and entered Narnia with Eustace, the *Queen Mary* was a fairly new ship, a national symbol for Britain, being used at the time as a troop transport ship during World War II.

Ch. 2, par. 60, poltroon: Coward; mean-spirited, worthless wretch.

Ch. 2, par. 64, corporal punishment: Corporal punishment, or "caning" (striking with a cane), in British schools was banned in 1998. It would have been common in the 1940s except in "progressive" schools like Experiment House (the name of Eustace's school supplied in the opening chapter of *The Silver Chair*).

Ch. 3, par. 6, I have never yet heard . . . some other book: The Narnian world seems "true" partly because of the sense that its history (like that of Tolkien's world) feels much larger than just what is presented in these seven stories. That sense is created particularly by references such as this one to characters and events of which the stories remain untold. Similarly, in *The Last Battle*, Jewel the Unicorn reminds Jill that in between visits by children from our world, for centuries and even millennia, peaceful kings came one after the other, and ordinary life went on, without anything dramatic or exciting occurring. The "Outline of Narnian History So Far As It Is Known" gives a glimpse of that historical sweep. And, just as the reader can look up Rabadash the Ridiculous "in a good History of Calormen (try the local library)," so good histories of Narnia are surely available — in the local libraries of Narnia if not of our world.

Ch. 3, par. 69, liege: The superior to whom one owes feudal allegiance and service (that is, one's "liege lord").

Ch. 3, par. 78, standing in to: Steering, or directing its course toward.

Ch. 3, par. 84, fief: Contraction of "fiefdom" — the estate or domain of a feudal lord.

Ch. 4, par. 4, postern: A side door, not the main entrance.

Ch. 4, par. 4, pike: A shafted weapon with an iron point or spike, a pikestaff.

Ch. 4, par. 27, putting the clock back: In *Mere Christianity* Lewis anticipates that some readers will dismiss what he is saying because it is only religion, which, after all, the world has tried already, and "you cannot put the clock back." Lewis writes in reply, "Would you think I was joking if I said that you can put a clock back, and that if the clock is wrong it is often a very sensible thing to do? But I would rather get away from that whole idea of clocks. We all want progress. But progress means getting nearer to the place where you want to be. And if you have taken a wrong turning, then to go forward does not get you any nearer. If you are on the wrong road, progress means doing an about-turn and walking back to the right road; and in that case the man who turns back soonest is the most progressive man."

Ch. 5, par. 2, buskins: See note on *PC* Ch. 4, par. 40.

Ch. 5, par. 2, jerkin: A close-fitting jacket, jersey, or short coat, often made of leather and often sleeveless.

Ch. 5, par. 4, reef: To lower a sail and secure it by tying it down.

Ch. 5, par. 4, cataract: Here, a violent downpour or rush of water, like that over a waterfall.

Ch. 5, par. 6, tiller: A bar or level attached to the head of a rudder, for turning the rudder in steering.

Ch. 5, par. 8, wireless: Ship-to-shore radio.

Ch. 5, par. 13, get two dozen: To receive twenty-four lashes by way of punishment.

Ch. 6, par. 1, blighter: A contemptible or unpleasant person.

Ch. 6, par. 55-56, tears . . . crocodiles: Crocodiles have long been said to weep either to allure victims for the purpose of devouring them or while (or after) devouring them. From this tradition the phrase "crocodile tears" has come to mean "false show of grief."

Ch. 7, par. 14, the turn of Fortune's wheel: In the Middle Ages, the "wheel of fortune" was used to image the belief in *mutability,* or constant change. Fortune is like a wheel that keeps turning: those presently at the top of the wheel should not be proud or complacent because inevitably their fortunes will decline and they will reach bottom.

Ch. 7, par. 36, bathe: Swim.

Ch. 7, par. 60, quoit: A ring thrown at an upright peg, in a game called quoits (similar to horseshoes).

Ch. 8, par. 4, coracle: A small boat made of hide stretched over a wicker framework.

Ch. 8, par. 14, cricket pitch: The "pitch," or area in which the bowler throws the ball toward the batter in the game of cricket, is 20.12 by 3.05 meters (about 65 by 10 feet).

Ch. 8, par. 14, the great Sea Serpent: One of the legends of the sea is the great sea serpent, reported to have been sighted by sailors from ancient times to the recent past and usually shown on old maps.

Ch. 8, par. 89, baccy: Slang abbreviation of *tobacco.*

Ch. 9, par. 38, parley: A conference between enemies under a truce.

Ch. 9, par. 64, and **Ch. 10, par. 1, they get visible,** and **to see the plates and dishes coming:** An inconsistency in the application of the physical laws of Lewis's Secondary World. In the first instance, a spear is invisible when held by the invisible Dufflepuds and becomes visible only when released; in the second, plates and dishes are visible when carried by the Dufflepuds. Each instance is very effective individually, but they are not compatible jointly.

Ch. 10, par. 4, mead: An alcoholic drink of fermented honey and water.

Ch. 10, par. 19, poor Bottom: An allusion to Bottom the Weaver in Shakespeare's *A Midsummer Night's Dream* (3.1.97); Bottom's head is changed to that of an ass by the prankster fairy, Puck.

Ch. 10, par. 21, had a strong feeling that she mustn't: Lucy has received from her parents and teachers the kind of sound moral education Lewis advocates in *The Abolition of Man,* so that she can rely on her "trained emotions" to lead her to the appropriate response when facing a moral choice.

Ch. 11, par. 32, Astrolabe: Instrument formerly used to take measurements and to solve other problems of practical astronomy.

Ch. 11, par. 32, Orrery: Mechanical model, usually clockwork, devised to represent the motions of the earth, the moon, and sometimes the planets around the sun.

Ch. 11, par. 32, Chronoscope: Instrument for observing and measuring time.

Ch. 11, par. 32, Poesimeter: A machine name invented by Lewis, with a pun on the meaning of *meter* in poetry.

Ch. 11, par. 32, Choriambus: The Latin name for a metrical foot (*choriamb* in English) — thus playfully extending the pun in the previous word.

Ch. 11, par. 32, Theodolind: Probably an adaptation of *theodolite,* a portable surveying instrument having a telescopic sight for establishing horizontal and sometimes vertical angles.

Ch. 11, par. 36, Monopod: Lewis drew two sketches of Dufflepuds to show Pauline Baynes, the illustrator of the Chronicles, how they should look. Lewis had undoubtedly seen drawings of monopods in medieval manuscripts. For a late example, see the drawing of a Skiapod in Malcolm Letts, *Sir John Mandeville: The Man and His Book* (London: Batchworth Press, 1949), illustration no. 8, opposite page 80. Mandeville, author of a popular fourteenth-century "travel" book, describes the Skiapods (from the Greek for *shade-foot*) as a cheerful race who lie on their backs and use their feet as umbrellas for protection from the sun.

Ch. 11, par. 53, brick: See note on *PC* Ch. 9, par. 57.

Ch. 11, par. 68, footballs: Known in the United States as soccer balls.

Ch. 12, par. 3, sleepers: Strong horizontal beams supporting a wall, joist, floor, or other main part of a structure.

Ch. 12, par. 47-48, Rhince: A misprint in the U.S. edition; should be "Rynelf."

Ch. 12, par. 60-70, changes in text: Lewis revised these paragraphs significantly in the U.S. edition. As the *Dawn Treader* emerges from the waters surrounding the terrifying Dark Island, where dreams come true, and shoots out into the sunlight, the British edition says that they blink their eyes and look around and they quickly realize there isn't and never had been anything to fear — and they begin laughing at themselves. Rynelf comments, "I reckon we've made pretty good fools of ourselves," and a moment later, when they look back, the Dark Island and the darkness have vanished forever. This version treats the episode itself as a dream, not as real. The effect is to diminish the seriousness of the adventure and of dreams themselves, which Lewis — who was bothered by bad dreams throughout his life — in all other cases took very seriously. By treating Rynelf's feeling as inconsequential, even as wrong, this version risks conveying to children that their feelings of fear in the face of danger (or anxiety or grief) are equally wrong.

The U.S. version replaces the above passage with this: "And just as there are moments when simply to lie in bed and see the daylight pouring through your window and to hear the cheerful voice of an early postman or milkman down below and to realise that *it was only a dream: it wasn't real*, is so heavenly that it was very nearly worth having the nightmare in order to have the joy of waking, so they all felt when they came out of the dark." This version preserves the nightmarish quality of the adventure, but by explicitly comparing it to a dream, retains the reality of the island and what they went through. The island does not vanish, but gradually grows smaller in the distance until they no longer can see it. Readers are much more deeply involved, imaginatively and emotionally. They cannot dismiss the island as unreal or as no longer existing: it is still there, and anyone who can get to Narnia still could get caught in it. More importantly, the inserted analogy, with its second-person pronoun, draws readers into the episode and evokes in them the same emotions the characters experienced. This is no laughing matter, as the earlier version risks making it.

The result is similar when Lord Rhoop asks Caspian to grant him a boon. In the British edition, Rhoop's request, that he never be brought there again, lacks the ring of authenticity. Of course they would not bring him back; there is no need to ask that. The revision for the U.S. edition adds greatly to the power and fearfulness of the episode. In this version Rhoop begs Caspian "never to ask me, nor to let any other ask me" what he had seen during the time he spent on the Dark Island, to which Caspian agrees readily, shudders, and adds that he would give up everything he owns rather than hear about what Rhoop experienced. Rhoop's request not to be asked leads readers to begin imagining what he might have seen, to substitute their own nightmares for Lord Rhoop's, and to shudder along with Caspian and agree that it was better not to be told.

In revising this passage, then, Lewis recognized a flaw in its artistry and psychology and corrected it admirably. It is regrettable that Lewis did not include these revisions — and the other changes as well — in reprints of the British editions. It is even more regrettable that Lewis's revisions were not used in the uniform edition of 1994; because they were not, most readers henceforth will read and know only the earlier, less effective wordings.

Ch. 12, par. 69 (par. 71 in the British and 1994 editions), grog: A mixture of rum and water, sometimes served hot.

Ch. 14, par. 20, star . . . is made of: Eustace raises the kind of issue that modern Western culture focuses on, looking at a star as a *thing*, a physical object, composed of analyzable substances. Ramandu's answer thrusts us into a larger, higher mode of conception, seeing stars as *living beings* to which we are intimately, inextricably related.

Ch. 14, par. 29, stint: Limitation or restriction.

Ch. 14, par. 40, quay: A landing place for ships, a wharf (pronounced *key*).

Ch. 15, par. 4, cutting: An open excavation cut through a hill to allow a train to pass on a level surface.

Ch. 15, par. 16 and **Ch. 16, par. 2, shoal:** A school of fish.

Ch. 15, par. 27, keel-hauled: A form of punishment in which a sailor is lowered on one side of a ship and dragged under the keel to the other side.

Ch. 15, par. 53, like a great round table: As the following paragraphs make clear, the Narnian world is flat, another instance of what is mythical for us (a flat world) being reality in Narnia, and vice versa (for a world to be round is mythical in Narnia).

Ch. 16, par. 3, shrouds: Ropes extending from a ship's masthead to keep the mast from swaying.

Ch. 16, par. 23, regent: A person who exercises the ruling power in a kingdom during the minority, absence, or disability of the sovereign.

Ch. 16, par. 67, how to get into your country: In answer to a question from young readers, Lewis responded, "The only way for us to [get to] Aslan's country is through death, as far as I know." Thus the use of a traditional symbol of death, a river, in the next paragraph.

The Silver Chair

The Silver Chair was the fifth book in order of composition, but it was the fourth to be published, to complete the group of three books dealing with Caspian. Lewis started work on it in the fall of 1950 and completed it by early March 1951. Roger Lancelyn Green's suggestion of *Night under Narnia* as title was rejected by the publisher as too gloomy. Other possibilities put forward included *The Wild Waste Lands, Gnomes under Narnia,* and *News under Narnia.* It was published in Britain by Geoffrey Bles on 7 September 1953 and in the United States by Macmillan on 5 October 1953.

Ch. 1, par. 2, should be allowed to do what they liked: As he described Experiment House, Lewis may well have had in mind Summerhill School, founded in Germany by A. S. Neill in 1921 and moved to Lyme Regis in southern England in 1923. Its basic premise is absolute freedom for the students: "All outside compulsion is wrong," Neill wrote; "inner compulsion is the only value." All lessons are optional. Teachers and classes are available at scheduled times, but the children can decide whether to attend or not. And rules of the school are made by majority vote in the community meetings, pupils and staff alike having equal votes. Controversial from its earliest days, it was depicted in the press as the "Do As You Please" school. Neill's approach to education became internationally famous upon publication of his best-selling book *Summerhill: A Radical Approach to Child Rearing* (New York: Hart Publishing Company, 1960).

Ch. 1, par. 24, hols: Holidays (vacations from school).

Ch. 2, par. 7, Trafalgar Square: A famous plaza in central London, constructed 1839-43 and named for Lord Nelson's naval victory in the Battle of Trafalgar (1805). The paved square is dominated by a 185-foot-high monument to Nelson. At the corners of its base are four bronze lions sculpted by Sir Edwin Landseer and cast by Baron Marochetti.

Ch. 2, par. 25, There is no other stream: Lewis's way of bringing in John 14:6 — "I am the way, the truth, and the life: no man cometh unto the Father, but by me."

Ch. 3, par. 2, quay: See note on *VDT* Ch. 14, par. 40.

Ch. 3, par. 2, forecastle: See note on *VDT* Ch. 2, par. 52.

Ch. 3, par. 2, circlet: A thin golden headband worn by a monarch on a daily basis, as opposed to the heavier crown appropriate for formal occasions.

Ch. 3, par. 4, fauns: See note on *LWW* Ch. 1, par. 27.

Ch. 3, par. 4, satyrs: See note on *PC* Ch. 4, par. 53.

Ch. 3, par. 4, centaurs: See note on *LWW* Ch. 12, par. 7.

Ch. 3, par. 18, dry up: Stop talking.

Ch. 3, par. 31, Regent: See note on *VDT* Ch. 16, par. 23.

Ch. 3, par. 62, graceful as a willow . . . moss in it: That is, a dryad (see note on *LWW* Ch. 2, par. 25).

Ch. 3, par. 87, blind poet: Probably an allusion to the blind minstrel Demodocus, who sings a poem about the fall of Troy to honor Odysseus in Book 8 of the *Odyssey*. This episode has given rise to the tradition that Homer himself was a blind bard.

Ch. 3, par. 87, the grand old tale of Prince Cor: The old tale is ancient in Narnian chronology, though the book relating it *(The Horse and His Boy)* was yet to be published. Lewis thus slips into the text an advertisement for the next book in the series.

Ch. 4, title and par. 23, parliament of Owls: An allusion to Geoffrey Chaucer's poem *A Parliament of Fowls*, composed between 1372 and 1386, in which an assembly of birds choose their mates on St. Valentine's Day.

Ch. 4, par. 6, guide's: Refers to the Girl Guides Association, an organization established in Britain in 1910 for girls between 10 and 16, corresponding to the Boy Scouts.

Ch. 4, par. 47, maying: Participating in the traditional celebrations of May Day, observing the return of spring by the gathering of wildflowers and green branches, the weaving of floral garlands, the crowning of a May king and queen, and the setting up of a decorated May tree, or Maypole, around which people danced.

Ch. 4, par. 47, ate and drank and were merry: Echoing the proverbial phrase "Eat, drink, and be merry, for tomorrow we die" (cf. Ecclesiastes 8:15), thus carrying a foreboding of ill.

Ch. 4, par. 47, physic: A medicine that purges.

Ch. 4, par. 48, blood of the stars flowed in her veins: See VDT Ch. 13, par. 77, and Ch. 14, par. 1 and 15.

Ch. 4, par. 48, worm: An archaic term for a serpent, snake, dragon.

Ch. 4, par. 50, the most beautiful lady: This description of the lady dressed in green draws upon the well-known tradition of *la belle dame sans merci*, the title of a poem by the medieval poet Alain Chartier about a beautiful but hardhearted temptress. It is most familiar in English literature through John Keats's ballad "La Belle Dame sans Merci" (1819).

Ch. 4, par. 56, one of the same crew: See note on SC Ch. 12, par. 3.

Ch. 5, par. 18, snipe: A long-billed wading bird.

Ch. 5, par. 18, bitterns: Wading birds of the heron family that inhabit reedy marshes.

Ch. 5, par. 18, bastioned: Fortified by erection of an earthwork faced with brick or stone.

Ch. 5, par. 59, Moor: Open land, high and rough but not mountainous.

Ch. 5, par. 64, bobance: Boasting, pride.

Ch. 5, par. 64, pantomime: An English dramatic performance based on a fairy tale or nursery story, performed especially during the Christmas holidays, without speech but with music, gestures, slapstick, and buffoonery and such standard character types as a pantomime "dame" played by a man, a leading boy played by a woman, and an animal played by actors dressed in a comic costume.

Ch. 6, par. 5, peewit: A bird of the plover family, inhabiting temperate areas, more commonly known as a lapwing.

Ch. 6, par. 14, cairn: A heap of stones set up as a landmark, monument, or memorial.

Ch. 6, par. 14, cock-shies: A game in which missiles are thrown at a convenient mark.

Ch. 6, par. 16, lammed: Beat, hit, whacked.

Ch. 6, par. 23, St. Paul's: Cathedral in the financial district of London, designed by Sir Christopher Wren and completed in 1710, famous for its dome rising nearly 366 feet above street level.

Ch. 6, par. 34, banneret: A small banner.

Ch. 7, par. 27, pat: Mastered perfectly or exactly.

Ch. 7, par. 37, portcullis: A strong, heavy frame of vertical and horizontal bars of iron that slides up and down in the gateway of a castle or fortress and can be quickly lowered as a defense against attack.

Ch. 7, par. 44, puttee: A long strip of cloth wound spirally round the leg from the ankle to the knee, worn as a protection and support to the leg.

Ch. 8, par. 14, possets: Drinks composed of hot milk curdled with ale, wine, or other liquor, often with sugar, spices, or other ingredients.

Ch. 8, par. 14, comfits: Confections made of fruit preserved with sugar; sugarplums.

Ch. 8, par. 14, caraways: Confections containing caraway seeds.

Ch. 8, par. 17, cock-a-leekie soup: Soup made of a cock boiled with leeks.

Ch. 8, par. 18, gasometer: A large tank used for holding gas.

Ch. 8, par. 39, bally: Pronounced to rhyme with *alley*. A euphemism for *bloody*, an epithet expressing anger or detestation, but often used just as an intensive (here, the equivalent of "stupid").

Ch. 9, par. 1, made love: Showed affection.

Ch. 9, par. 1, scullery: Room off a kitchen where cooking utensils are cleaned and stored.

Ch. 9, par. 1, scullions: Kitchen servants who do menial tasks.

Ch. 9, par. 4, hooters: The horns of motor vehicles.

Ch. 9, par. 19, blamey: Blasted, confounded.

Ch. 9, par. 25, joint: A large piece of meat, usually with a bone; in this case, one course of a meal.

Ch. 9, par. 48, shingle: Small roundish stones or pebbles, as can be found on a beach.

Ch. 10, par. 4, few return: An echo of the words of the Sibyl of Cumae to Aeneas in Virgil's *Aeneid* (6.88): "Easy is the descent to Hell; the door of dark Dis stands open day and night. But to retrace your steps and come out to the air above, that is work, that is labor!"

Ch. 10, par. 46, Hamlet: The character Hamlet, in Shakespeare's *Hamlet* (ca. 1599-1601), is traditionally costumed in black; his mother asks him to "cast thy nighted color off" (1.2.68).

Ch. 10, par. 50, nosegay: Literally, a bunch of flowers or herbs having a sweet smell; here, a metaphor for perfection.

Ch. 11, par. 4, fie: An expression of rebuke; in this case, to dismiss taking a matter seriously (with "gravity").

Ch. 11, par. 19, curious silver chair: John Cox in a fine essay points to the "siluer seat" in the underground Cave of Mammon in Spenser's *The Faerie Queene* as a likely source of the Green Witch's chair.

Ch. 12, par. 3, Witch-queen: The 1994 mass-market paperback of *The Silver Chair* in the U.S. states incorrectly, in the "Cast of Characters" feature at the front of the book, that the Queen of Underland is another embodiment of Jadis, the witch in *The Magician's Nephew* and *The Lion, the Witch and the Wardrobe*. The oldest owl suggests in Chapter 4 that the White Witch and the Queen of Underland are of the same nature but are not the same person. The fact that the Queen of Underland is killed by Prince Rilian is further evidence that she is not the White Witch. According to *The Lion, the Witch and the Wardrobe,* Aslan killed the White Witch in battle ("the Witch was dead"); in that case she could not be the Queen of Underland many hundreds of years later.

Ch. 12, par. 23, ration-books: Books of stamps, issued to families during World War II, permitting the holders to purchase scarce items such as sugar, butter, coffee, and meat. Ration books would have been in use in 1942, the year in which the action of this book is set.

Ch. 12, par. 52, judge's wig: Since the late 1600s high-court judges in England have worn wigs along with their judicial robes to add to the dignity and formality of court proceedings.

Ch. 12, par. 63, blub: Weep or cry; short for *blubber.*

Ch. 12, par. 64, look to the lady: An allusion to Shakespeare's *Macbeth* 2.3.127, where Banquo says these words after Lady Macbeth pretends to faint upon hearing that Duncan, King of Scotland, has been murdered in her house.

Ch. 13, par. 2, four strangers: This is a slip in the original British and U.S. texts; it has been corrected to "three" in the 1994 uniform edition.

Ch. 13, par. 26, funk: A coward.

Ch. 13, par. 26, ratty: Ill-tempered, nasty.

Ch. 13, par. 26, used Christian names: Tolkien writes in a letter to his publisher, "I belong to a generation which did not use Christian names outside the family. . . . Even C. S. Lewis never called me by a Christian name (or I him)."

Ch. 13, par. 36, an old song about Corin Thunder-fist: See note on *SC* Ch. 3, par. 87.

Ch. 13, par. 45, Play the knave: Act dishonorably or deceitfully, be a base and crafty rogue.

Ch. 14, par. 1, squib: Firecracker.

Ch. 14, par. 3, Bism: Lewis's adaptation of the Greek *byssos,* meaning "bottom" or "the lowest deep," perhaps influenced by the English *chasm.*

Ch. 14, par. 38, slit in a pillar-box: The slot for depositing letters in English postal boxes (often round, pillar-shaped).

Ch. 16, par. 20, pavender: "A beautiful rainbow-coloured [Narnian] fish" (*PC* 30).

Ch. 16, par. 28, nine names of Aslan: According to Paul Ford, of the nine names known by the centaurs, we are given only four: Aslan, the Great Lion, the son of the Emperor-Beyond-the-Sea, and the King above all High Kings.

The Horse and His Boy

The Horse and His Boy was the fourth of the Chronicles to be written, but the fifth to be published (by Geoffrey Bles in Britain on 6 September 1954 and by Macmillan in the United States on 5 October 1954). Lewis began work on it in spring 1950; on 26 July, Roger Lancelyn Green read the finished manuscript. Lewis's first choice of title, *Narnia and the North*, was rejected by Geoffrey Bles. Lewis suggested several others: *The Horse and the Boy, The Desert Road to Narnia, Cor of Archenland, The Horse Stole the Boy, Over the Border,* and *The Horse Bree*. Bles replied, "I like best *The Horse and the Boy*, but what about *The Horse and his Boy*, which is a little startling and conveys the idea of your other title *The Horse Stole the Boy*?"

    Ch. 1, par. 6, scimitar: A short, curved, single-edged sword, used especially in the Middle East.

    Ch. 1, par. 6, bosses: Decorative protrusions, in their simplest form rounded.

    Ch. 1, par. 26, thymy: Having the scent of the shrubby, fragrant herb thyme.

    Ch. 1, par. 26, plashing glens: Narrow mountain valleys with streams splashing noisily through them.

    Ch. 2, par. 3, gorse: Bree does not seem to realize that landing in a spiny gorse bush is not the ideal way to break a fall.

    Ch. 2, par. 4, copse: A thicket of small trees and underbrush.

    Ch. 2, par. 7, meat pasty: See note on *PC* Ch. 12, par. 87.

    Ch. 2, par. 14, rum: See note on *PC* Ch. 11, par. 23.

    Ch. 2, par. 75, cob: A short-legged, stout variety of horse, suitable to be ridden by heavy persons.

    Ch. 3, par. 24, ghouls: See note on *LWW* Ch. 13, par. 16.

    Ch. 4, par. 1, battlements: Alternating high and low extensions of stone or brick at the top of the wall of a fortified building, used for defense against assailants.

    Ch. 4, par. 12, litter: A means of transportation consisting of a couch or chair shut in by curtains and carried on men's shoulders.

    Ch. 4, par. 18, sweetmeat: Sweet food, such as sugared cakes or pastry, confectionery, preserved or candied fruits, or sugared nuts.

Ch. 4, par. 19, arcades: Arches forming a covered avenue.

Ch. 4, par. 32, hangdog: Base, sneaking, despicable.

Ch. 4, par. 32, scape: Transgression due to thoughtlessness.

Ch. 4, par. 32, avouch: To acknowledge or take responsibility for an action.

Ch. 4, par. 48, hastilude: Spear-play, or a kind of combat, for sport or exercise.

Ch. 5, par. 23, planting an orchard: See PC Ch. 2, par. 34.

Ch. 5, par. 33, minim: A monetary unit in Calormen.

Ch. 5, par. 43, galley: See note on VDT Ch. 2, par. 42.

Ch. 5, par. 50, snipe: See note on SC Ch. 5, par. 18.

Ch. 5, par. 50, fools: Dishes composed of fruit stewed, crushed, and mixed with milk, cream, or custard.

Ch. 5, par. 63, stoup: Here, a large jar holding a liquid.

Ch. 6, par. 22, staring him out of countenance: Making him feel uneasy or disconcerted.

Ch. 7, par. 32, punts: Shallow, flat-bottomed boats, broad and square at both ends, propelled by pushing a long pole against the bottom of a river or other shallow body of water.

Ch. 8, par. 1, jade: A contemptuous name for a horse of inferior breed, it is also used as a term of reprobation applied to a woman.

Ch. 8, par. 40, apophthegms: British variant of *apothegm*. Terse, pointed sayings, embodying important truths in few words.

Ch. 9, par. 14, scullion: See note on SC Ch. 9, par. 1.

Ch. 9, par. 18, quailed: Became cowed or discouraged; gave way through fear.

Ch. 9, par. 26, grease his oats: Literally, spoil by mixing grease in the grain; here, an equine metaphor for upsetting one's plans.

Ch. 9, par. 47, cataract: Here, a waterfall.

Ch. 10, par. 3, fetlock: A projection on a horse's leg where the tuft of hair grows, above and behind the hoof.

Ch. 10, par. 6, fallow deer: A species smaller than the stag or red deer, named for its light brown color.

Ch. 10, par. 35, March: Boundary or frontier of a country, district, or region.

Ch. 10, par. 42, hot mash: Bran, meal, or the like mixed with hot water and given as a warm food to animals.

Ch. 11, par. 61, Myself . . . Myself . . . Myself: This is the only place in the Chronicles where Lewis brings in specifically the Christian doctrine of the Trinity, of three divine persons — Father, Son, and Holy Spirit — in one divine nature. Each "Myself" is spoken in an appropriate way: the first so powerful that it causes the earth to shake; the second clear and gay; the third like spirit or wind.

Ch. 11, par. 66, High King above all kings: Perhaps an allusion to "King of kings and Lord of lords" in Revelation 19:16.

Ch. 12, par. 49, all's well: Probably an echo of Shakespeare's line "All's well that ends well" (5.1.25) from the play by that name (c. 1601–1605), though it could also be alluding to a well-known affirmation of the doctrine of Providence by Julian of Norwich (1342–c. 1416), whose mystical thought Lewis admired: "All will be well and all manner of thing will be well."

Ch. 12, par. 51: heart's-scald: Literally, heartburn; here, a metaphor for vexation.

Ch. 12, par. 51, lief: Gladly, happily.

Ch. 12, par. 53, cordial: See note on *LWW*, Ch. 10, par. 46.

Ch. 13, par. 1, goosecap: Simpleton.

Ch. 13, par. 17, funk: Flinch or shrink or try to back out of through fear.

Ch. 13, par. 24, full career: Short gallop at full speed.

Ch. 13, par. 34, hauberk: See note on *PC* Ch. 8, par. 47.

Ch. 14, par. 22, a Beast just like: As God the Son became incarnate as a man in our world ("true man," the Creeds insist), so in Lewis's Otherworld of Talking Beasts it is appropriate he should take the form of a true beast.

Ch. 14, par. 45, halberd: Weapon consisting of a sharp-edged blade ending in a point, and a spearhead, mounted on a handle five to seven feet long.

Ch. 14, par. 48, cambric: A kind of fine white linen originally made at Cambrai in Flanders.

Ch. 14, par. 63, brick: See note on *PC* Ch. 9, par. 57.

Ch. 14, par. 63, Centaur: See note on *LWW* Ch. 12, par. 7.

Ch. 14, par. 79, heraldry: See note on *PC* Ch. 5, par. 1.

Ch. 15, par. 19, noisome: Offensive or disgusting, smelly, noxious.

Ch. 15, par. 21, Faugh!: An exclamation of abhorrence or disgust.

Ch. 15, par. 24, pajock: A peacock or vain pretender. Lewis probably remembered the word — rarely used — from Shakespeare's *Hamlet* (3.2.280-82): "This realm dismantled was / Of Jove himself, and now reigns here / A very, very — pajock."

Ch. 15, par. 47, estres: Quarters, inner rooms.

The Magician's Nephew

Lewis began to write a story of Narnia's origins soon after completing *The Lion, the Witch and the Wardrobe* in March 1949. Two chapters, now called "The Lefay Fragment," have survived in manuscript and can be found in Walter Hooper's *Past Watchful Dragons* 48-65. Lewis abandoned that effort, however, because he wasn't satisfied with it and because the idea for a different story came to him, the story that became *Prince Caspian*. After completing *The Silver Chair*, he again turned his attention to the origins of Narnia. By the end of May 1951, he had written the first half of *The Magician's Nephew*, and by the end of October he had finished three-fourths of it. But Roger Lancelyn Green criticized parts of it, and Lewis put it aside to consider whether and how to revise it. Not until the spring of 1953 did he return to it, and not until early in 1954 did he finish it, after completing *The Last Battle*. It was published by The Bodley Head in Britain on 2 May 1955 and by Macmillan in the United States on 4 October 1955.

Ch. 1, par. 2, Holmes: The famous fictional detective of Sir Arthur Conan Doyle's stories lived at 221B Baker Street between 1881 and 1904.

Ch. 1, par. 2, Bastables: The six Bastable children were characters in a series of books by E. Nesbit, starting with *The Story of the Treasure Seekers*, published in 1899.

Ch. 1, par. 2, Eton collar: A broad, stiff white collar formerly worn outside the jacket by students at Eton College — hence the name.

Ch. 1, par. 23, coiner: One who coins money; here, specifically a maker of counterfeit coins.

Ch. 1, par. 24, the man at the beginning of *Treasure Island:* The pirate Billy Bones in Robert Louis Stevenson's novel (1883).

Ch. 1, par. 28, cistern: A tank placed in a high part of a building from which water flows through pipes to faucets below.

Ch. 1, par. 28, ginger-beer: A drink similar to ginger ale in the United States.

Ch. 1, par. 58, Hoovers: Vacuum cleaners. W. H. Hoover began producing Hoover "suction sweepers" in 1908; because his products dominated the market, his name came to be used for vacuum cleaners generally.

Ch. 1, par. 60, bunk: Be off; get out of here.

Ch. 1, par. 63, pantomime demon: A stock character (villain) in British pantomime (see the note on *SC* Ch. 5, par. 64) who often ascends to the stage through a trapdoor.

Ch. 1, par. 76, duffer: An incapable and inefficient person or, as in this case, a stupid or foolish person. The British and 1994 editions have **buffer**, a British slang term for a foolish or incompetent person.

Ch. 2, par. 28, Atlantis: A legendary island said to be rich and powerful more than three thousand years ago, and situated in the Atlantic Ocean, west of Europe; now sunk.

Ch. 2, par. 51, showing the white feather: Acting like a coward.

Ch. 3, par. 56, the famous Professor Kirke: The professor's name was not given in *LWW*. It is probably a tribute to Lewis's tutor, W. T. Kirkpatrick (see above, p. 7).

Ch. 3, par. 58, St. Paul's: See note on *SC* Ch. 6, par. 23.

Ch. 5, par. 22, Charn: Lewis may have derived the name of this dead city from the now obsolete word *charnel* — a burial place, cemetery.

Ch. 5, par. 64, bosh: Nonsense, trash.

Ch. 6, par. 43, We'll call it Pax: We'll make peace, or declare a truce. (Cf. note on *LWW* Ch. 3, par. 30.)

Ch. 6, par. 46, frockcoat: A man's close-fitting, knee-length, double-breasted coat with a vent in the back.

Ch. 6, par. 46, eye-glass: A monocle.

Ch. 6, par. 47, dem: Euphemistic form of *damn*.

Ch. 6, par. 50, hansom: A hansom cab, a low-hung, two-wheeled horse-drawn vehicle holding two persons inside with the driver mounted on an elevated seat behind.

Ch. 6, par. 53, deucedly: Damnably, exceedingly. The use of genteel oaths is part of Uncle Andrew's characterization (cf. the final line in the book).

Ch. 7, par. 13, *sal volatile*: Ammonium carbonate, the chief ingredient in smelling salts, used to restore people who have fainted.

Ch. 7, par. 34, cove: Fellow or chap.

Ch. 8, par. 1, cross-bars of the lamp-post: Lewis has in mind the Victorian lamppost with a crossbar to steady the lamplighter while igniting the gas lamp.

Ch. 8, par. 1, stick of barley-sugar: A candy, usually in twisted sticks, made from boiling sugar in an extract of barley.

Ch. 8, par. 4, brick: See note on *PC* Ch. 9, par. 57.

Ch. 8, par. 27, the Underground: The first section of the London Underground was opened in 1863, using steam engines. By 1900 it had become an extensive network using electric engines and carrying approximately 50 million passengers a year.

Ch. 8, par. 37, it was the stars . . . singing: Alluding to the Music of the Spheres — see Peter Schakel, *Imagination and the Arts in C. S. Lewis* 104-5 (chapter 5 discusses the importance of music in Lewis's life and works generally). On Lewis's use of song in his creation story, see also Charles Huttar, "C. S. Lewis's Narnia and the 'Grand Design'" 124.

Ch. 8, par. 41, a Magic different from hers and stronger: Aslan's Magic is akin to what Tolkien calls "the elvish craft," a creative magic, which he contrasts to the manipulative power of a "mere Magician," who can only produce alterations in the Primary World.

Ch. 9, par. 5, Yeomanry: A volunteer cavalry force in the British army, originally formed at the time of the French Revolution and consisting chiefly of yeomen, farmers who own the land they cultivate; the force has now been amalgamated with the Volunteers to form the Territorial Army. Andrew clearly thinks of himself as a gentleman — that is, of a higher social class than his cousin.

Ch. 9, par. 36, two at a time: Perhaps an echo of the Noah story (Genesis 6:19).

Ch. 10, par. 2, Fauns, Satyrs, Naiad daughters: See notes on *LWW* Ch. 1, par. 27; *PC* Ch. 4, par. 53; and *PC* Ch. 4, par. 11.

Ch. 10, par. 7, jackdaw: A small Eurasian crow with a gray nape, proverbial for its talkativeness and ability to imitate the sound of words and its propensity for collecting objects that catch its eye.

Ch. 10, par. 57, Prep. school: In Britain, a junior school that prepares students for a higher school or college.

Ch. 10, par. 57, Tally-ho! Tantivy!: Hunting cries, the first being the cry raised by huntsmen on catching sight of the quarry in a fox hunt, the second urging the group to ride full tilt, to go all out.

Ch. 11, par. 1, Norfolk suit: A suit consisting of a Norfolk jacket (modeled on a hunting coat introduced by the Duke of Norfolk in the 1880s) and knee breeches.

Ch. 11, par. 15, Tapir: A mammal of tropical America somewhat resembling the swine but more nearly related to the rhinoceros, having a short, flexible trunk.

Ch. 11, par. 17, half-sovereign: British gold coin worth ten shillings (a *sovereign* was equivalent to a pound).

Ch. 11, par. 17, half-crown: British silver coin worth two shillings and sixpence (a *crown* was equivalent to five shillings).

Ch. 11, par. 17, sixpence: A British silver coin worth six pennies.

Ch. 11, par. 30, for a bath: See note on *VDT* Ch. 7, par. 36.

Ch. 11, par. 63, name all these creatures: An echo of Genesis 2:19-20.

Ch. 11, par. 66, use a spade: Alludes to the medieval rhyme, "When Adam delved, and Eve span / Who was then a gentleman?" (referring to original equality vs. the later development of class distinctions).

Ch. 11, par. 73, cockney: A native of the East End district of London, speaking the distinctive dialect of this area.

Ch. 12, par. 1, blub: See note on *SC* Ch. 12, par. 63.

Ch. 12, par. 18, curvetted: Leaped with his forelegs raised equally together and hind legs springing forward.

Ch. 12, par. 27, rum go: Strange turn of events, unexpected course of action.

Ch. 12, par. 31, moorland: See note on *SC* Ch. 5, par. 59.

Ch. 13, par. 2, honesty: A plant of the mustard family, having clusters of purple flowers and semitransparent satiny pods.

Ch. 13, par. 3, cataract: Here, a cascade.

Ch. 13, par. 12, climb my wall and **par. 19, must have climbed in over the wall:** Alluding to the walls around Paradise in Milton's *Paradise Lost* (4.143), which Satan overleaped (4.181) with ease, and to John 10:1: "He that entereth not by the door . . . but climbeth up some other way . . . is a thief."

Ch. 13, par. 16, Could it be wrong to taste one? and **par. 22, you will miss some knowledge:** Alluding to the temptation in Eden (Genesis 3:5-6).

Ch. 13, par. 17, a wonderful bird: See note on *LB* Ch. 16, par. 31.

Ch. 13, par. 18, hammered into boys' heads: Digory's parents seem to have adhered to the principles Lewis advocated in *The Abolition of Man,* that "the little human animal" must be trained to have the proper moral responses, "to feel pleasure, liking, disgust, and hatred at those things which really are pleasant, likeable, disgusting, and hateful."

Ch. 13, par. 24, the apple of life: Lewis has conflated the two trees of Eden, that of life and that of forbidden fruit (see Genesis 3:22). The tree reappears in *The Last Battle* 169-70.

Ch. 13, par. 24, I shall never grow old or die: Jadis's claim to have gained immortality by eating fruit from the tree of life is confirmed by Aslan in Chapter 14, paragraph 34. It apparently is a guarantee only of protection from aging and "natural" death, but not from violent death, just as other gods (Balder, Osiris, even Aslan) can be killed though they would not die of natural causes. Likewise, Tolkien's Elves can be killed, even though the gift of death has not been given to them.

Ch. 14, par. 1, Well done: Alluding to Matthew 25:21: "Well done, thou good and faithful servant: thou hast been faithful over a few things, I will make thee ruler over many things: enter thou into the joy of thy lord."

Ch. 14, par. 5, River-Nymphs: See notes on *LWW* Ch. 2, par. 25, and Ch. 4, par. 11.

Ch. 15, par. 14, wan: (in the U.S. editions) Pallid, sickly, unhealthily pale, especially a human face. **Thin**, in the British and 1994 editions, is perhaps preferable since the next word is "pale."

Ch. 15, par. 29, frowsy: Musty, having a "close," unpleasant smell from being ill-ventilated or unwashed.

Ch. 15, par. 34, devilish: Note the double meaning — Uncle Andrew means "exceedingly," but "like a devil in character or actions" is equally applicable.

The Last Battle

Lewis began working on *The Last Battle* in the fall of 1952; he completed it in March 1953. It was first called *The Last Chronicle of Narnia;* another title considered was *Night Falls on Narnia* (from ch. 14, par. 26). It was published in Britain by The Bodley Head on 19 March 1956, and in the United States by Macmillan on 4 September 1956. It was awarded the Carnegie Medal for the best children's book of 1956.

Ch. 1, par. 1, panniers: Large baskets for carrying goods, provisions, and other commodities, slung in pairs across the back of a pack animal.

Ch. 1, par. 16, hearthrug: A fairly large rug laid before a fireplace to protect the carpet or floor.

Ch. 2, par. 10, Centaurs: See note on *LWW* Ch. 12, par. 7.

Ch. 2, par. 13, page: A boy or lad employed as a servant or attendant.

Ch. 2, par. 18, written in the skies, and **The stars never lie:** Consistent with the medieval-era setting Lewis creates for Narnia, astrology is treated as a legitimate science.

Ch. 2, par. 24, the holy trees: Not trees that are worshipped, which was not done in Narnia, but talking trees growing in Lantern Waste, a place of special significance as the location of the Tree of Protection (paragraph 56), planted by Digory at Narnia's beginning, which guarded Narnia from the witch Jadis for almost nine hundred years.

Ch. 2, par. 25, Dryad: See note on *LWW* Ch. 2, par. 25.

Ch. 2, par. 33, fell: Fierce, deadly.

Ch. 2, par. 36, dried his sword very carefully: See note on *LWW* Ch. 12, par. 37.

Ch. 3, par. 1, traces: The pair of leather straps by which the collar of a horse or other draft animal is connected with the vehicle the animal is pulling.

Ch. 3, par. 3, scimitars: See note on *H&B* Ch. 1, par. 6.

Ch. 3, par. 9, faugh!: See note on *H&B* Ch. 15, par. 21.

Ch. 3, par. 23, circlet: See note on *SC* Ch. 3, par. 2.

Ch. 4, par. 18, Wood-Nymphs: Dryads (see note on *LWW* Ch. 2, par. 25).

Ch. 5, par. 31, battlements: See note on *H&B* Ch. 4, par. 1.

Ch. 5, par. 37, garrison: Fortress or stronghold.

Ch. 5, par. 50, firkin: A small cask containing a quarter of a barrel of liquid.

Ch. 6, par. 6, guide: See note on *SC* Ch. 4, par. 6.

Ch. 6, par. 9, Fauns: See note on *LWW* Ch. 1, par. 27.

Ch. 6, par. 24, rive: Slit or cut.

Ch. 6, par. 50, jiggered: A mild oath, substituted for a stronger one.

Ch. 6, par. 55, malapert: Presumptuous, impudent, saucy.

Ch. 6, par. 59, mattocks: Digging tools shaped like pickaxes with one end broad instead of pointed.

Ch. 7, par. 2, manikins: Little men.

Ch. 7, par. 16, said Jill impatiently: A paragraph break (perhaps unintended) occurs after this phrase in the U.S. edition, but not in the British and 1994 editions. Thus paragraph numbering differs for the rest of the chapter.

Ch. 7, par. 23 (British and 1994 editions, 22), It's all a trick: Changed in the U.S. edition from **It's all a plant** [a scheme or plot to defraud], "all a blooming [euphemism for *bloody*, with a pun on a plant blooming] plant."

Ch. 7, par. 25 (British and 1994 editions, 24), moke: British slang for *donkey*.

Ch. 7, par. 34 (British and 1994 editions, 33), churl: Villain, base fellow: a term of contempt.

Ch. 7, par. 34, give . . . a lie to (U.S. edition), give . . . the lie to (British and 1994 editions, 33): Accuse a person of lying.

Ch. 7, par. 48 (British and 1994 editions, 47), made to clean and polish it: See note on *LWW* Ch. 12, par. 37.

Ch. 7, par. 54 (British and 1994 editions, 53), scurvy: Discourteous, contemptible.

Ch. 7, par. 54 (British and 1994 editions, 53), enlightened: The Tarkaan seems to be the product of a Calormene movement parallel to the Enlightenment in Europe, a philosophical movement in the seventeenth and eighteenth centuries characterized by supreme faith in the power of reason. Grounded in a skeptical attitude and a materialistic epistemology, it applied a rational and scientific approach to all subjects, including religion.

Ch. 8, par. 1 and 5, Tash: Lewis describes Tash as a pagan god with characteristics antithetical to those of Aslan; he is cruel, hateful, unforgiving. The worship of Tash, therefore, includes what Lewis in his essay "Religion without Dogma?" calls "the obscenities and cruelties of paganism." In our world such gods are not real, and even in Narnia the Lamb doesn't believe Tash actually exists. But in Narnia other figures mythical in our world have turned out to be real, and so does Tash.

Ch. 8, par. 13, demons: Devils in the sense of false gods (not "the devil," Satan), as in *Paradise Lost*, Book 1.

Ch. 8, par. 27, rucked: Rumpled, caught in small folds.

Ch. 8, par. 29, old Narnian marching song: For the entire song, see Lewis's "Narnian Suite," part 2: "March for Drum, Trumpet, and Twenty-one Giants," in *Poems*, ed. Walter Hooper (London: Geoffrey Bles, 1964), 7.

Ch. 8, par. 51, leagues: Units measuring distance, usually estimated roughly at about 3 miles.

Ch. 9, par. 13, I've got the wind up: I'm in a state of nervous anxiety or fear.

Ch. 9, par. 24, rum: See note on *PC* Ch. 11, par. 23.

Ch. 9, par. 29, bathchair: Wheelchair.

Ch. 9, par. 36, biscuit: A kind of crisp, dry bread prepared in thin, flat cakes; close to *cracker* in the United States.

Ch. 12, par. 48, And this is my brother: In the U.S. edition, a line is unintentionally omitted from this paragraph. The British and 1994 editions read: "'And this,' he said, 'is the Lord Digory who was with her on that day. And this is my brother, King Edmund: and this my sister, the Queen Lucy.'"

Ch. 12, par. 50, no longer a friend of Narnia: An extension of the characterization in *The Voyage of the "Dawn Treader"* where Susan is described as not a good student, but trying to seem older than she is. Here Lewis appears to be indicating that Susan also is no longer a friend of Aslan, thus using her to make the point that some people abandon their faith and will not reach heaven. In reply to a child who inquired about Susan, he wrote, "The books don't tell us what happened to Susan. She is left alive in this world at the end, having by then turned into a rather silly, conceited young woman. But there is plenty of time for her to mend, and perhaps she will get to Aslan's country in the end — in her own way. I think that whatever she had seen in Narnia she *could* (if she was the sort that wanted to) persuade herself, as she grew up, that it was 'all nonsense.'"

Ch. 13, par. 14, hack: A cut or gash in the skin caused by a kick with the toe of a boot.

Ch. 13, par. 14, rugger: Rugby, a sport somewhat similar to American football.

Ch. 13, par. 33, a Stable once had: Referring to the stable in which Jesus was born (Luke 2:7).

Ch. 13, par. 59, baccy: See note on VDT Ch. 8, par. 89.

Ch. 13, par. 61, like your sauce: Typical of your impertinence or sauciness.

Ch. 13, par. 72, in their own minds: Compare to these lines from *The Great Divorce:* "Hell is a state of mind. . . . And every state of mind, left to itself, every shutting up of the creature within the dungeon of its own mind — is, in the end, Hell." Uncle Andrew's experience in *The Magician's Nephew* is similar; no matter how beautifully the Lion sings, Uncle Andrew convinces himself he can hear nothing but roaring.

Ch. 14, par. 10, Satyrs, Fauns: See note on LWW Ch. 1, par. 27.

Ch. 14, par. 10, Monopods: See VDT chapters 10-11.

Ch. 14, par. 41, blown: Out of breath.

Ch. 15, par. 1, Know, O Warlike Kings: Notice that Emeth, like

Aravis in *The Horse and His Boy,* has learned to tell stories in "the grand Calormene manner."

Ch. 15, par. 6, the Flaming Mountain of Lagour: Not mentioned elsewhere; part of Calormene mythology.

Ch. 15, par. 6, I account as service done to me: This passage suggests that Lewis, theologically, was an "inclusivist," not a "universalist" on the one hand or an "exclusivist" on the other. An inclusivist allows for the possibility that God will extend grace to those who earnestly seek the Truth and live virtuous lives even though they have not heard of Christianity. Universalists (like Lewis's "mentor" George MacDonald) believe that God's love and grace are so all-encompassing that ultimately all people will yield to them and be saved. (Lewis was not able to accept this position because it denies human freedom, the freedom to refuse God's love and grace.) Exclusivists believe that only those who know, believe in, and accept Jesus by name will be saved.

The belief that he needed to accept the exclusivist position seems to have been one of the reasons Lewis "ceased to be a Christian" in his teens. As he put it in *Surprised by Joy,* in the classics, "especially in Virgil, one was presented with a mass of religious ideas" which his teachers assumed to be "a mere farrago of nonsense, though our own, by a fortunate exception, was exactly true." He later came to believe that in some senses "Christianity fulfilled Paganism or Paganism prefigured Christianity."

He expands on that possibility in *Mere Christianity:* "[It] used to puzzle me . . . that this new life should be confined to people who have heard of Christ and been able to believe in Him[.] But . . . God has not told us what His arrangements about the other people are. We do know that no man can be saved except through Christ; we do not know that only those who know Him can be saved through Him. . . . People in other religions . . . led by God's secret influence to concentrate on those parts of their religion which are in agreement with Christianity . . . thus belong to Christ without knowing it. . . . Many of the good Pagans long before Christ's birth may have been in this position." See also his letters to Mrs. Arnold dated 31 January 1952 and to Mrs. Ashton dated 8 November 1952.

Ch. 15, par. 6, Yes I have been seeking: "Yes" is a misprint in the older U.S. editions; the correct reading is "Yet."

Ch. 15, par. 32, Ettinsmuir: See note on *LWW* Ch. 14, par. 39, and *SC* Ch. 5, par 59. *Muir* is an older form of *moor*.

Ch. 15, par. 36, a shadow or a copy: In this paragraph Lewis summarizes briefly and explicitly Plato's idealistic philosophy, the theory that things perceived in our world are imitations (copies, shadows) of originals called *Forms* or *Ideas*. Ideas are permanent, perfect, unchanging, and thus are the only real objects of knowledge in the universe. In contrast, things in our world are imperfect and changing, and therefore essentially unreal.

Human souls existed in the realm of Ideas before being "imprisoned" in physical bodies through birth. Until souls are sufficiently corrupted by the physical world to forget their place of origin, they constantly long to return to it. Thus Jewel's words in paragraph 39 apply in both Platonic and Christian senses.

Ch. 15, par. 36, what *do* they teach them: Part of Lewis's critique of modern education. The Professor said the same thing twice in *LWW*, pp. 40 and 153.

Ch. 16, par. 24, circlet: See note on *SC* Ch. 3, par. 2.

Ch. 16, par. 31, Phoenix: A mythical Arabian bird, only one of which existed at a given time. After living 500 years, the bird set fire to its nest, leaped into the fire, and was consumed, then rose from its own ashes as a new bird. It is a traditional symbol for Christ. (Presumably this is the same bird that was sitting in the tree in *The Magician's Nephew*, Ch. 13, par. 17.)

Ch. 16, par. 31, in a tree: See note on *MN* Ch. 13, par. 24. On the reappearance of the tree, see Revelation 22:14.

Ch. 16, par. 31, a King and Queen so great and beautiful: Compare to Lewis's description in *A Preface to "Paradise Lost"* (Ch. 16) of the greatness of Adam and Eve in Paradise, the King and Queen of Earth before whom we would quickly fall to our knees were we to encounter them.

Ch. 16, par. 37, like an onion: except that as you . . . go in . . . each circle is larger than the last: Lewis here chooses a more homely image to do what Dante did with the Celestial Rose in the closing cantos of *Paradiso* (esp. canto 28), as each writer struggles to express a divine paradox. In his essay "Dante's Similes," Lewis described it this way: "The universe is turned inside out and the circumference is found to be the centre." And in

The Discarded Image, he explained, "The universe is thus, when our minds are sufficiently freed from the senses, turned inside out."

Ch. 16, par. 38, as if she were looking through a telescope: Lucy's improved sight is similar to that Dante experiences in *Paradiso* 30.58ff. (see also 1.53). (This and the preceding are among the many notes supplied by Charles Huttar.)

Ch. 16, par. 42, quay: See note on *VDT* Ch. 14, par. 40.

Ch. 16, par. 46, cataract: Waterfall. The image here is more like that of Yosemite, which drops nearly half a mile in two segments, than that of Niagara.

Ch. 16, par. 52, Shadow-Lands (U.S. edition), Shadowlands (British and 1994 editions): See the note on *LB* Ch. 15, par. 36. This is the source of the title of the movie and play about Lewis's life (see below, p. 166).

Sources and Notes

B ooks by C. S. Lewis are cited from the first British editions except in the case of the Chronicles of Narnia, where the Macmillan editions published in the United States reflect his last revisions (see above, pages 13-15).

The Chronicles of Narnia are cited by page numbers; for locating equivalent pages in other editions, see pages 192-94. Books by Lewis that are available in only one edition are cited by page numbers. Those other than the Chronicles that exist in reprints with different pagination include a chapter or section reference.

The following brief references are used in citing the works referred to most frequently in these Sources and Notes.

WORKS BY LEWIS

AofM   *The Abolition of Man, or Reflections on Education with Special Reference to the Teaching of English in the Upper Forms of Schools.* The Riddell Memorial Lectures, University of Durham, Fifteenth Series. London: Oxford University Press, 1943.

Collected Letters   *Collected Letters*, edited by Walter Hooper. Vol. 1: *Family Letters 1905-1931.* London: HarperCollins, 2000. Vol. 2: *Books, Broadcasts and War 1931-1949.* London: HarperCollins, 2004.

EinC   *An Experiment in Criticism.* Cambridge: Cambridge University Press, 1961.

God in the Dock *God in the Dock: Essays on Theology and Ethics.* Edited by Walter Hooper. Grand Rapids: Eerdmans, 1970.

GD *The Great Divorce.* London: Geoffrey Bles — The Centenary Press, 1946. (Cited by page number, and by the chapter numbers added in the U.S. edition.)

H&B *The Horse and His Boy.* New York: Macmillan, 1954.

LB *The Last Battle.* New York: Macmillan, 1956.

Letters *Letters of C. S. Lewis* (1966), edited by W. H. Lewis. Revised and enlarged edition, edited by Walter Hooper. London: Fount, 1988.

Letters to Children *Letters to Children,* edited by Lyle W. Dorsett and Marjorie Lamp Mead. New York: Macmillan, 1985.

LWW *The Lion, the Witch and the Wardrobe.* New York: Macmillan, 1950.

MC *Mere Christianity.* London: Geoffrey Bles, 1952.

MN *The Magician's Nephew.* New York: Macmillan, 1955.

OnS *On Stories and Other Essays on Literature.* Edited by Walter Hooper. New York: Harcourt Brace Jovanovich, 1982.

OOW *Of Other Worlds: Essays and Stories.* Edited by Walter Hooper. London: Geoffrey Bles, 1966.

PPL *A Preface to "Paradise Lost."* London: Oxford University Press, 1942.

PC *Prince Caspian: The Return to Narnia.* New York: Macmillan, 1951.

SbyJ *Surprised by Joy: The Shape of My Early Life.* New York: Harcourt, Brace & World, 1955.

SC *The Silver Chair.* New York: Macmillan, 1953.

TST *They Stand Together: The Letters of C. S. Lewis to Arthur Greeves (1914-1963).* Edited by Walter Hooper. New York: Macmillan, 1979.

VDT *The Voyage of the "Dawn Treader."* New York: Macmillan, 1952.

OTHER WORKS

Ford, Companion Ford, Paul. *Companion to Narnia* (1980). Rev. ed. San Francisco: HarperSanFrancisco, 1994.

Hooper, *C. S. Lewis*   Hooper, Walter. *C. S. Lewis: A Companion and Guide.* London: HarperCollins, 1996.

Hooper, *Past Watchful Dragons*   Hooper, Walter. *Past Watchful Dragons.* New York: Collier, 1979.

Green and Hooper   Green, Roger Lancelyn, and Walter Hooper. *C. S. Lewis: A Biography.* New York: Harcourt Brace Jovanovich, 1974.

Tolkien, "On Fairy-Stories"   Tolkien, J. R. R. "On Fairy-Stories." In *Essays Presented to Charles Williams*, edited by C. S. Lewis, 38-89. London: Oxford University Press, 1947.

Tolkien, *Letters*   *The Letters of J. R. R. Tolkien.* Edited by Humphrey Carpenter. New York: Houghton Mifflin, 1981.

Sayer   Sayer, George. *Jack: C. S. Lewis and His Times.* San Francisco: Harper & Row, 1988.

NOTES

Chapter 1: The Story-maker and His Stories

3   **"I am sure . . . to bear leaves":** Lewis, TST 385.

3   **Many aspects of his life:** The information in this chapter about Lewis's life comes mostly from his autobiography *Surprised by Joy* and from George Sayer's excellent biography *Jack: C. S. Lewis and His Times.*

3   **"story-maker" creating imaginary worlds:** Tolkien, "On Fairy-Stories" 60.

4   **"dressed animals" and "knights in armour":** SbyJ 21, 20 (ch. 1).

4   **"Balder the beautiful . . . regions of northern sky":** SbyJ 23 (ch. 1).

4   **stories . . . about an imaginary country:** About a dozen Animal-Land and Boxen stories have been published in *Boxen: The Imaginary World of the Young C. S. Lewis*, ed. Walter Hooper (San Diego: Harcourt Brace Jovanovich, 1985).

5   **On two visits . . . *Encyclopedia Boxoniana*:** Hooper, Introduction, *Boxen* 21.

5   **in *Surprised by Joy* . . . reminiscing about the stories:** SbyJ 13-14, 19-20, 21-22, 79-82 (ch. 1, 5).

5   **"With my mother's death . . . from my life":** SbyJ 27 (ch. 1).

7   **even mentioning suicide:** Sayer 45-46.

7   **"everyone's poem . . . for physical beauty," "seeming to have a life
           of its own":** "Edmund Spenser," *Major British Writers*, ed. G. B. Harrison,
           enlarged edition, 2 vols. (New York: Harcourt, Brace and World, 1954),
           1.97, 98.

7   **"I have at last come . . . have I enjoyed it":** *TST* 93.

7   **On a Saturday evening in 1915 or 1916:** *Surprised by Joy* says this oc-
           curred on an evening in October 1915 (p. 169, ch. 11). However, in a letter
           to Arthur Greeves that editor Walter Hooper has dated Tuesday, 7 March
           1916 (*TST* 92), Lewis says it occurred the previous Saturday.

7-8   **"A few hours later . . . a great frontier":** *George MacDonald: An Anthol-
           ogy*, ed. C. S. Lewis (London: Geoffrey Bles, 1946), 20.

8   **"a new quality . . . in a certain sense, baptized":** *SbyJ* 169, 171 (ch. 11).

8   **"If you thought of Lewis . . . thought of poetry":** Barfield, "C. S.
           Lewis" (1964), *Owen Barfield on C. S. Lewis*, ed. G. B. Tennyson
           (Middletown, Conn.: Wesleyan University Press, 1989), 5-6. Lewis met
           Barfield, who shared his interests in poetry, myth, and imagination, at
           Oxford. Lewis was deeply influenced by Barfield's ideas, especially those
           of Barfield's first book, *Poetic Diction: A Study in Meaning* (London: Faber &
           Faber, 1928).

9   **"a smooth, pale . . . a smack or so":** *All My Road Before Me: The Diary of
           C. S. Lewis, 1922-27*, ed. Walter Hooper (London: HarperCollins, 1991), 393.

9   **after an evening meeting:** *TST* 317.

9   **the Inklings:** For an account of the Inklings and the importance of this
           group in Lewis's life, see Humphrey Carpenter, *The Inklings: C. S. Lewis,
           J. R. R. Tolkien, Charles Williams, and Their Friends* (London: Allen & Unwin,
           1978).

10   **"It is God's myth . . . are men's myths":** *TST* 427.

10   **"the 'scientifiction' of H. G. Wells":** *SbyJ* 40 (ch. 2).

11   **Lewis said "Perelandra!":** Green and Hooper 201-2.

11   **Lewis met Joy Davidman Gresham:** The story of Lewis's marriage
           and the death of his wife has been dramatized (rather romantically) in
           Shadowlands, which originated as a largely factual made-for-TV movie in
           1985, was revised into a play with successful runs in London in 1989-90
           and New York in 1990-91, and was revised again into a Hollywood movie
           in 1994. For a discussion of the different versions, see Peter J. Schakel,

"The Importance of Shadows in *Shadowlands*," *Seven: An Anglo-American Literary Review* 11 (1994): 25-29.

12   **"to re-edit the books . . . didn't tie up)":** Quoted in Green and Hooper 432.

Chapter 2: Controversies over Texts and Reading Order

13   **"The series was not planned . . . never remember dates":** Lewis to Laurence Krieg, 23 April 1957, *Letters to Children* 68-69.

14   **"far too stupid . . . up himself":** *VDT*, Bles edition, p. 12 (ch. 1).

14   **"quite incapable . . . up himself":** *VDT*, Macmillan edition, p. 5.

14   **uniform worldwide edition of the seven Chronicles:** After the original hardcover editions in Britain and the United States and the original paperback reprints, the Chronicles were reprinted in numerous formats and special editions prior to 1994, following the British and Macmillan texts, respectively. The best account of the publishing record can be found in Hooper, *C. S. Lewis* 452-56.

14   **by Pauline Baynes:** The choice of illustrator was left to Lewis, and he selected Pauline Baynes, who after World War II began illustrating books professionally. In the late 1940s she left a portfolio with Allen & Unwin, publisher of Tolkien's *The Hobbit* and about to bring out his *Farmer Giles of Ham*. When Tolkien rejected illustrations the publisher had chosen for *Farmer Giles*, they showed him Baynes's drawings. He liked what he saw, and she did a set of illustrations that Tolkien felt exactly suited the book. Lewis presumably learned about her from Tolkien (though Baynes says Lewis told her that he went into a bookshop and asked an assistant to "recommend someone who could draw children and animals" — Hooper, *Past Watchful Dragons* 77). In December 1949, Geoffrey Bles showed Lewis the initial drawings, and Lewis sent Baynes a note congratulating her on them, especially their vigorous detail (Lewis, *Collected Letters* 2.1009). See also Wayne G. Hammond, "Pauline Baynes," in *British Children's Writers, 1914-1960*, ed. Donald R. Hettinga and Gary D. Schmidt, Dictionary of Literary Biography, vol. 160 (Detroit: Gale Research Inc., 1996), 36-44; Hooper, *Past Watchful Dragons* 76-80; and Nancy-Lou Patterson, "An Appreciation of Pauline Baynes," *Mythlore* 7, no. 3 (Autumn 1980): 3-5.

16-17   **"for the first . . . should be read in":** Hooper, *Companion* 453.

17   **"I think I agree . . . anyone reads them":** Lewis to Laurence Krieg, 23
         April 1957, *Letters to Children* 68.

17   **"the order in which . . . *Magician's Nephew*]":** Green and Hooper 320.

17   **"is not necessarily . . . perfect, judge":** "On Criticism" (1966), OOW 57
         (*OnS* 140).

18-19   **"Narnia? What's . . . the eastern sea":** *LWW* 9.

19   **"They say Aslan . . . felt quite different":** *LWW* 54.

19   **"something jump in his inside":** *LWW* 54.

19   **"This is a story about . . . Narnia first began":** *MN* 1.

20   **"Narnia, Narnia, Narnia . . . Be divine waters":** *MN* 103.

21   **it unquestionably does make a difference:** A further reason for treat-
         ing *The Lion, the Witch and the Wardrobe* as the first in the series is its catchy,
         imaginative title, which surely contributed significantly to the success of
         the first book, and thus of the series. Imagine yourself in 1950, seeing a
         new book on the shelf with the title of any of the other six Chronicles.
         Would you feel inclined to pick up a book entitled *Prince Caspian* or *The
         Silver Chair*? I suspect many people would not — *The Voyage of the "Dawn
         Treader"* or *The Horse and His Boy*, maybe, but surely not *The Magician's
         Nephew*. *The Lion, the Witch and the Wardrobe* evokes just the right mixture
         of interest and curiosity. What witch? Why a wardrobe? What do these
         three items have to do with each other? The rhythm of the phrase and
         the alliteration fix the title in the mind.

         When Walden Media decided to film one of the Chronicles, they
         chose this book first instead of *The Magician's Nephew* in part because the
         story has better graphic potential and provides a better introduction to
         the series, but also because of its title. *The Lion, the Witch and the Wardrobe*
         is the most widely recognized title of the series: the Chronicles are in a
         significant way identified with it. For that reason the full title of the
         movie includes both the book title and the series title: *The Chronicles of
         Narnia: The Lion, the Witch and the Wardrobe*.

21   **preferred by a number of Lewis scholars:** See Ford, *Companion* xix-xx;
         Evan K. Gibson, *C. S. Lewis, Spinner of Tales* 194-95; Margaret Patterson
         Hannay, *C. S. Lewis* 23-71; Colin Manlove, *The Chronicles of Narnia* 30-31;
         Doris T. Myers, *C. S. Lewis in Context* 227n; Peter J. Schakel, *Reading with the*

Heart 143-45, and *Imagination and the Arts in C. S. Lewis* 40-52. (For publishers and dates, see pages 195-96.)

Chapter 3: The Storytelling: Fairy Tale, Fantasy, and Myth

25   **"I wrote fairy tales . . . I had to say":** Lewis, "Sometimes Fairy Stories May Say Best What's to Be Said" (1956), OOW 37 (*OnS* 47).

25   **"the first qualification . . . meant to be used":** *PPL* 1 (ch. 1).

25   **"All my seven Narnian books . . . a story about it'":** "It All Began with a Picture . . ." (1960), OOW 42 (*OnS* 53).

26   **"This book is about . . . in the country":** Hooper, *Companion* 402.

26   **The date of the *Dark Tower* manuscript is disputed:** Hooper says the unfinished manuscript of *The Dark Tower* was "probably written in 1939" (*C. S. Lewis* 402; see also his preface to *The Dark Tower and Other Stories*, ed. Walter Hooper [New York: Harcourt Brace Jovanovich, 1977], 8). Hooper's assumption is that Lewis began *The Dark Tower* shortly after publication of *Out of the Silent Planet* (1938), as the time-travel sequel mentioned in its final paragraph: "If there is to be any more space-travelling, it will have to be time-travelling as well" (*OSP* 264). John D. Rateliff has argued recently that Lewis was setting up not his own time-travel sequel, but one to be written by Tolkien (see Tolkien, *Letters* 29, 342, 347, 378), and that *The Dark Tower* was begun after *That Hideous Strength* (1944), not after *Out of the Silent Planet*. See "The Lost Road, The Dark Tower, and *The Notion Club Papers*: Tolkien and Lewis's Time Travel Triad," in *Tolkien's Legendarium: Essays on the History of Middle-earth*, ed. Verlyn Flieger and Carl F. Hostetter (Westport, Conn.: Greenwood Press, 2000), 198-218.

26   **"In the Author's mind . . . impulse complete":** "Sometimes Fairy Stories May Say Best What's to Be Said," OOW 35 (*OnS* 45).

26   **Lewis told . . . Chad Walsh:** Walsh, *C. S. Lewis: Apostle to the Skeptics* (New York: Macmillan, 1949), 10. In a letter to Mr. and Mrs. E. L. Baxter dated 10 September 1947, Lewis wrote, "I have tried one [a fairy tale] myself but it was, by the unanimous verdict of my friends, so bad that I destroyed it" (*Collected Letters* 2.802). No other information remains about that story, whatever it was.

26-27   **"Everything began . . . enamoured of it":** "Sometimes Fairy Stories May Say Best What's to Be Said," OOW 36-37 (*OnS* 46-47).

27 **"one of the highest forms of literature":** Tolkien, in notes accompanying a letter to the Houghton Mifflin publishing company, 30 June 1955, *Letters* 220.

28 **takes place in the realm of Faërie:** Tolkien, "On Fairy-Stories" 42.

28 **not literature just for children:** Tolkien, "On Fairy-Stories" 58-66; Lewis, "On Three Ways of Writing for Children" (1952), *OOW* 26 (*OnS* 35), and "Sometimes Fairy Stories May Say Best What's to Be Said," *OOW* 37-38 (*OnS* 47-48); "On Juvenile Tastes" (1958), *OOW* 39-41 (*OnS* 49-51).

28 **satisfy a sense of longing:** Tolkien, "On Fairy-Stories" 62-63.

28 **"primal desire":** Tolkien, "On Fairy-Stories" 45.

28 **"desire for our own far-off country":** "The Weight of Glory" (1941), *Transposition and Other Addresses* 23. (*The Weight of Glory and Other Addresses*, ed. Walter Hooper, revised and expanded edition [New York: Macmillan, 1980], 6.) See also *MC* 108 (3.10).

29 **"prison":** Tolkien, "On Fairy-Stories" 76.

29 **"the noise, stench . . . injustice, [and] death":** Tolkien, "On Fairy-Stories" 79.

29 **"Good and evil meet . . . the major difference":** Frederick Buechner, *Telling the Truth: The Gospel as Tragedy, Comedy, and Fairy Tale* (San Francisco: Harper & Row, 1977), 82.

29 **"drab blur of triteness or familiarity":** Tolkien, "On Fairy-Stories" 74.

30 **"joyous 'turn' . . . the walls of the world":** Tolkien, "On Fairy-Stories" 81.

30 **"the peculiar quality . . . echo of *evangelium*":** Tolkien, "On Fairy-Stories" 83.

31 **The Wood that Time Forgot:** Green and Hooper 305.

31 **the making or glimpsing of Other-worlds:** Tolkien, "On Fairy-Stories" 63.

31 **"strangeness" . . . "wonder":** Tolkien, "On Fairy-Stories" 67.

31 **"Secondary Worlds" . . . "Primary World":** Tolkien, "On Fairy-Stories" 60.

32 **"man may, if he pleases . . . own postulates, incredible":** George MacDonald, *A Dish of Orts: Chiefly Papers on the Imagination, and On Shakespeare*, enlarged edition (London: Sampson Low Marston, 1893), 314.

32 **an act of "sub-creation":** Tolkien, "On Fairy-Stories" 60.

32   **more difficult . . . than writing realistic fiction:** Tolkien, "On Fairy-Stories" 67.

32   **"Primary Belief" . . . "Secondary Belief":** Tolkien, "On Fairy-Stories" 60-61.

32   **"that willing suspension of disbelief":** *Biographia Literaria,* vol. 7, Pt. 2 of *The Collected Works of Samuel Taylor Coleridge,* ed. James Engell and W. Jackson Bate (Princeton: Princeton University Press, 1983), 6.

32   **"This suspension of disbelief . . . has for us failed":** Tolkien, "On Fairy-Stories" 60.

33   **"survey the depths . . . other living things":** Tolkien, "On Fairy-Stories" 44.

33   **"an enlargement of our being . . . as with our own":** *EinC* 137.

33   **"I saw the bright . . . the bright shadow":** *SbyJ* 170-71.

33   **Carlingford Mountains . . . he had ever seen:** Walter Hooper, quoted in Douglas Gilbert and Clyde S. Kilby, *C. S. Lewis: Images of His World* (Grand Rapids: Eerdmans, 1973), 143.

34   **"I had very little idea . . . whole story together":** "It All Began with a Picture . . . ," *OOW* 42 (*OnS* 53).

34   **"total (unanalysable) effect":** Tolkien, "On Fairy-Stories" 57.

34   **"deals with impossibles and preternaturals":** *EinC* 44.

34   **"permanent and fundamental":** Tolkien, "On Fairy-Stories" 77.

35   **"not knowing, but . . . *about which* truth is)":** "Myth Became Fact" (1944), *God in the Dock* 66.

35   **"panning the vein of spirit out of sense":** Tolkien, "Mythopoeia" (line 40), *Tree and Leaf, Including the Poem "Mythopoeia"* (London: Unwin Hyman, 1988), 98.

35   **"the story of Christ . . . *it really happened":*** *TST* 427.

35   **"The heart of . . . is the miracle":** "Myth Became Fact," *God in the Dock* 66-67.

36   **"arouses in us . . . such mythopoeic art:** Preface, *George MacDonald: An Anthology,* ed. C. S. Lewis (London: Geoffrey Bles, 1946), 16-17.

36   **"A fairytale is not . . . is not an allegory":** MacDonald, *A Dish of Orts* 317.

36   **"always excepting . . . particular and topical"**: Tolkien to W. H.
          Auden, 7 June 1955, Tolkien, *Letters* 212.

36   **"Tolkien's book is not . . . any other way"**: Lewis to Fr. Peter Milward,
          22 September 1956, Tolkien, *Letters* 458.

37   **"You are mistaken . . . a different thing"**: Lewis to a fifth-grade class
          in Maryland, 29 May 1954, *Letters to Children* 44-45.

37   **"supposition"**: Lewis to Mrs. Hook, 29 December 1958, *Letters* 475.

37   **"We spoil countless . . . whose sake it exists"**: MacDonald, *A Dish of
          Orts* 322, 321-22.

37-38   **"sort of religious experience . . . came to have any"**: "On Stories,"
          OOW 16 (*OnS* 15-16).

Chapter 4: *The Lion, the Witch and the Wardrobe*

39   **"When I say 'magic' . . . their own accord'"**: Lewis, *Letters to Malcolm:
          Chiefly on Prayer* (London: Geoffrey Bles, 1964), 134 (letter 19).

39   **"Faërie . . . may perhaps . . . laborious, scientific magician"**: Tolkien,
          "On Fairy-Stories" 43.

39   **"produces a Secondary . . . can enter"**: Tolkien, "On Fairy-Stories" 70-
          71.

40   **"elvish craft"**: Tolkien, "On Fairy-Stories" 70.

41   **when the Professor . . . wider possibilities**: *LWW* 37-40.

41   **"It's — it's a magic wardrobe"**: *LWW* 19.

41   **"some magic in the house . . . into Narnia"**: *LWW* 42.

41   **set out on a mission**: The seven Chronicles are constructed like medi-
          eval romances, with knights in armor (in this case, children) being sent
          out on missions and quests. Each book is structured as an adventure,
          with suspense and excitement as a basic, and very important, level of ap-
          peal. Each involves danger to the children, or to Narnia, or both, and un-
          certainty and anxiety over whether, and how, disaster will be averted.

42   **Emperor-Beyond-the-Sea**: *LWW* 64. The title is sometimes given as
          the "Emperor-over-Sea."

43   **"good and terrible at the same time"**: *LWW* 103.

43   **"Every traitor belongs . . . a right to a kill"**: *LWW* 114.

43   **"Deep Magic from the Dawn of Time":** *LWW* 108.

43   **"the Law of Human Nature . . . need to be taught":** MC 4 (1.1).

43   **Old Testament tablets of stone:** Exodus 24:12; 32:15-20; 34:1-5.

43   **"in letters deep as . . . World Ash Tree":** *LWW* 114. See Annotations, page 126 above.

43   **"Emperor's magic . . . Emperor-Beyond-the-Sea":** *LWW* 115, 114.

43   **"Work against . . . to him again":** *LWW* 115.

43   **"Unless I have blood . . . fire and water":** *LWW* 114.

44   **"Deeper Magic from *before* the Dawn of Time":** *LWW* 127.

44   **"It is after you have realised . . . begins to talk":** MC 24-25 (1.5).

44   **"The Passion and . . . not exactly like":** Lewis to [Patricia], 8 June 1960, *Letters to Children* 93. Also, "[Aslan] is an invention giving an imaginary answer to the question, 'What might Christ become like if there really were a world like Narnia and He chose to be incarnate and die and rise again in *that* world as He actually has done in ours?' This is not allegory at all": Lewis to Mrs. Hook, 29 December 1958, *Letters* 475. For further discussion of why the Chronicles should not be regarded as allegories, see Schakel, *Reading with the Heart*, 3-5, and Charles Huttar, "The Heresy of Allegorizing Narnia: A Rejoinder," *CSL: The Bulletin of the New York C. S. Lewis Society* 11, no. 3 (January 1980): 1-3.

44-45   **"God is the Lord, of angels, and of men — and of elves":** Tolkien, "On Fairy-Stories" 84.

45   **The account . . . really did happen:** "Myth Became Fact," *God in the Dock* 66-67.

45   **"Any amount of . . . their knowing it":** Letter to Sister Penelope, 9 July [August] 1939, *Collected Letters* 2.262.

46   **"C. S. Lewis, the . . . figure to be emulated":** *Time*, 12 April 2004, 61.

46   **"a good many different . . . quite secondary":** MC 43 (2.4).

46   **"on the face . . . very silly theory":** MC 45 (2.4).

46   **"According to that . . . God let us off":** MC 43 (2.4).

46   **one of the things . . . acceptance of Christianity:** MC 43 (2.4); *SbyJ* 64-65 (ch. 4).

46   **"What possible point . . . someone who has not":** MC 45 (2.4).

46-47   **"For every treachery . . . is my property":** *LWW* 114.

47   **"renounced . . . brother's blood":** *LWW* 115.

47   **"footing the bill" . . . climb out of the hole:** MC 45 (2.4).

47   **regain a clear view . . . triteness or familiarity":** Tolkien, "On Fairy-Stories" 74.

47   **no longer able to experience its full potency:** "Supposing that by casting all these things into an imaginary world, stripping them of their stained-glass and Sunday school associations, one could make them for the first time appear in their real potency? Could one not thus steal past those watchful dragons? I thought one could" ("Sometimes Fairy Stories May Say Best What's to Be Said," OOW 37 [*OnS* 47]).

47   **"the Stone Table . . . end to end":** *LWW* 131.

47   **the veil in the Temple tearing:** Matthew 27:51.

47   **"proper use":** *LWW* 109.

47   **Law by itself . . . that gives life:** Romans 8:2.

47-48   **"she would have known . . . working backwards":** *LWW* 132-33.

48   **"conversation which Edmund never forgot":** *LWW* 112.

48   **he apparently learned about that only later:** In the final chapter, Lucy whispers to Susan, "Does he know . . . what Aslan did for him?" and Susan replies, "Hush! No. Of course not," and adds that he shouldn't be told: "It would be too awful for him" (*LWW* 147). Apparently he does find out later, for he tells Eustace, after hearing how the latter was freed from his dragon skin, about Aslan, "the great Lion, . . . who saved me and saved Narnia" (*VDT* 91). But at this point he knows only that Aslan is good and that he loves Aslan.

48   **"thinking about himself . . . looking at Aslan":** *LWW* 113.

48   **"not only healed . . . look you in the face":** *LWW* 146.

48   **"Edmund was a graver . . . Edmund the Just":** *LWW* 150.

48   **"courtyard full of statues . . . like a zoo":** *LWW* 135, 137.

48   **"And that is precisely . . . come to life":** MC 126 (4.1). During the time Lewis wrote the earlier Chronicles, he was also revising the published versions of his BBC radio talks from the 1940s into *Mere Christianity* (published in 1952, two months before *The Voyage of the "Dawn Treader"*).

Chapter 5: *Prince Caspian*

50   **"I believe there is . . . not seen it myself":** MC 49 (2.5).

50   **"Many of the elements . . . practised in daily life":** Tolkien, "On Fairy-Stories" 56.

51   **"This is magic":** PC 3.

51   **"a little use of simple magic":** PC 72.

51   **"a very magical place . . . most deeply magical of all":** PC 74, 79.

51   **"White Magic":** PC 81.

51   **incantations to call up evil spirits:** PC 142.

51   **calls the tree-people to life:** PC 115.

51   **exudes from Aslan's mane:** PC 119.

51   **creates the feast of plenty:** PC 177.

51   **bestowed by Aslan . . . into our world:** PC 183.

51   **"How it all comes back":** PC 12.

51   **"It brought back — oh, such lovely times":** PC 15.

51   **the apple orchard they had helped plant:** PC 16 (cf. H&B 57).

51   **the ancient treasure chamber:** PC 20.

51   **"the Golden Age in Narnia":** PC 44.

51   **"battles and hunts and feasts":** PC 23.

52   **to blow the ancient horn of Queen Susan:** PC 51.

52   **"I wish . . . in the Old Days":** PC 34.

52   **"a King like . . . Peter of old":** PC 44.

52   **"raised in very ancient times":** PC 74.

52   **"to belong to an even older Narnia":** PC 75.

52   **"a great longing . . . talk in Narnia":** PC 96.

52   **"fairy tales," "old wives' tales":** PC 34, 74.

52   **"We don't change . . . in Aslan himself":** PC 57.

53   **"I never quite believed . . . believed all right":** PC 28.

53   **"There never were . . . Do you hear?":** PC 35.

53   **a rejection . . . knows to be true:** PC 42.

53   **"gone sour inside . . . and hating":** PC 145.

53	**he will believe in anything:** PC 63.
53	**doesn't believe in . . . or in Aslan:** PC 66, 80, 57.
53	**"We want power . . . on our side":** PC 140.
53	**Nikabrik might have turned out better:** PC 145.
54	**Peter declares . . . to join Caspian:** PC 90.
54	**"We're lost":** PC 102.
54	**"You're bigger . . . find me bigger":** PC 117.
54-55	**"Christ never meant . . . a five-year-old":** MC 61 (3.2).
55	**"I couldn't have left . . . must follow me alone":** PC 117-19.
55	**"I believe my eyes, your Majesty":** PC 151.
56	**"Will the others see . . . Later on, it depends":** PC 118.
56	**the dwarfs do not see Aslan:** LB 138-40.
56	**Orual is unable to see the palace:** Till We Have Faces, Part 1, Ch. 10.
56	**as the experience of Uncle Andrew demonstrates:** MN 111-12 ("What you see and hear depends a good deal on where you are standing").
56	**they are just following Lucy:** PC 124.
56	**"I really believed . . . breathe on you'":** PC 126-28.
56	**"The Dwarf flew up . . . did not feel so":** PC 129.
57	**Peter remembers the language:** PC 147.
57	**Peter's courtesy as "a Knight":** PC 162.
57	**"'To arms, Narnia. Treachery!' Peter shouted":** PC 163.
57	**"silenced the beasts . . . the dwarfs and fauns":** PC 42.
57	**"a youth, dressed only . . . in his curly hair":** PC 131.
57	**"the streams would run . . . for weeks on end":** LWW 12.
58	**"No other festival in Greece . . . the general rejoicing":** Edith Hamilton, Mythology (Boston: Little, Brown and Company, 1942), 73-74.
58	**"long-lost days of freedom":** PC 43.
58	**"It may have been . . . he was blindfolded":** PC 131.
58	**Aslan declares a holiday:** PC 165.
58	**"unnecessary and uncomfortable":** PC 168.
58-59	**"a tired-looking girl . . . very like pigs":** PC 168.
59	**"Chained dogs broke their chains":** PC 168.

59   **"The boy, who . . . and joined them":** *PC* 168.

59   **"Why I do declare . . . breakfast this morning":** *PC* 170.

59   **"one of the magical places":** *PC* 181.

59   **reaction of the Telmarines . . . the door first:** *PC* 184.

59   **"through that arch . . . moment's delay":** *PC* 184.

59   **"to seek adventures . . . a kinglier look":** *PC* 52, 69.

Chapter 6: *The Voyage of the "Dawn Treader"*

60   **"There have been times . . . anything else":** Lewis, *The Problem of Pain* (London: Centenary Press, 1940), 133 (ch. 10).

60   **"satisfying it while . . . it unbearably":** Tolkien, "On Fairy-Stories" 62.

60   **"desired dragons . . . profound desire":** Tolkien, "On Fairy-Stories" 63.

60   **"intense longing . . . unnameable something":** Preface to the third edition of *The Pilgrim's Regress* (London: Geoffrey Bles, 1943), 7, 9.

60   **"an unsatisfied desire . . . any other satisfaction":** *SbyJ* 23-24 (ch. 1).

61   **"Most of us . . . secret country [is] real":** *VDT* 3.

61   **"If you spent . . . till you get there":** *VDT* 11.

61   **"arresting strangeness":** Tolkien, "On Fairy-Stories" 67.

62   **seven noble lords:** *VDT* 16 (cf. *PC* 49).

62   **"little bit of a thing":** *VDT* 23.

63   **"If Caspian had been . . . made this suggestion":** *VDT* 30.

63   **understanding of the slave trade from the inside:** *VDT* 48.

63   **a show of power . . actually possess:** *VDT* 38.

63   **"You're to go on . . . I'm to go back":** *VDT* 203.

64   **"called Eustace . . . in model schools":** *VDT* 1.

64   **"liners and motor-boats and aeroplanes":** *VDT* 24.

64   **the inability of the slave traders to get rid of him:** *VDT* 51.

64   **has been "pretty beastly":** *VDT* 91.

64   **behaving like a "monster":** *VDT* 75.

64   **he must first undress:** *VDT* 88-89.

64	**"the beastly stuff"**: *VDT* 89.
65	**"a different boy"**: *VDT* 92.
65	**"Lucy sees him most often"**: *VDT* 91.
65	**"no title page or title"**: *VDT* 126.
65	**"You couldn't turn back . . . pages could not"**: *VDT* 130.
65	**"a girl standing . . . exactly like Lucy"**: *VDT* 127.
65	**"much more than a picture. It [is] alive"**: *VDT* 129.
66	**"the loveliest story"**: *VDT* 130.
66	**a cup, a sword . . . and a green hill**: *VDT* 131.
66	**he will keep telling it to her**: *VDT* 133.
66	**a Dryad said over his cradle**: *VDT* 17.
66	**"something that cannot . . . in this world"**: MC 107 (3.10).
66-67	**"desire for my . . . do the same"**: MC 108 (3.10).
67	**"the most valiant . . . Beasts of Narnia"**: *VDT* 12.
67	**"to look for things . . . honour and adventures"**: *VDT* 150.
67	**"full of forlorn hopes . . . and last stands"**: *VDT* 55.
67	**"go on . . . into the world"**: *VDT* 174.
67	**in Aslan's country**: *VDT* 207.
67	**"the White Witch . . . while the world lasts"**: *VDT* 168.
67	**"all were very hungry"**: *VDT* 169.
67	**only those who believe**: *VDT* 169 ("you can only believe — or not").
67	**"eaten [by birds . . . renewed, every day"**: *VDT* 170.
67	**"It is set here by [Aslan's] bidding"**: *VDT* 169.
68	**a coracle, a tiny boat**: *VDT* 93.
68	**"go on alone"**: *VDT* 206.
68	**"a brightness you . . . dark glasses on"**: *VDT* 205.
68	**"No one in that boat . . . into Aslan's country"**: *VDT* 206.
68	**he gets into the coracle**: *VDT* 206.
68	**no one in Narnia . . . there ever since**: *VDT* 207.
68	**the sky — solid and . . . joins the earth**: *VDT* 207.
68	**the door into Aslan's country**: *VDT* 210.

69   **"open the door in the sky":** *VDT* 209.

69   **"How can we live . . . know me better there":** *VDT* 209.

69   **across a river:** *VDT* 209.

Chapter 7: *The Silver Chair*

71   **"Obedience is the road to freedom":** Lewis, "Membership" (1945), *Transposition and Other Addresses* 39 (*The Weight of Glory* 113).

71   **"Few attempt such . . . most potent mode":** Tolkien, "On Fairy-Stories," 68.

71   **"boys and girls . . . what they liked":** *SC* 1.

72   **"a place where animals . . . have in fairy tales":** *SC* 4.

72   **"a different world . . . That Place":** *SC* 9.

72   **"dreadfully thirsty . . . come and drink":** *SC* 14, 16.

72   **"If any man thirst . . . and drink":** John 7:37.

72   **"Whosoever drinketh . . . into everlasting life":** John 4:14.

72   **"most refreshing . . . ever tasted":** *SC* 17.

73   **gives Jill four signs:** *SC* 19.

73   **"when thou liest . . . thou risest up":** Deuteronomy 6:7 (also, 11:18).

73   **"First, the descent . . . a higher world":** Northrop Frye, *The Secular Scripture: A Study of the Structure of Romance* (Cambridge, Mass.: Harvard University Press, 1976), 97.

73   **"as green as poison":** *SC* 47.

74   **"to kill it and be avenged":** *SC* 47.

74   **"the most beautiful . . . is sure is "evil":** *SC* 48-49.

74   **"We think this may be one of the same crew":** *SC* 50.

74   **rule the Narnians through Rilian:** *SC* 134-35.

74   **"an inwardly optimistic . . . of immense integrity":** Hooper, *Past Watchful Dragons* 81.

75   **A beautiful lady . . . knight in black armor:** *SC* 73.

75   **"steaming baths, soft beds":** *SC* 74.

75   **"how lovely it [will] be to get indoors":** *SC* 77-78.

75	**"for [their] Autumn Feast":** SC 93 (echoing SC 75).
75	**"We'll have no man-pies to-morrow":** SC 114.
75	**tells her to go . . . forgotten them all:** SC 98.
75-76	**"written in great letters . . . a gigantic city":** SC 99.
76	**"UNDER ME":** SC 100.
76	**"back on the right . . . instructions again":** SC 126.
76	**to remain "steady":** SC 140.
76-77	**"Quick! I am sane . . . a man again":** SC 140.
77	**"It's the Sign . . . what *are* we to do?":** SC 141.
77	**"there *are* no accidents":** SC 131.
77	**"You see, Aslan . . . following the Sign":** SC 142-43.
77	**Half of the children's . . . back to his father:** SC 144.
77	**"She is a nosegay of all virtues":** SC 129.
77	**"How do you . . . such man here":** SC 130.
77	**"the toy and lap-dog":** SC 140.
77	**"I know myself . . . son of Narnia":** SC 147.
77	**"There never was any world but mine":** SC 150.
78	**"'Tis a pretty . . . no sun, no Aslan":** SC 153-54.
78	**"The lamp is . . . but a tale":** SC 152.
78	**"invention about truth . . . that is with God":** Humphrey Carpenter, *Tolkien: A Biography* (Boston: Houghton Mifflin, 1977), 146.
78	**"a real though unfocussed . . . human imagination":** *Miracles* 161n. (ch. 15).
78	**"I've seen the sky full of stars":** SC 150.
78-79	**"Suppose we *have* only . . . isn't any Narnia":** SC 155.
79	**Perelandra:** The world Lewis created in *Perelandra* (1943).
79	**"half of [his] heart" in Bism:** SC 177.
79	**"Aslan will be our good lord":** SC 163 and 181.
79	**"in the heart of Narnia":** SC 186.
80	**the Great Snow Dance:** SC 186.
80	**"solemn, triumphal music":** SC 201.
80	**"Suddenly the King's head fell back":** SC 201.

80   **"a tune to break your heart"**: *SC* 202.

80   **"to bring [them] Home"**: *SC* 202.

80   **the king lying . . . drank living water**: *SC* 203.

80   **"a very young man, or a boy"**: *SC* 204.

80   **"most people have [died], you know"**: *SC* 205.

81   **"the steep, earthy slope"**: *SC* 7.

81   **"loathsome Garrett twins"**: *SC* 206.

81   **"an Inspector . . . happily ever after"**: *SC* 207.

81   **"for the better . . . quite a good school"**: *SC* 207.

81   **"quite as well as they did"**: *SC* 205.

Chapter 8: *The Horse and His Boy*

82   **"If we are made . . . what we find"**: Lewis, "The Weight of Glory,"
      Transposition and Other Addresses 23 (*The Weight of Glory* 6).

82   **"Most good 'fairy-stories' . . . shadowy marches"**: Tolkien, "On
      Fairy-Stories" 42.

84   **"Why, I might be anyone!"**: *H&B* 7.

84   **"By the rivers . . . remembered Zion"**: Psalm 137:1.

84   **"desire for our own far-off country"**: "The Weight of Glory," 23 (*The
      Weight of Glory* 6).

84   **"the desire for . . . till after death"**: *MC* 108 (3.10).

85   **"Narnia and the North"**: e.g., *H&B* 14.

85   **North in paradisal terms**: "North" is a relative term in the Chronicles,
      not an absolute. For Shasta in Calormen, Narnia, to the North, is
      paradisal; for those in Narnia, the North is an area in which giants live
      and from which evil witches come (see *SC* 50, 61; *MN* 155).

85   **"pure 'Northernness' . . . my own country"**: *SbyJ* 74-75 (ch. 5).

85   **the grass stops suddenly, the sand begins**: *H&B* 68.

85   **"it look[s] absolutely dead"**: *H&B* 107.

85   **"that everyone who . . . is more important"**: *H&B* 46.

85   **soft grass . . . a nightingale**: *H&B* 112-13.

85   **"long-lost captive[s] . . . home and freedom"**: *H&B* 179.

86	**"Funny to think . . . in the saddle!":** *H&B* 13.
86	**"low, bad habits":** *H&B* 18.
86	**"try to look less like a princess":** *H&B* 43.
87	**"Instead of being grave . . . chatted and laughed":** *H&B* 47.
87	**"the very nicest kind of grown-up[s]":** *H&B* 49.
87	**"He had, you see . . . free-born people behave":** *H&B* 60.
87	**"Who are you? . . . exactly like himself":** *H&B* 64.
87	**"clothes and parties and gossip":** *H&B* 82.
88	**"common little boy . . . not good enough":** *H&B* 25, 27.
88	**"It's not Nice . . . get to Narnia":** *H&B* 86.
88	**"I feel just like . . . that we're free":** *H&B* 114.
88	**"a very sensible mare":** *H&B* 39.
88	**sets the pace the rest of the way:** *H&B* 115.
89	**"Must go back! Must help!":** *H&B* 120.
89	**"[Shasta] ran in the . . . little human boy":** *H&B* 127.
89	**"he knows nothing . . . with his sword":** *H&B* 160-61.
89	**"You're not quite . . . decent sort of Horse":** *H&B* 127-28.
90	**"Who *are* you? . . . Myself":** *H&B* 139.
90	**"I am":** Exodus 3:14.
90	**"After one glance . . . needn't say anything":** *H&B* 140.
90	**a powerfully numinous moment:** Aslan has been present a number of other times in the book, but none of those occasions creates a sense of awe and wonder because we (and the characters) don't know that the lion or the cat is Aslan.
90	**"A new and different . . . came over him":** *H&B* 139.
90	**"I say," she exclaims . . . any such thing as Luck":** *H&B* 125.
90	**several other times in the book:** *H&B* 37, 138, 142.
91	**"Ye thought evil . . . much people alive":** Genesis 50:20.
91	**"rather a fool":** *H&B* 170.
91	**"The scratches . . . what it felt like":** *H&B* 171.
92	**"I'd sooner be eaten . . . Joy shall be yours":** *H&B* 170.
92	**"returning to home and freedom":** *H&B* 179.

92   **"You are the foul fiend of Narnia":** *H&B* 185.

92   **"Forget your pride . . . these good kings":** *H&B* 184.

92   **"the most peaceable . . . had ever known":** *H&B* 188.

Chapter 9: *The Magician's Nephew*

94   **"Either the stream . . . like creation":** Lewis, "The Laws of Nature" (1945), *God in the Dock* 78.

94   **"In O[xford] I wrote a cosmogonical myth":** Tolkien to Christopher Bretherton, 16 July 1964, *Letters* 345.

94   **"your grandfather was a child":** *MN* 1.

94   **"In those days . . . Lewisham Road":** *MN* 1.

94   **"fairy blood in her":** *MN* 17.

95   **"the vulgar devices . . . scientific magician":** Tolkien, "On Fairy-Stories" 43.

95   **"some devilish queer people":** *MN* 18.

95   **"not an art . . . a technique":** Tolkien, "On Fairy-Stories" 71.

95   **power, domination:** Tolkien, "On Fairy-Stories" 71.

95   **"Some of them . . . like little bombs":** *MN* 19.

95   **"You're simply . . . ones in the stories":** *MN* 22.

95   **"the Wood Between the Worlds":** *MN* 25.

95   **"in-between place":** *MN* 30.

96   **"Any pool . . . try that one":** *MN* 33.

96   **dead, cold, and empty:** *MN* 39.

96   **"taller than the people of our world":** *MN* 43.

96   **"stiff with enchantments":** *MN* 42.

96   **"Make your choice . . . followed if you had":** *MN* 44.

96   **"bide the danger":** *MN* 44.

97   **"Ours . . . is a high and lonely destiny":** *MN* 16, 55.

97   **the words sound . . . Jadis says them:** *MN* 55.

97   **have a greedy look:** *MN* 12, 56.

97   **"That's what . . . bought them myself":** *MN* 19.

97	**"They were all . . . do my will"**: MN 55.
97	**"paid a terrible price"**: MN 54 (cf. MN 18: "for nothing").
97	**lacking "the Mark"**: MN 50, 62.
97	**"pantomime demon"**: MN 10.
97	**"spoke the Deplorable . . . beneath the sun"**: MN 54.
97	**"near the end of its life"**: MN 52.
97	**the as yet "empty world"**: MN 85.
98	**"elvish craft . . . desire and purpose"**: Tolkien, "On Fairy-Stories" 70-71.
98	**deep voice of the earth**: MN 87.
98	**looked older than ours**: MN 52.
98	**laughing and full of joy**: MN 90.
98	**"Narnia, Narnia, Narnia, awake"**: MN 103.
98	**swells into humps . . . shake itself off**: MN 101.
98	**drawn from several creation stories**: See Charles A. Huttar, "C. S. Lewis's Narnia and the 'Grand Design,'" in *The Longing for a Form: Essays on the Fiction of C. S. Lewis,* ed. Peter J. Schakel (Kent, Ohio: Kent State University Press, 1977), 123-26.
98	**creator of our world**: See John 1:3 and Hebrews 1:2.
99	**at the same steady pace**: MN 95.
99	**"until you saw the Singer himself"**: MN 90.
99	**"Creatures, I give . . . myself"**: MN 105.
99	**"that all the things . . . the Lion's head'"**: MN 94.
99	**"Christianity . . . them right again"**: MC 31 (2.1).
99	**"evil will come of that evil"**: MN 121.
100	**the benevolent land he intends it to be**: MN 158.
100	**"Soon she will . . . well again"**: MN 145.
100	**"the most terrible choice"**: MN 145 (cf. MN 54).
100	**"false and hollow"**: MN 147.
100	**the accolade "Well done"**: MN 149.
100	**"That world is . . . had never been"**: MN 159.
100	**"strong and cruel empire"**: MN 158.

101   **"a secret as evil . . . than the Empress Jadis":** MN 160.

101   **"Outline of Narnian History So Far As It Is Known":** First published in Walter Hooper, "Past Watchful Dragons: The Fairy Tales of C. S. Lewis," *Imagination and the Spirit: Essays in Literature and the Christian Faith Presented to Clyde S. Kilby*, ed. Charles Huttar (Grand Rapids: Eerdmans, 1971), 298-301. Reprinted in Hooper, *Past Watchful Dragons* 41-44, and Hooper, *C. S. Lewis* 420-23.

101   **"in the country . . . Hole like this":** MN 2.

101   **"It was a hard . . . All hard stones":** MN 110.

101   **"You were a country . . . for me there":** MN 110.

101   **"use a spade . . . out of the earth":** MN 123.

101   **"more like the country . . . of a cockney":** MN 124.

101   **"great big house . . . better and better":** MN 165.

102   **"like a miracle":** MN 163.

102   **"live happily ever after":** MN 165.

Chapter 10: *The Last Battle*

103   **"Our lifelong nostalgia . . . our real situation":** Lewis, "The Weight of Glory," *Transposition and Other Addresses* 30 (*The Weight of Glory* 15-16).

103   **"Probably every writer . . . in the real world":** Tolkien, "On Fairy-Stories" 82-84.

104   **"whatever its own . . . adventure, morality, fantasy":** Tolkien, "On Fairy-Stories" 43.

104   **"how easily they . . . you'll be sorry":** LB 4.

104   **"'You *are* unkind . . . look at the coat":** LB 8.

105   **"to make Narnia . . . worth living in":** LB 30.

105   **"to do us good . . . *are* their business":** "Is Progress Possible?" (1958), in *God in the Dock* 314.

105   **"Two wars necessitated . . . choice or chance":** "Is Progress Possible?" 313.

105   **"we want to be free . . . what I tell you":** LB 30.

105   **"Tash and Aslan . . . you know Who":** LB 31.

105   **"you know Who":** LB 6.

105-6   **"I have some definite . . . opposed to the world":** "Cross-Examination" (1963), in *God in the Dock* 265.

106   **"so 'broad' or 'liberal' . . . Christian at all":** "Christian Apologetics" (1945), in *God in the Dock* 89.

106   **"'I just wanted to know . . . said the Tarkaan":** LB 75-76.

106   **finds himself present in a room:** LB 42-43.

106   **had buried years before:** MN 164.

106   **"The Dwarfs are for the Dwarfs":** LB 71, 112, 139.

107   **"The snowdrops were over . . . Narnian marching song":** LB 82.

107   **"In the last days of Narnia":** LB 1.

107   **"terrible things written in the skies":** LB 15.

107   **"horrible thoughts aris[ing] in [his] heart":** LB 20.

107   **"much evil came of their rashness":** LB 20.

107   **"Gloom and fear reigned over Narnia":** LB 58.

107   **"except Aslan's own country":** LB 84.

107   **"Narnia is no more":** LB 86.

108   **"might mistake him for a lion":** LB 9.

108   **"dreadful midnight meetings":** LB 75.

108   **"black as pitch":** LB 75.

108   **"clouding over":** LB 76.

108   **"pitch-black":** LB 136.

108   **"fighting for Narnia . . . by British Railways!":** LB 91.

109   **"pass through that . . . indeed a grim door":** LB 120.

109   **"much older than we are here":** LB 130.

109   **"unstiffened":** LB 130.

109-10   **"crowns on their heads . . . glittering clothes":** LB 124.

110   **"the country where everything is allowed":** LB 129.

110   **"the freshest grapefruit . . . orange was dry":** LB 129.

110   **"There stood his . . . Lion, Aslan himself":** LB 137.

110   **"If I find in myself . . . till after death":** MC 108 (3.10)

110   **"This is my real . . . knew it till now":** LB 162.

110	**"Seeing is believing":** *LB* 99.
110-11	**"They will not let us . . . in that prison":** *LB* 139-40.
111	**"pitch-black, poky . . . of a stable":** *LB* 136.
111	**"Narnia is not dead. This is Narnia":** *LB* 160.
111	**"That had a beginning . . . of the real Narnia":** *LB* 160.
111	**"like places in a story . . . want to know":** *LB* 161.
111	**"This is still Narnia . . . Narnia down below":** *LB* 170.
111	**"I can't describe it . . . know what I mean":** *LB* 162.
112	**"at the end of the world":** *SC* 124.
112	**"He will have a new one":** *LB* 142.
112	**"just crept . . . during the fighting":** *LB* 113.
112	**"spreading blackness . . . emptiness":** *LB* 142.
112	**"a foaming wall of water":** *LB* 147.
112	**"and instantly . . . total darkness":** *LB* 149.
112	**"the ice-cold . . . covered with icicles":** *LB* 149.
112	**the Icelandic myths he loved:** See above, page 4.
112	**"young and merry" again:** *LB* 168.
112	**Lucy referred to earlier:** *LB* 133.
113	**"far bigger inside than it was outside":** *LB* 170.
113	**"cool mixture . . . with white flowers":** *LB* 169.
113	**no longer looking like a lion:** *LB* 173.
113	**can't find words to express them:** *LB* 173.
113	**"live happily ever after":** *MN* 165.
113	**"they all lived happily ever after":** *LB* 173.

Chapter 11: The Stories Told: Fairy-land and Its Effects

114	**"Supposing that by . . . thought one could":** Lewis, "Sometimes Fairy Stories May Say Best What's to Be Said," *OOW* 37 (*OnS* 47).
114	**"elvish craft":** Tolkien, "On Fairy-Stories" 68.
115	**"I hear you've been . . . he's talking about?":** Green and Hooper 307.

115   **"It is sad that . . . of my sympathy"**: Tolkien to David Kolb, S.J., 11 November 1964, *Letters* 352.

115   **"an astonishing . . . the following lines"**: Sayer 47.

116   **"Always winter but never Christmas"**: *LWW* 14.

116   **Recovery, in Tolkien's sense**: Tolkien, "On Fairy-Stories" 74-75.

117   **"Do you really mean . . . is more probable"**: *LWW* 40.

117   **"There are laws . . . shame and the like"**: *Out of the Silent Planet* (London: Bodley Head, 1938), 226 (ch. 20). Lewis thus adheres to George MacDonald's dictum that "in the moral world . . . [an author] must invent nothing. He may not, for any purpose, turn its laws upside down. . . . In physical things a man may invent; in moral things he must obey and take their laws with him into his invented world as well" (*A Dish of Orts* 315).

117   **"Men more frequently . . . reminded than informed"**: Samuel Johnson, *The Rambler* (No. 2), ed. W. J. Bate and Albrecht B. Strauss, the Yale Edition of the Works of Samuel Johnson, vol. 3 (New Haven: Yale University Press, 1969), 14. Paraphrased in *Mere Christianity*, 3.3: "People need to be reminded more often than they need to be instructed."

118   **primarily concerned with what we desire**: Tolkien, "On Fairy-Stories" 62.

118   **story-maker proved . . . successful subcreator**: Tolkien, "On Fairy-Stories" 60.

Annotations to the Chronicles

121   **I have noted some allusions**: Ford, *Companion*, lists 70 items under the "Biblical Allusions" entry, with *allusions* defined as "indirect hints." A good many of them seem to me to be accidental parallels or broad resemblances rather than examples of deliberate allusiveness.

122   **he told Chad Walsh**: Walsh, *C. S. Lewis: Apostle to the Skeptics* (New York: Macmillan, 1949), 10.

122   **read two chapters . . . end of the month**: Green and Hooper 307.

122   **Lewis and Mrs. Moore . . . 2 September 1939**: Lewis to his brother, 2 September 1939, *Collected Letters* 2.270 and note.

122   **"Outline of Narnian History So Far As It Is Known":** See above, page 185.

122   **Paul Ford suggests:** Ford, *Companion* 164.

125   **Maugrim, Fenris:** See Ford, *Companion* 189.

125   **"I pronounce it Ass-lan":** Lewis to [Carol], 22 January 1952, *Letters to Children* 29.

126   **"breaking the magic . . . into his place":** Green and Hooper 241.

126   **"what a horrid messy business *that* will be":** PC 101.

126   **dries his sword after wading:** LB 18.

126   **"back in the sheath . . . clean and polish it":** LB 74.

127   **Paul Ford thinks:** Ford, *Companion* 366, 447-48.

128   **What, he asked, would it be like:** Green and Hooper 309.

132   **"in the bowels of the earth . . . kings of metals and mines":** *Encyclopedia Britannica*, 11th ed., s.v. "Dwarf."

133   **"devilish queer people":** MN 18.

133   **"little, peddling Magician . . . in [her] blood":** MN 64, 34, 64.

133   **"if spoken . . . who spoke it":** MN 54.

134   **"as part . . . wine in a moment":** *Miracles* 163 (ch. 15).

135   **"was written obviously in the heat of inspiration with hardly a correction":** Green and Hooper 310.

135   **Paul Ford suggests:** Ford, *Companion* 178n.

136   **"Outline of Narnian History So Far As It Is Known":** See above, page 185.

137   **peaceful kings came one after another:** LB 83.

137   **"Outline of Narnian History So Far As It Is Known":** See above, page 185.

137   **"in a good History . . . local library)":** H&B 188.

137   **"you cannot put . . . would you think . . . most progressive man":** MC 22 (1.5).

139   **"trained emotions":** AofM 13 (Lecture 1, para. 16).

139   **drew two sketches of Dufflepuds:** The drawings are reproduced in Walter Hooper, "Past Watchful Dragons: The Fairy Tales of C. S. Lewis," in *Imagination and the Spirit: Essays in Literature and the Christian Faith Pre-*

sented to Clyde S. Kilby, ed. Charles Huttar (Grand Rapids: Eerdmans, 1971), 313.

142 **"The only way . . . as far as I know":** Lewis to a fifth-grade class in Maryland, 29 May 1954, *Letters to Children* 45.

142 **Roger Lancelyn Green's suggestion:** Green and Hooper 311.

142 **"All outside compulsion . . . the only value":** The Summerhill School website, www.summerhillschool.co.uk/pages/history.html.

146 **points to the "siluer seat":** John Cox, "Epistemological Release in *The Silver Chair,"* in *The Longing for a Form: Essays on the Fiction of C. S. Lewis,* ed. Peter J. Schakel (Kent, Ohio: Kent State University Press, 1977), 162-63.

146 **"the Witch was dead":** *LWW* 145.

147 **"I belong to a generation . . . Christian name (or I him)":** Tolkien to Rayner Unwin, 15 December 1965, *Letters* 365.

147 **"A beautiful . . . [Narnian] fish":** *PC* 30.

147 **the nine names . . . all High Kings:** Ford, *Companion* 60.

148 **"I like best . . . *Stole the Boy*?":** Green and Hooper 311-12.

150 **"All will be well . . . will be well":** Quoted by Lewis in "The Psalms" (ca. 1958?), *Christian Reflections,* ed. Walter Hooper (Grand Rapids: Eerdmans, 1967), 123.

153 **"C. S. Lewis's Narnia and the 'Grand Design'":** In *The Longing for a Form: Essays on the Fiction of C. S. Lewis,* ed. Peter J. Schakel (Kent, Ohio: Kent State University Press, 1977).

153 **"the elvish craft . . . in the Primary World:** Tolkien, "On Fairy-Stories" 70-71.

155 **"the little human . . . disgusting, and hateful":** *AofM* 10 (Lecture 1, para. 10).

156 **planted by Digory at Narnia's beginning:** *MN* 149.

158 **"the obscenities . . . of paganism":** "Religion without Dogma?" (1946), *God in the Dock* 143.

158 **doesn't believe Tash actually exists:** *LB* 31.

159 **not a good student . . . than she is:** *VDT* 3.

159 **"The books don't tell . . . it was 'all nonsense'":** Lewis to Martin, 22 January 1957, *Letters to Children* 67.

159 **"Hell is a state . . . in the end, Hell":** *GD* 63 (ch. 9).

159   **no matter how ... nothing but roaring:** MN 112. (See also MN 153.)

159   **"the grand Calormene manner":** H&B 30-31.

160   **"ceased to be a Christian":** SbyJ 61 (ch. 4).

160   **"especially in Virgil ... prefigured Christianity":** SbyJ 64 (ch. 4).

160   **"[It] used to puzzle me ... saved through Him":** MC 51 (2.5).

160   **"People in other ... in this position":** MC 164 (4.10).

160   **letter to Mrs. Arnold dated 31 January 1952:** Letters 418.

160   **Mrs. Ashton dated 8 November 1952:** Letters 428.

161   **"The universe is turned ... be the centre":** "Dante's Similes," Studies in Medieval and Renaissance Literature, ed. Walter Hooper (Cambridge: Cambridge University Press, 1966), 74.

161   **"The universe is thus ... turned inside out":** The Discarded Image: An Introduction to Medieval and Renaissance Literature (Cambridge: Cambridge University Press, 1964), 116.

Table for Converting Page References to Chapter Numbers

Quotations from the Chronicles of Narnia are from the Macmillan hardbound editions published in the United States (1950-56); the page references are to those editions. The table below will enable readers using other editions to find the references by chapter and approximate location within the chapter.

The Lion, the Witch and the Wardrobe

Pp. 1-7: ch. 1

Pp. 8-17: ch. 2

Pp. 18-25: ch. 3

Pp. 26-34: ch. 4

Pp. 35-42: ch. 5

Pp. 43-50: ch. 6

Pp. 51-61: ch. 7

Pp. 62-70: ch. 8

Pp. 71-80: ch. 9

Pp. 81-89: ch. 10

Pp. 90-98: ch. 11

Pp. 99-107: ch. 12

Pp. 108-16: ch. 13

Pp. 117-26: ch. 14

Pp. 127-35: ch. 15

Pp. 136-44: ch. 16

Pp. 145-54: ch. 17

Prince Caspian

Pp. 1-9: ch. 1   Pp. 94-106: ch. 9
Pp. 11-23: ch. 2   Pp. 107-21: ch. 10
Pp. 24-32: ch. 3   Pp. 122-33: ch. 11
Pp. 33-45: ch. 4   Pp. 134-45: ch. 12
Pp. 46-58: ch. 5   Pp. 146-56: ch. 13
Pp. 59-68: ch. 6   Pp. 157-71: ch. 14
Pp. 69-81: ch. 7   Pp. 172-86: ch. 15
Pp. 82-93: ch. 8

The Voyage of the "Dawn Treader"

Pp. 1-14: ch. 1   Pp. 107-19: ch. 9
Pp. 15-28: ch. 2   Pp. 120-33: ch. 10
Pp. 29-40: ch. 3   Pp. 134-46: ch. 11
Pp. 41-53: ch. 4   Pp. 147-58: ch. 12
Pp. 54-66: ch. 5   Pp. 159-70: ch. 13
Pp. 67-80: ch. 6   Pp. 171-83: ch. 14
Pp. 81-92: ch. 7   Pp. 184-95: ch. 15
Pp. 93-106: ch. 8   Pp. 196-210: ch. 16

The Silver Chair

Pp. 1-13: ch. 1   Pp. 107-18: ch. 9
Pp. 14-25: ch. 2   Pp. 119-32: ch. 10
Pp. 26-38: ch. 3   Pp. 133-45: ch. 11
Pp. 39-51: ch. 4   Pp. 146-58: ch. 12
Pp. 52-64: ch. 5   Pp. 159-70: ch. 13
Pp. 65-79: ch. 6   Pp. 171-82: ch. 14
Pp. 80-92: ch. 7   Pp. 183-94: ch. 15
Pp. 93-106: ch. 8   Pp. 195-208: ch. 16

The Horse and His Boy

Pp. 1-14: ch. 1

Pp. 15-28: ch. 2

Pp. 29-40: ch. 3

Pp. 41-53: ch. 4

Pp. 54-66: ch. 5

Pp. 67-77: ch. 6

Pp. 78-90: ch. 7

Pp. 91-102: ch. 8

Pp. 103-15: ch. 9

Pp. 116-28: ch. 10

Pp. 129-40: ch. 11

Pp. 141-53: ch. 12

Pp. 154-66: ch. 13

Pp. 167-79: ch. 14

Pp. 180-91: ch. 15

The Magician's Nephew

Pp. 1-13: ch. 1

Pp. 14-24: ch. 2

Pp. 25-35: ch. 3

Pp. 36-47: ch. 4

Pp. 48-58: ch. 5

Pp. 59-69: ch. 6

Pp. 70-81: ch. 7

Pp. 82-91: ch. 8

Pp. 92-103: ch. 9

Pp. 104-14: ch. 10

Pp. 115-25: ch. 11

Pp. 126-37: ch. 12

Pp. 138-48: ch. 13

Pp. 149-58: ch. 14

Pp. 159-67: ch. 15

The Last Battle

Pp. 1-11: ch. 1

Pp. 12-23: ch. 2

Pp. 24-33: ch. 3

Pp. 34-43: ch. 4

Pp. 44-54: ch. 5

Pp. 55-65: ch. 6

Pp. 66-76: ch. 7

Pp. 77-86: ch. 8

Pp. 87-96: ch. 9

Pp. 97-106: ch. 10

Pp. 107-16: ch. 11

Pp. 117-27: ch. 12

Pp. 128-40: ch. 13

Pp. 141-52: ch. 14

Pp. 153-62: ch. 15

Pp. 163-74: ch. 16

Further Reading

Books on the Chronicles

Ditchfield, Christian. *A Family Guide to Narnia: Biblical Truths in C. S. Lewis's The Chronicles of Narnia*. Wheaton, Ill.: Crossway Books, 2003. A guide to using the Chronicles devotionally.

Duriez, Colin. *A Field Guide to Narnia*. Downers Grove, Ill.: InterVarsity Press, 2004. Provides background information and an A-Z guide to names and details.

Ford, Paul F. *Companion to Narnia: A Complete Guide to the Enchanting World of C. S. Lewis's The Chronicles of Narnia*, 4th edition. San Francisco: HarperSanFrancisco, 1994. An indispensable encyclopedia of information relating to the Chronicles.

Holbrook, David. *The Skeleton in the Wardrobe: C. S. Lewis's Fantasies: A Phenomenological Study*. Lewisburg, Pa.: Bucknell University Press, 1991. A Freudian analysis of the Chronicles.

Hooper, Walter. *Past Watchful Dragons: The Narnian Chronicles of C. S. Lewis*. New York: Collier, 1971. Valuable background information, now incorporated into his *C. S. Lewis: A Companion and Guide*.

Karkainen, Paul A. *Narnia Explored: The Real Meaning behind C. S. Lewis's Chronicles of Narnia*. Old Tappan, N.J.: Fleming H. Revell, 1979. Readings of the books as Christian allegories.

Lindskoog, Kathryn. *Journey into Narnia*. Pasadena, Calif.: Hope Publishing House, 1998. An expansion of *The Lion of Judah in Never-Never Land* (Grand

Rapids: Eerdmans, 1973), in which she examines the theology of God, man, and nature in the Chronicles; this book adds materials for teachers and questions for discussion.

Manlove, Colin. *The Chronicles of Narnia: The Patterning of a Fantastic World*. New York: Twayne, 1993. Valuable literary readings of each of the Chronicles.

Sammons, Martha C. *A Guide through Narnia*. Wheaton, Ill.: Harold Shaw Publishers, 1979. Encyclopedia-type entries on a variety of themes and topics in the Chronicles.

Schakel, Peter J. *Imagination and the Arts in C. S. Lewis: Journeying to Narnia and Other Worlds*. Columbia: University of Missouri Press, 2002. A study of Lewis's theory of imagination and the importance of the imaginative arts in Lewis's life and in the Chronicles.

————. *Reading with the Heart: The Way into Narnia*. Grand Rapids: Eerdmans, 1979. Online at www.readingwiththeheart.com. A study of archetypal symbols, patterns, and themes in the Chronicles and of thematic connections between the Chronicles and *Mere Christianity*.

Selected Books with Sections on the Chronicles

Christopher, Joe R. *C. S. Lewis*. Boston: Twayne, 1987.

Gibson, Evan K. *C. S. Lewis, Spinner of Tales: A Guide to His Fiction*. Washington, D.C.: Christian University Press, 1980.

Glover, Donald E. *C. S. Lewis: The Art of Enchantment*. Athens: Ohio University Press, 1981.

Hannay, Margaret Patterson. *C. S. Lewis*. New York: Ungar, 1981.

Hart, Dabney Adams. *Through the Open Door: A New Look at C. S. Lewis*. Tuscaloosa: University of Alabama Press, 1984.

Hooper, Walter. *C. S. Lewis: A Companion and Guide*. London: HarperCollins, 1996.

Howard, Thomas. *The Achievement of C. S. Lewis: A Reading of His Fiction*. Wheaton, Ill.: Harold Shaw Publishers, 1980. Reissued as *C. S. Lewis, Man of Letters: A Reading of His Fiction*. San Francisco: Ignatius Press, 1990.

Kilby, Clyde S. *The Christian World of C. S. Lewis*. Grand Rapids: Eerdmans, 1964.

Myers, Doris T. *C. S. Lewis in Context*. Kent, Ohio: Kent State University Press, 1994.

Walsh, Chad. *The Literary Legacy of C. S. Lewis.* New York: Harcourt Brace Jovanovich, 1979.

Selected Articles and Essays on the Chronicles

Alexander, Joy. "'The whole art and joy of words': Aslan's Speech in the Chronicles of Narnia." *Mythlore* 24, no. 1 (Summer 2003): 37-48.

Beyer, Doug. "What the Mutter with Magic? Its Use in the Writings of C. S. Lewis." *The Lamp-Post of the Southern California CS Lewis Society* 24, no. 4 (Winter 2000-01): 4-14.

Brady, Charles A. "Finding God in Narnia." *America* 96 (1956): 103-5.

Cox, John D. "Epistemological Release in *The Silver Chair*." In *The Longing for a Form: Essays on the Fiction of C. S. Lewis,* edited by Peter J. Schakel, 159-68. Kent, Ohio: Kent State University Press, 1977.

Hall, Thomas G. "Narnia: The Gospel According to C. S. Lewis." *Cresset* 38 (1975): 29-33.

Huttar, Charles A. "C. S. Lewis's Narnia and the 'Grand Design.'" In *The Longing for a Form: Essays on the Fiction of C. S. Lewis,* edited by Peter J. Schakel, 119-35. Kent, Ohio: Kent State University Press, 1977.

———. "The Heresy of Allegorizing Narnia: A Rejoinder." *CSL: The Bulletin of the New York C. S. Lewis Society* 11, no. 3 (January 1980): 1-3.

Johnson, William G., and Marcia K. Houtman. "Platonic Shadows in C. S. Lewis' Narnia *Chronicles*." *Modern Fiction Studies* 32 (1986): 75-87.

Khoddam, Salwa. "Balder the Beautiful: Aslan's Norse Ancestor in *The Chronicles of Narnia*." *Mythlore* 22, no. 3 (Winter 1999): 66-75.

Montgomery, J. W. "The Chronicles of Narnia and the Adolescent Reader." *Journal of Religious Education* 54 (1959): 418-28.

Murrin, Michael. "The Multiple Worlds of the Narnia Stories." In *Word and Story in C. S. Lewis,* edited by Peter J. Schakel and Charles A. Huttar, 232-55. Columbia: University of Missouri Press, 1991.

Myers, Doris T. "Growing in Grace: The Anglican Spiritual Style in the Chronicles of Narnia." In *The Pilgrim's Guide: C. S. Lewis and the Art of Witness,* edited by David Mills, 185-202. Grand Rapids: Eerdmans, 1998.

———. "Spenser's Faerie Land as a Key to Narnia." Lecture delivered at Wheaton College, 24 September 1998.

Nicholson, Mervyn. "Confusion of Tongues in *The Silver Chair.*" *The Lamp-Post: Bulletin of the Southern California C. S. Lewis Society* 18, no. 2 (1994): 15-27.

————. "C. S. Lewis and the Scholarship of Imagination in E. Nesbit and Rider Haggard." *Renascence* 51 (1998): 41-62.

————. "What C. S. Lewis Took from E. Nesbit." *Children's Literature Quarterly* 16, no. 1 (1991): 16-22.

Patterson, Nancy-Lou. "Narnia and the North: The Symbolism of Northernness in the Fantasies of C. S. Lewis." *Mythlore* 4, no. 2 (December 1976): 9-16.

Ruud, Jay. "Aslan's Sacrifice and the Doctrine of Atonement in *The Lion, the Witch and the Wardrobe.*" *Mythlore* 23, no. 2 (Spring 2001): 15-22.

Taliaferro, Charles. "A Narnian Theory of Atonement." *Scottish Journal of Theology* 41 (1988): 75-92.

Tixier, Eliane. "Imagination Baptized, or, 'Holiness' in the Chronicles of Narnia." In *The Longing for a Form: Essays on the Fiction of C. S. Lewis,* edited by Peter J. Schakel, 136-58. Kent, Ohio: Kent State University Press, 1977.

For a comprehensive list of writings on Lewis through June 1972, see Joe R. Christopher and Joan K. Ostling, *C. S. Lewis: An Annotated Checklist of Writings about Him and His Works* (Kent, Ohio: Kent State University Press, 1973). For a comprehensive list of writings on Lewis from 1972 to 1988, see Susan Lowenberg, *C. S. Lewis: A Reference Guide, 1972-1988* (New York: G. K. Hall, 1993). Studies of Lewis's literary works since 1988 can be found in the annual *MLA International Bibliography* (New York: Modern Language Association of America).

Index

Unlabeled titles are by Lewis.